Last Bonanza Kings

BOOKS BY THE AUTHOR

BIOGRAPHY

Last Bonanza Kings: The Bourns of San Francisco

Frémont: Explorer for a Restless Nation

HISTORY

Sand in a Whirlwind: The Paiute Indian War of 1860

The El Dorado Trail: The Story of the Gold Rush Routes Across Mexico

FICTION

The Taste of Time

EDITED WORKS

Thomas S. Martin: With Frémont to California and the Southwest in 1845–1849

Hozial H. Baker: Overland Journey to Carson Valley and California

J. Ross Browne: A Dangerous Journey

J. Müller: California, Land of Gold or Stay at Home and Work Hard

John Yates: A Sailor's Sketch of the Sacramento Valley in 1842

George D. Brewerton: Incidents of Travel in New Mexico

FEROL EGAN

Last Bonanza Kings

The Bourns of San Francisco

UNIVERSITY OF NEVADA PRESS / RENO & LAS VEGAS

University of Nevada Press, Reno, Nevada 89557 USA
www.unpress.nevada.edu

Manufactured in the United States of America
Design by Carrie Nelson House

Library of Congress Cataloging-in-Publication Data
Egan, Ferol.
Last bonanza kings : the Bourns of San Francisco /
by Ferol Egan.
p. cm.
Includes bibliographical references and index.
ISBN 978-0-87417-319-2 (cloth : alk. paper)
1. San Francisco (Calif.)—Biography. 2. Bourn, William, b. 1813. 3. Bourn, William, 1857–1936. 4. Pioneers—California—San Francisco—Biography. 5. Businessmen—California—San Francisco—Biography. 6. Bourn family. 7. San Francisco (Calif.)—History. I. Title.
F869.S353B684 1998 98-10998
979.4'04'0922—dc21 CIP
[b]

The paper used in this book meets the requirements of American National Standard for Information Sciences—Permanence of Paper for Printed Library Materials, ANSI/NISO Z39.48-1992 (R2002).
Binding materials were selected for strength and durability.

University of Nevada Press Paperback Edition, 2009
ISBN 978-0-87417-786-2 (pbk. : alk. paper)
ISBN 978-0-87417-849-4 (ebook)

This book has been reproduced as a digital reprint.

This book is dedicated to Arthur William Bourn Vincent,

and the late Francis Bourn Hayne.

As descendants of William Bourn I and II, they did not let the

memories, correspondence, and papers of these

remarkable California pioneers vanish.

CONTENTS

ILLUSTRATIONS

following page 94

1

Planting the Seed

There were eleven ships in the Winthrop Fleet that set sail from England to the New World in 1630. For twenty-one-year-old Jared Bourn of Bobbingworth, Essex, it was an adventure he would probably remember for the rest of his life. Although he sailed aboard the *Arbella,* the flagship of the fleet, young Bourn had signed on as an indentured servant, obligated to pay for his passage by working for Puritan elder William Colborne for five years. At the end of his service, he was to receive some land to mark his change of position from indentureship to that of a freeman. Yet during the first weeks at sea, after the departure on April 8, 1630, from Yarmouth, Isle of Wight, there must have been times when he wondered why he had given up a yeoman's life in Bobbingworth, for the ship offered far less comfort than he had known at home, and during turbulent seas, most passengers were seasick and feared for their lives.

Quarters aboard the vessels of the fleet were tight at best. On the *Arbella,* seamen had their quarters in the high forecastle deck, and the poop deck on the stern contained the cabins for the ship's officers and the leaders of the Puritans. In between these tall structures—"between decks"—were some very rough cabins to accommodate women and children. The men who sailed as future landowners or servants had to make do with hammocks.

Food supplies consisted of cured beef; beef tongues in brine; salted codfish; brown and white biscuits that were dry to begin the voyage and soon became moldy; a quarter barrel of butter to spread on the biscuits; oatmeal; dried peas, and mustard seeds to make the peas more palatable; and flour, salt, and suet that were used by the cook to make a dull diet into something the passengers would eat. Liquid for drinking was limited to 3,500 gallons of water and 10,000 gallons of beer, which was used to prevent scurvy. To keep themselves warm in the cold winds blowing off the Atlantic Ocean, the passengers had only heavy clothing and the small amount of warmth that drifted from the cook's stove, for which there were only eight thousand pieces of firewood for the entire voyage.[1]

To Jared Bourn and the other pioneers bound for the New World aboard the *Arbella* and the other ships of Governor John Winthrop's fleet, this westward voyage proved to be much rougher than they had ever imagined. During the hours of darkness, the only light available aboard the *Arbella* was given off by four lanterns and six dozen candles. Toilet facilities consisted of whatever pots were available, or the pitching and rolling deck with only the railing to hold on to while taking care of natural needs.

John Winthrop and the other Puritan leaders of the Massachusetts Bay Colony were courageous people. Most of them came from a strong middle class, and they left comfortable lives in England to escape the Romish changes that they saw taking place in the Anglican Church. So they put their faith to the test by sailing westward with a new vision of a life apart from a faith that they believed had failed them. In every sense, the Puritans were true believers willing to risk their lives for their religion. The Moses of this fleet of believers was forty-two-year-old John Winthrop, an influential man of means and education. He was a dignified and controlled individual whose temperament kept him from making impulsive moves.[2] Winthrop's religion controlled his actions, for he was convinced that his decision to journey with other religious followers was an act of God.

As for Jared Bourn and others like him, their reasons for sailing westward were as much for a better economic future as for religious beliefs. The nature of society in England confined Bourn to a social class that would never receive an opportunity to advance, but in the New World he could hope to break away from such constrictions. Even though his knowledge of the land they were sailing to as pioneers was very limited, he did know that Governor John Winthrop had obtained a charter from Charles I that seemed grand in every sense of the word.

What this New World meant to these members of the Massachusetts Bay Colony was that the land they were going to settle ran from a few miles south of the Charles River to a point within a few miles north of the Merrimack River. Between these two points on the map, there appeared to be unlimited future opportunity to move westward as far as the South

Seas.[3] True, most of the map had great blank spaces; and places such as the South Seas, or even the names of rivers, mountains, and the first settlements in New England were either without meaning or vaguely understood when these pioneers signed or made their mark for the voyage westward. Still, there was to be freedom from the Crown, and the ultimate chance to fulfill their wildest dreams once they set foot on the shoreline of the New World.

2 As the 350-ton *Arbella* sailed west across the Atlantic, she pitched and rolled and dropped in and out of great troughs of waves that threatened to drown the ship. During this voyage of the Great Fleet, two hundred pioneers died without ever hearing the lookout call: "Land Ho!" For young Bourn and the other healthy and strong men aboard, the voyage became a floating funeral, because the strong had to carry the dead to the deck railing and let the bodies slide into the sea as one of the Cambridge ministers quickly read services before the pitching and rolling ship was caught by another wave that might sweep the burial party overboard.

Within the eleven ships of the fleet, there were seven hundred passengers, yet somehow one hundred passengers managed to jump ship before the two sections of the fleet reached the open sea. As for those voyagers who were buried at sea, their passage to the New World became a chartered trip to the world of the dead.[4]

The first part of the Great Fleet reached Salem Harbor on June 13, 1630—a voyage of just over two months. The second half of the fleet sailed from the Isle of Wight in May of that same year and reached the New World during the month of July. Four of the ships carried cargo, including materials the immigrants would need in their new homeland and livestock to add to the limited number of farm animals in New England.

Altogether, four hundred settlers of the Massachusetts Bay Colony reached New England between June and July of 1630. Of those who set foot on the rocky shoreline, some died from lingering illness within the first weeks of their arrival. Others were put to work building this new homeland, and this meant even harder work than they had known in England. Worst of all, the nature of the country was alien to them. They had come from a land that was fertile, green, and cultivated. Here, the soil was thin; rocks were everywhere; and the forests that bordered the communities were thick and almost foreboding. The immigrants felt uneasy about this wild land, which seemed endless in its dimensions. To add to its strangeness, they heard stories about tribes of Indians who lived in the depths of the forest; and these people who were nearby, but out of sight and unknown, became the grist for nightmares. What were these people like? Would they resent the arrival of new settlers in a land they surely looked upon as theirs, and if they did, would they become an unseen foe, always lurking just out of sight?

3 Once the immigrants of the Winthrop Party located the area that would eventually become Boston, the hard work of carving out a city in the wilderness began. As an indentured servant, a young man possessed of good health and strength, Jared Bourn and others like him put in long hours of hard work in the construction of a village that was based upon a master plan designed to provide both security and solidarity.

The concept of this planned settlement was an adaptation of a medieval village. There was to be a village green and a meetinghouse, which were to be the center of life for the families who lived in the surrounding dwellings. For farming, livestock grazing, trees for lumber, firewood, and even for shipbuilding, a much larger allotment of land was marked off for the settlers. However, this land was beyond the village, and to make use of it, the settlers walked back and forth to plant or pick crops, to take care of the livestock, to fell trees and mill lumber, and to gather the firewood needed for use in the village homes. Even though this daily travel back and forth took time, the overall village plan kept the settlers in close touch with each other and within the watchful vision of community leaders who maintained a close-knit social structure centered around the church and the Puritan elders.

In addition, this closeness of community served the settlers of the Bay Colony as a home base as some of them gradually moved westward into Connecticut or southwest to Long Island.[5]

One bit of good fortune for the Puritans was the presence of the nearby forests of the Boston area, which provided timber for those New England pioneers like Bourn, who arrived in America with the trade of ship building as part of their heritage. They built ships for their own use as well as for other countries, which liked the ships that came from New England. Within a few years after the settlement of Boston, New England ships were flying the flags of England, Spain, and Portugal. Along with the construction of ships for sale, the Puritans made a good business of selling clapboards, well-made spars and masts, shingles, and cooperage staves.

Freedom came at a hard price for the Puritans, but they endured the icy winters, tolerated the thin, rocky soil, and became a people noted for their hard work, their religious purity, and their ability to adapt to a land where only the toughness of spirit and body became the equation for survival.

4 On April 22, 1634, twenty-six-year-old Jared Bourn was admitted to the church in Boston. By this time, he was a married man, and he and his wife, Mary, had the beginning of a family. Just a little more than a year later, Bourn completed his indentureship to Elder William Colborne and became a freeman. At this time, he was granted a lot in Boston at "what is now the corner of Washington and Essex Streets."[6]

Two years later, Jared was granted eight acres outside Boston. Here, he moved into a region that was still the frontier. The nearby forests were thick and wild, and the area was the homeland of the Indians. The boundaries of Bourn's property were the Robert Houlton land to the southwest; Cedar Swamp on the northwest; the Muddy River on the southeast; and the John Briggs land to the northeast.[7]

Bourn worked hard at improving his land, and in 1643, he took on the additional job of constable at Muddy River (today's Roxbury, Massachusetts). But at the end of one year as constable, tragedy struck: Bourn's wife, Mary, died on March 30, 1644.[8]

As a widower trying to raise his family and carve out his future in the wilderness, Bourn needed another wife to take over his home and the responsibility of raising the children. There was not much time for mourning before he married Frances Brayton, and in 1651, she gave birth to Jared Bourn II.

During this period of Bourn's life, he became restless. Like many of the early settlers of America, he felt the need to keep on the move, to explore the land just beyond in the hope that it might improve his lot in life. The move took the Bourn family to Portsmouth, Rhode Island. Here, Bourn served as a representative in the colonial legislature from 1654 to 1655.[9]

But Rhode Island apparently did not appeal to Jared Bourn. There is no indication as to why he decided to move back to Massachusetts, but he returned with his family, and they settled in Swansea. Soon, there were rumors of a possible war with various Indian tribes, which in southern New England were of the Algonquian-speaking people and were able to understand other tribes of the region. The combination of the Narragansets,

Nipmucs, Wampanoags, Mohegans, Pequots, Pocomtucs, and others meant that the Indians of southern New England totaled some twenty thousand persons, compared to about forty thousand English settlers in that area.[10]

Bourn realized that there was good reason to fear a possible uprising of the Indians, for the English settlers had taken a great amount of their land, disrupted the game in the forests, and insisted upon trying to Christianize the Indians and make them into second-class citizens within the land the tribes rightfully considered to belong to them. As the years passed and rumors of a possible Indian uprising persisted, Bourn decided that some form of protection against an attack was needed. While some of his neighbors wondered why he was so concerned, Bourn followed his own belief and built a stone blockhouse at Mattapoisett (now known as Gardiner's Neck). And though his neighbors poked fun at what he was doing, Bourn took whatever was said behind his back as nothing when compared to the very real possibility that the nearby tribe of Wampanoags under the leadership of King Philip, the remaining son of the late Chief Massasoit, was not happy about the steady increase of English settlers into their homeland.

Twenty years passed between Jared Bourn's return to Massachusetts and the uprising of King Philip and his warriors. But on June 8, 1675, the final affront to the tribe took place when three Wampanoags were tried and hanged by English settlers for a murder they had not committed. Three days later, word reached Swansea that armed Indians under Philip's leadership were getting ready for war.[11]

Between June 18 and 19, 1675, King Philip's warriors killed John Winslow at Swansea. By June 20, Swansea came under very heavy attack. Settlers fled for their lives and left their homes to be looted and burned. The survivors of this first attack took refuge at either the Miles Garrison house or Jared Bourn's blockhouse. These were the nearest places of protection in this outbreak of a war that only men such as Garrison and Bourn had been wise enough to foresee.[12]

What the fearful settlers taking cover in the two blockhouses did not know was that King Philip and his Wampanoag warriors had been joined by three thousand Nipmucs to make this Indian army a powerful force in any battle. By June 24, the troops that had been stationed at Swansea were moved into the blockhouses both for their own protection and for the protection of the settlers in case the warriors decided to mount an all-out attack.[13]

The settlers and soldiers were under siege, but somehow word of their situation reached other settlements. At once, more militia soldiers were sent to help the besieged village. But by the time these soldiers reached Swansea, the Indians had vanished into the forest, where they were joined by the chieftainess of the Weetamoes from Pocasset in southeastern Rhode Island.[14]

During the next year, other tribes joined King Philip, and the war against the settlers of New England spread across the land in a series of raids that resulted in the death of several thousand persons. Settlers scattered and left homes, belongings, and cleared fields as they fled for their lives. Communities became burnt-out ruins; gardens and market crops were destroyed; and once-thriving areas such as Deerfield, Brookfield, Quinsigamond (today's Worcester), Warwich, Wickford, and Simsbury were almost totally destroyed in a hit-and-run war. It was like a forest fire crowning from treetop to treetop as it built its own winds of fury. Even such towns as Springfield, Westfield, and Providence were partially put to the torch in this exhausting war between militia units and bands of Indian warriors who knew the lay of the land far better than the English settlers.

Still, the constant state of war took a heavy toll on the federation of Indian tribes that made up King Philip's army. The need to take care of their own families and to make sure that their villages were safe caused a growing trend of desertion by warriors from other tribes. Finally, King Philip was left with only the remaining warriors from his own tribe. But Philip was having a hard time trying to keep them in line. The breaking point came on August 12, 1676, when one of the Wampanoags, whose brother had been killed by Philip for suggesting that it was time to seek a truce with the settlers, guided Captain Benjamin Church and his "army" of eighteen men from Plymouth, combined with twenty-two Indians, to the outskirts of King Philip's camp just as dawn was breaking. When the men of King Philip's army realized they had been discovered, they made a break for cover. As they did, the militiamen opened fire. And in the final battle of this bloody war, it was one of King Philip's former warriors who shot and killed the Indian leader.[15]

Captain Church had King Philip's body decapitated and quartered.[16] As a final act of brutality toward the Wampanoags, the settlers sold King Philip's widow and son into slavery in the West Indies.

This war that Jared Bourn saw from its very beginning to its barbaric finish was won at a cost that did terrible damage to New England's economy. Farming, shipbuilding, fur trading, and the export trade to Barbados suffered badly. Yet the Indians suffered even more. The settlers now believed that, by right of conquest, all Indian land belonged to them. In addition, they placed Indians on poor lands and refused to recognize any of their claims. Mistreatment of all tribes became commonplace after the war. Even those Indians who had fought on the side of the settlers suffered a bitter existence in a country that had once been their homeland.[17]

5 Jared Bourn was sixty-seven years old when King Philip's War ended. Considering that in 1676 life-spans tended to be short, Bourn was a very old man for that period. Still, he was active and not dependent upon relatives and children for support and care. When his wife, Frances, died and he became a widower for the second time, he looked for a new wife once a suitable period of mourning had passed. Within a year he married for the third time.

In his remaining years, Jared sired more children, and by the time of his death, sometime during 1681, seventy-two-year-old Jared Bourn left behind children by three wives to carry the Bourn name into the next century. Among the many direct descendants were such men as Jared Bourn II and Francis Bourn I, II, and III. From Francis Bourn III (1766–1826) and his wife Mary Bowers (1764–1830) came William Bowers Bourn I. He was born on June 21, 1813, at Somerset, Massachusetts.[18]

Like Jared, William Bourn was destined to carry on the pioneer experience. For his life was to be a very real part of the epic American journey into the frontier.

2

Westward Vision

William Bowers Bourn was a tall, handsome young man who was no more than seventeen years old when the call of the sea roared into his ears. As a sixth-generation descendant of Jared Bourn, young William could point with pride to his pioneer ancestry, but as the sixth of seven children of Francis Bourn III and Mary Bowers, there was not time for young William to consider the history of the Bourns in America.[1] To young William Bourn, Jared was only a vague memory pictured in his mind through family tales.

William was more interested in the world of men who made their fortunes by braving the waters of the open sea. For Massachusetts men, the sea was a way out of back-breaking labor in fields that were not very productive. By the time Bourn was old enough to consider what he would do to make his way in the world, Massachusetts men had already become famous as shipbuilders, sea captains, export and import merchants, and owners of sailing ships that traveled to ports in Newfoundland and Nova Scotia, where the offshore waters teemed with fish, which were traded in the West Indies for molasses for New England's many rum distilleries. During Bourn's youthful years, there were over sixty distilleries running in Massachusetts. Rum was the drink of the taverns, and it had replaced beer as the drink of choice.[2]

During these early years of sea trade, the merchants who backed the vessels on their long voyages somehow avoided the African slave trade. Still, "most Boston merchants owned slaves as house servants, and bought and sold them like other merchandise." Trade was carried on in South America for the products of the Dutch West Indies, and timber and even mahogany came from Honduras to be traded or sold in the London market. As early as the late 1700s, Massachusetts ships were sailing all the way to the Pacific Coast, where they traded for furs in the Northwest, hunted whales in the South Pacific, and even established trade with China. Missionaries from Massachusetts reached Hawaii by 1819, when William Bourn was only six years old, and by the time he was nine, sailing ships from Massachusetts were making regular stops in California. There they traded goods for cattle hides and tallow at such ports as San Diego, where "each firm maintained salt-vats, where seamen and Kanakas cured the hides and stored them until a shipload was accumulated." The same hide and tallow trade was also carried on with Buenos Aires, Montevideo, and Chile. Other ships made stops and traded for coffee beans at ports in Brazil, Haiti, and Cuba. The economy of Massachusetts derived its greatest income from the wide-ranging sea trade of its maritime fleet.[3]

At seventeen, William Bourn became involved in the sea trade as a way to earn his fortune. His first venture involved the purchase of a field of onions which he sent to Bermuda on a small trading vessel.[4] This was the beginning for Bourn, and within the next few years, as his profits grew, he began to send other cargoes from such ports as Providence and Salem to New Orleans, Bermuda, and Cuba. By this point in his life, Bourn became known as a sharp, trustworthy businessman. He was even given a letter of credit for a considerable sum in Cuba, where he was respected for his honesty and shrewdness. In the latter 1830s, he established an office for his maritime ventures in New Orleans. Here, he was closer to Havana and in the right location for the inland trade in furs from the Rocky Mountains, as well as the cotton and produce crops that came down the Mississippi River on large rafts and aboard paddle-wheelers that went as far upstream as the confluence of the Missouri and Mississippi Rivers, and even up the Missouri River into the heart of the fur trade country at the confluence of the Yellowstone and Missouri Rivers.[5] Although the major headquarters of trade for this inland river traffic was St. Louis, anything that had a potential market out of a seaport had to come to New Orleans, where Bourn and other sea traders had their offices. At New Orleans, it was easy to meet other shipowners whose vessels carried cargoes down the Mississippi River. Such cargoes were sold in the trading ports of the East Coast, Havana, the West Indies, South America, the Pacific Coast, and even northeast across the Atlantic to London and the ports of the European mainland.

By the time he was thirty-two, William Bourn had earned a solid reputation in business. He conducted his affairs with economy and already owned property free and clear of any debt.[6] As his business continued to grow and spread up the eastern coastline, he decided in 1847 to open a shipping office in New York City at 163 Maiden Lane. Here, he became a close friend of Captain George Chase, a sea-going man from Salem, Massachusetts, who was living at that time in Yonkers, New York.

Bourn and Chase liked and trusted each other, and they decided to go into business together.[7] But more than business entered into their relationship, for William Bourn had met his partner's daughter, Sarah Esther Chase, and the couple began to see each other on a regular basis.

By late 1848 and early 1849, one of the great events in the history of the United States became known in New York. Gold had been discovered in Mexican California in the tailrace of Captain John Sutter's sawmill in the foothills of the Sierra Nevada. By early 1849, the first of the swarms of men infected with "gold fever" headed for California by land and by sea. To Bourn and Chase, this was their chance to realize returns on investments lucrative beyond their wildest dreams. Even though William and Sarah were engaged to be married, Captain Chase and Bourn got the clipper ship *Robert Fulton* loaded with goods and some passengers bound for California. Before the forthcoming marriage of William and Sarah, the *Robert Fulton* set sail from New York on May 25, 1849, without Bourn, but with Captain Chase at the helm for the long voyage around the Horn and up the Pacific Coast to San Francisco and the golden land of California.[8]

2

Twenty-three days after William Bourn and Sarah Chase were married on July 20, 1849, at the Episcopal Church of the Holy Trinity in Brooklyn, New York, the *Robert Fulton,* with Captain George Chase at the helm, struck the point of a small island off the northeast point of Lively Island in the East Falklands.

As the winter snows blew across the Falklands and darkness began to approach, Captain Chase and his crew got all the passengers ashore. Then with the help of both crew members and some passengers, they saved as much of the cargo as possible—a cargo consisting of tools, framed doors and windows, paint, putty, bags of nails, cases of locks and fastenings, ladders, joists, and other building materials. When this was accomplished, Captain Chase sent his first and second mates by rowboat to Port Stanley.

Upon their return in a whaleboat, Captain Chase and the others made their way to Stanley to report the wreck to Governor George Rennie. Chase sold salvage rights to the wrecked vessel and acquired another ship. On October 31, 1849, he set sail again for California.[9]

Despite the difficulties at the Falkland Islands, Captain Chase and his crew managed to make the hard voyage 'round-the-Horn, enduring the fiercely cold weather and the rough seas and huge swells that caused the ship to roll and plunge between great waves that threatened to drown the vessel in the icy depths. Continuous winds blew against the prow of the ship and put the decks awash with water that felt as though it had come directly from the South Pole to threaten any hope of rounding the tip of South America.

Once around the Cape, the voyage up the Pacific Coast was not easy either. The current was coming from north to south, and though the weather began to grow warmer once the ship was free of the frigid climate of Cape Horn, the vessel had to tack back and forth as it sailed the rough waters of the Pacific.

One of the first stops on the voyage northward to California was Valparaíso, Chile. Here, the passengers and crew strolled the wide streets between adobe buildings and ate food that had much more flavor than the usual fare at sea, which consisted of potatoes, salt meat, dried fish, and hardtack. The ship replenished its food stores and purchased citrus fruit to add to the diet of the passengers in order to prevent an outbreak of scurvy.

After the stop at Valparaíso, Captain Chase got the best he could out of his ship, for his passengers were getting bored. All they had to do was to play cards, keep journals, or try a hand at fishing which, for the most part, was not very profitable. Another port of call was Callao, Peru, a walled Spanish city that served as the seaport for Lima, some seven to ten miles into the mountains. Callao was a dirty hole of a city, but some passengers hired horses and rode upward to Lima, considered a place of great beauty.

Captain Chase did not put into any other ports on the Pacific Coast once he sailed from Callao. He did not even stop at such Mexican seaports as Acapulco and Mazatlán.

The long voyage of seventeen to eighteen thousand nautical miles finally ended in the latter part of 1849 when Captain Chase sailed through the Golden Gate and entered San Francisco Bay. While the bay was a grand harbor, San Francisco was a ramshackle city built on brown, largely barren hills. Even more disappointing was the first sight of the jumble of tents, flimsy houses, unimposing hotels, and business houses that operated in tents, wooden shacks, or derelict ships. The waterfront was crowded with ships abandoned by earlier arrivals, and the upper part of today's Montgomery Street was composed of sandy hills. As Captain Chase found a place to anchor his ship, he saw that many of the deserted ships were being used as places of business; other vessels had been stripped of masts and even decks to be used as lumber in this treeless city.

After Captain Chase had unloaded his cargo, he discovered that prices in San Francisco were much higher than he had anticipated for most imported goods, especially for items in short supply. He also found that qualified craftsmen commanded wages that ran between ten and fifteen dollars per day. Equally high were prices for decent rooms and quality meals.

Chase wrote to his son-in-law, William Bourn, suggesting that it would be profitable to send another ship to California with passengers and the goods from the East that were in short supply in this Gold Rush city, as well as items needed in the gold-mining country of the foothills of the Sierra Nevada. Tools that might sell he deemed hard to judge, because the price for such items fluctuated wildly, depending upon which were in short supply. Still, San Francisco was a growing community in need of building materials and milled boards as well as prefabricated houses, which sold for a very high price.[10]

3 When William Bourn received Captain Chase's letter in the latter part of 1849, he requested Captain W. P. Hunter to assist him in getting a vessel ready for a voyage to California.[11] As Bourn explained, the ship would be loaded with the type of cargo that Captain Chase had suggested as good-selling items for California.

Between Bourn's initial letter to Captain Hunter and the loading of most of the cargo aboard the sailing ship *Powhatan,* as well as the booking of some passengers bound for California, a Captain Tucker was placed in charge of the *Powhatan.* He was at the helm when the ship set sail from New York harbor a few days before Christmas of 1849 to make a slow voyage before its first stop, March 23, 1850, at Rio de Janeiro.[12]

This port's business was much more formal than most ports on either the Atlantic or Pacific coast of South America. Here, Brazilian officials boarded the ship as representatives of both the Health and Customs Services.[13] No persons were allowed to board or go ashore from an incoming sailing ship until cabins and cargo had passed inspection by Brazilian officials. When this was completed, it was not unusual for a whole fleet of boats from the port to draw near the anchored ship or ships. No doubt, this happened to the *Powhatan,* and its crew and passengers were besieged by tradesmen with goods for sale; pitchmen for shops, hotels, and restaurants ashore; and reporters from newspapers who wanted stories about the voyage up to this point, as well as any news of the outer world.

The passengers had to wait for clearance the next day before they were allowed to go ashore. Most of them were impressed with the beauty of Rio as a city. They enjoyed the chance to dine in restaurants that served fine steaks, roasted chickens, hams, and fresh fruit such as bananas and oranges served on a bed of lettuce and watercress. To top the meals that the passengers enjoyed, there were bottles of claret and Madeira, and rich coffee made from freshly ground beans. But this treat was all too short. Before the crew and passengers wished to end their visit, they were back on the deck of the *Powhatan,* watching the outline of Rio de Janeiro fade from view as their ship struck its southern course toward Cape Horn. The voyage ahead of them was not to be as delightful as that which they had enjoyed up to their stop at Rio. Even for men who had some knowledge of the crossing from the Atlantic to the Pacific, the cold, rough weather of the passage 'round the Horn made a lasting impression on the memories of voyagers. So, too, most passengers never forgot the slow voyage up the Pacific Coast, against prevailing currents and winds.

During the endless days, the passengers grew bored and restless with life aboard so crowded a ship. It carried 15 passengers in better quarters, but 147 passengers had to make do with steerage. In addition, the cargo left little room for anybody to move about. The major items consisted of 100,000 shingles, 100 tons of coal, 80,000 bricks, and 10,000 feet of milled lumber.[14]

Finally, to the joy of both passengers and crew, the *Powhatan* sailed through the Golden Gate on July 29, 1850, and entered San Francisco Bay after a voyage of 228 days.[15]

San Francisco did not offer a vision of beauty. The city was no more than a jumble of tents and wooden shacks, and the harbor was crowded with the deserted ships of earlier arrivals, most of whom were already somewhere in the Gold Country of the Sierra Nevada foothills. The derelicts made it clear to any new arrival that this harbor city was only a jumping-off place. Bad as it appeared, it *was* land, and that made this crude city more than inviting to men who had endured the cramped quarters and short rations of such a long voyage.[16]

Once the men were ashore and found themselves walking the dirt streets and board sidewalks in search of living quarters, food, and the needed supplies to take to the Gold Country, they quickly discovered that prices were much higher than they had expected. It took time to find a place to stay while the would-be miners gathered some knowledge of which diggings to strike out for in search of that quick fortune they hoped to find. Often, rented quarters were in crowded tents or expensive hotel rooms; meals also were costly. But the city was filled with saloons, gambling houses, and ladies of the evening who plied their trade in this twenty-four-hour pleasure dome designed to let some residents reap a fortune without ever having to engage in the hard work of prospecting and mining. San Francisco was an exciting port of call for the passengers of all ships. Here weary sea voyagers heard astounding stories of gold strikes by some of the first chasers of the golden dream, men who had already made genuine fortunes in the rich foothill country east of San Francisco.

4 While the passengers of the *Powhatan* found their land legs in San Francisco, Captain George Chase conferred with the agent that William Bourn had sent to handle the merchandising of the cargo. But even as Captain Chase decided that it would be more efficient to sell the cargo right off the ship, he began to see that the agent who was to handle this job was losing his grasp of reality and would not be able to handle the job he had been hired to do.

Realizing that he would need help for this and for all the opportunities he saw in this Gold Rush port, Captain Chase wrote to Bourn and asked him to close the New York business and take the shortest available route to California. As Chase pointed out in his letter, San Francisco promised to be a most lucrative center for men of imagination and business enterprise. Between the two of them, there were opportunities that they could exploit as they worked together in the many business ventures that awaited men willing to risk capital and put in the time and work that could easily lead to the building of fortunes.[17]

3

Bound for California

By the time Captain Chase's letter reached William Bourn at his waterfront office in New York, a shorter, faster route to California had been developed across the Isthmus of Panama. Such enterprising men as William Henry Aspinwall and his cousin, William Edgar Howland, were involved in a steamship business that carried passengers and freight between New York and other ports, such as New Orleans, to Chagres, Panama. Beyond Chagres, businesses like the Pacific Mail Steamship Company made agreements with officials in Panama to have mail, freight, and passengers cross the sixty-mile Isthmus by way of the Chagres River. Then, from the river's mountain headwaters at Gorgona, travelers went by muleback to Panama City on whatever remained of the old road constructed by the Spanish during their heydays of plundering the mineral wealth of the New World.[1]

Bourn talked over his reasons for making this journey to California with his wife, and Sarah Chase Bourn agreed that he should go alone so he could learn the nature of the journey and what living conditions were like in San Francisco. However, the understanding between them was that once Will located a proper dwelling, Sarah would take whatever route he suggested and join him in San Francisco. Information about opportunities in San Francisco and in the goldfields, as they learned through her father's correspondence and through newspapers, told them that California was the future, the land in which to make one's fortune.

The fare from New York to Chagres fluctuated during the latter part of 1850, varying between $275 for cabin accommodations to as low as

$60 for steerage tickets.[2] The voyage to the Isthmus sometimes included stops in Cuba, where the steamers loaded additional coal. Other steamers came down the coast from New York to New Orleans and then cut over to Chagres. The voyage to this port was short when compared with the time it took to sail around the Horn or to take one of the overland trails to California.

To William Bourn, the voyage to Chagres was an easy one aboard a steamship. He enjoyed being at sea, and he took in every view with a feeling of adventure. He disembarked off the coast at Chagres and was taken into port by one of the smaller boats that had to unload steamers in the stream because of shallow water. Bourn must have been as disappointed as all other passengers who first saw the old city. After passing the crumbling fortress of San Lorenzo (which had never been repaired since the pirate Henry Morgan tried his best to destroy it), all passengers were unloaded at Chagres, which was not much more than a collection of hovels at the edge of a muggy, hot tropical jungle.[3]

The unhealthy climate of Chagres was an encouragement to make arrangements as quickly as possible for passage up the Chagres River. Native canoes hollowed out of single logs carried two to four passengers, who were protected from the hot sun by canopies. These *bongos,* as the natives called them, provided passage to the headwaters of the Chagres River. Would-be passengers had to bargain with the boatmen, and during Bourn's Panama passage, the going rate for space aboard a dugout canoe was about $10. The native boatmen were a mixture of Indians, blacks, and mixed-bloods who were usually part Spanish and part Indian.[4]

The trip upriver was slow, usually about a mile per hour, but to the Gold Rush passengers who had never been in a tropical rain forest, the journey must have been filled with both curiosity and some fear. The jungle had tree branches overhanging the water, and there was the constant sound and sight of monkeys and brilliant-plumed birds that filled the air with their squawks and whistles as they lit on branches beside brightly colored tropical flowers.[5]

This upriver trip of thirty-nine and a half miles to the village of Gorgona depended upon skilled boatmen who knew how to avoid eddies and rushing currents and were adept at keeping their boats close to the bank. In shallower water they made good use of their poles. Overnight stops were made at primitive native villages along the river. Here, many passengers made do with whatever food was available and tried to sleep on cots or hammocks during a night filled with jungle noises that ranged from the buzzing of insects to the howling of animals that were either predators or prey or both.

Some Americans who headed upriver had the good sense to carry their own food, such as dried beef, boiled ham, sea biscuits, and even bottles of claret or jugs of whiskey. Many of these travelers also carried pistols and rifles for protection and found delight in shooting alligators in the river or killing monkeys that foraged through trees of the green jungle.[6]

2 After the voyage up the Chagres River, William Bourn and others who made this jungle crossing found themselves in the village of Gorgona, a place with little to offer in the way of beauty or local color. There were a few rough American-style frame buildings used for hotels and warehouses, but the rest of this village consisted of cane huts covered with mud and long palm leaves. They served as dwellings for the local Indians who made their living as boatmen on the Chagres River or as muleteers on the trail from Gorgona to Panama City.[7]

A night's lodging at Gorgona cost between $10 and $15. Although this was not a great price, what it bought was not worth even that. If a man was lucky, he might have a rough bed for the night, but if he did not manage to get to Gorgona early enough, he might have to sleep in a crowded room or in a large tent with a hammock for a bed. Worse yet, there might be a dozen or more strangers in the same quarters. As for anything that resembled a decent meal, the offerings at Gorgona were eaten only because the pangs of hunger demanded some kind of food.

The journey from Gorgona to Panama City was downhill all the way for twenty-two miles, but Bourn and the other men bound for Panama City first had to bargain for mules and guides. The cost ran between $10 and $20 for the trip.

Once a traveler had secured a mule and a guide, the downhill journey was hardly an easy trip. The trail from Gorgona to Panama City had been a stone-paved road when Spanish pack mules carried Peruvian silver and gold up the mountains to the Chagres River. Here, the precious cargo was loaded aboard *bongos* for the downstream voyage to the port of Chagres for shipment to Spain. When William Bourn made this crossing, things had changed for the worse. The first two miles west of Gorgona were fairly easy traveling across tableland. After that, the trail wound downward through a dense forest where overhanging branches shut out the sunshine. On this rough, narrow trail, riders heard their guides shout at the mules to keep them moving, because stretches of trail had crumbled away, leaving shallow holes. The mules carefully placed their hooves to avoid slipping and sliding into the deep ravines at the trail's edge. If the guides heard a shout from a party coming uptrail, they bunched their mules in a wider part of the path so the upward-bound party would be able to pass. At such a halt, the guides and their customers checked their firearms in case they had to use them, because this jungle trail was noted for raids upon parties—especially those returning from Panama City with California gold—but bandits had also killed men just for their mules and supplies.

Leaving Gorgona at daybreak, Bourn and the other emigrants arrived on the outskirts of Panama City late in the day. As the trail became a road, they saw carts loaded with produce bound for the city, passed mules loaded with wood, and saw adobe houses two and three stories tall. Then they crossed a moat, and the road ran beneath the arched and towered gateway of the Puerta de Tierra, which had a stone cross and bell and served as the entrance to Panama City.[8]

Panama City was crowded with men either bound for California or returning from the goldfields with the luck of their prospecting mirrored in their faces. The city was located on a promontory with two sides facing the sea, protected by cannons facing the harbor, while the land boundary to the rear of the city was protected by the moat and a high wall. After what emigrants had seen of Panama since their first landing at Chagres, Panama City must have looked like a breath of civilization. The city was nearly two centuries old, and its great stone buildings, paved streets, churches, and cathedral were impressive when compared to Chagres.[9]

When Bourn arrived in Panama City, it was home to at least eight thousand Panamanian natives, plus an additional two to three thousand Americans, most of them waiting to catch a ship northward to California. In addition, there was a smaller contingent of Americans making arrangements to cross Panama to Chagres, where they could obtain passage aboard a steamship back to the United States.[10]

Living in Panama City was anything but easy for California-bound emigrants. The hotels were usually filled, and the places that most men could afford were much like the terrible lodgings in Gorgona. Some men found sleeping quarters in private homes. These fortunate travelers took their meals in restaurants and enjoyed a comfortable existence during their stay at Panama City.[11]

The best restaurant food usually consisted of ham, beans, chicken, eggs, and rice. Although beef was also available, it was avoided by customers who had been forewarned or who had the misfortune of having tried a meal of this stringy, tough, nearly tasteless meat that surely had come from cattle that had done a great amount of walking to find enough grass to keep them alive. Also, some of this meat was on the verge of turning rotten or had already turned bad enough to have the odor of spoiled meat.[12]

There were many Americans in business in Panama City, and their occupations varied from running restaurants and hotels to gambling houses and saloons, where a good deal of drinking and betting took place. In these gambling casinos, it was not unusual for shootings or knifings to take place over what a man might consider a suspicious turn of the card.

Travelers often had to wait a long time for a ship, and California-bound men became uneasy as their money began to run short. They had already paid as much as $300 for first-class steamer accommodations, or $100 for second- to third-class cabins, if they were lucky. If there was a run on steamer space, steerage could cost as much as $85 to $100. But even first-class staterooms were not what a passenger might expect. Such a room "contained three berths, one above another, together with a cushioned locker which could accommodate another passenger; each room had a mirror, toilet stand, washbowl, water bottles and glasses. . . . Outside the staterooms, the saloons were furnished with long tables, at which the passengers sat for meals and which could be used for reading or writing between meals."[13]

Steerage aboard any of the steamships making the run between San Francisco and Panama City offered little comfort. In steerage, passengers had no private rooms, and often there was no segregation of the sexes. Berths were arranged in three tiers, one above another, with no more than two and a half feet between the upper berth and the deck. In addition, these berths were nothing more than narrow canvas bags just over six feet long and about thirteen inches wide.[14] One or two toilets served the first and second class, and steerage passengers were lucky if they had a single toilet in their area. The shipowner's idea was to cram as many paying passengers into the steerage hole as possible. (The passengers' comfort was not taken into consideration.) The profits made by transporting Gold Rush people to California became yet another way of making a profit by mining the would-be miners.

Even with a ticket in one's pocket, time passed slowly for people waiting for a ship to take them to California. Panama City was overcrowded, and there were cases of cholera, yellow fever, and dysentery that took a toll of men on their way to the goldfields. Even men who managed to remain healthy sometimes lost their California grubstake at the Monte tables or on bets made at cock fights.

When a steamer bound for San Francisco put into port, excitement ran high. But a man with ticket in hand could not be certain that he would be one of the California-bound passengers, for sometimes more tickets were sold than there was space available aboard the steamship. When this kind of error occurred, some of the ticket holders found they would have to remain in Panama City until the next steamer put into port. But William Bourn was lucky. Like all other aspects of his Panama crossing, boarding a ship for San Francisco fell into place as though it were only natural that it should be that way.

3 Because the design of the early Gold Rush steamers—such as the *California,* the *Oregon,* the *Isthmus,* the *Antelope,* and the *Columbus*—was fairly uniform, the ship that William Bourn sailed aboard from Panama City's harbor no doubt had upper decks that ran unobstructed from stem to stern, except for the deckhouse amidship where the navigation room and officers' quarters were located.[15] If the weather was warm—and it generally was—and no storm threatened, the passengers spent most of their time on the open upper decks, taking walks, playing games, or resting beneath canvas awnings to avoid the glare of the sun. In these shaded spots, some played cards, some read or took time to write their impressions of their journey in journals or in letters to be mailed home from harbors where the steamers dropped anchor during the two- to three-week voyage.

Among the harbors that were stops for these steamers were San Juan del Sur, Nicaragua, and the Mexican ports of Acapulco, Manzanillo, San Blas, and Mazatlán. In many of these ports of call, ships took on tropical fruits, vegetables, and other fresh foods to stretch their supplies. Also, at such stops on the northward voyage, the captains purchased coal and wood for the boiler room to be sure the engines did not run out of fuel. By 1851, however, most ships limited their ports of call to either Acapulco or Manzanillo, for both harbors always had supplies on hand, and Manzanillo also was noted for its export of silver bullion.[16]

North of Mazatlán, the weather became much cooler, and beyond San Diego it was not unusual to hit rough seas and stormy weather. Then, from Monterey to San Francisco, navigation often became difficult as great fogbanks enveloped the ships. Here, passengers aboard the steamships suddenly found themselves out of the dreadful heat south of the Tropic of Cancer and in cold winds and damp fog that chilled them to the bone. To add to the discomfort of the voyage, the food, which had already been suspect for its freshness, now no longer left any doubt as to its unfitness for human consumption.

Conditions aboard the Panama steamers were often so bad that passengers wrote angry letters to San Francisco newspapers once they had stepped ashore in California. Their complaints ranged from crowded conditions, rotting food, and filthy conditions in their quarters and the dining saloon, to the lack of enough toilets to come even close to handling the passengers' sanitary needs during the voyage.

Under such intolerable conditions, William Bourn must have been more than happy when he received notice that they were approaching the entrance to the Golden Gate. Even a relatively brief fourteen- to seventeen-day voyage aboard such a ship was a hardship never to be forgotten.

4 Sometime during the early fall of 1850, William Bourn arrived in San Francisco. His trip from New York via the Isthmus and then by steamship to San Francisco took around thirty-three days. And though there were discomforts during the voyages from New York to Chagres and from Panama City to San Francisco, these were not difficult for Bourn, who was accustomed to going to sea in much smaller vessels than the steamships operated by Howland and Aspinwall.

Although Bourn left no record of what it was like to sail through the Golden Gate and enter San Francisco Bay, four years later, when Sarah Bourn sailed into the harbor, she described all that she saw. To her, the passage was "a perfect archway . . . formed by rocks . . . but after having passed through one feels . . . secure, so beautifully is the harbour protected by the adjacent islands and coast."[17]

William Bourn's view of San Francisco was of a confusion of deserted ships, bare hills covered with wooden and canvas buildings, and the general appearance of a temporary city carelessly thrown together to provide immediate shelter without any plans for the future. And in a very real way, this *was* the nature of the city during the beginning years of the Gold Rush.

On the waterfront, Bourn was greeted by his father-in-law, Captain George Chase, who had been meeting all incoming ships for almost a month as he awaited Bourn's arrival. Chase and Bourn made their way to one of their own ships anchored with hundreds of others in the bay.[18] Here, Chase explained to Bourn that they would make their home aboard the ship until all their cargo had been sold. After that, there were business opportunities for them in San Francisco, in the mining country, and even in the shipment of cargo and passengers to such inland ports as Stockton and Sacramento.

To William Bourn, San Francisco offered great excitement and the potential for making his fortune. Still, he did not think it a city in which to raise a family, so when he wrote to Sarah, he made it clear that it would be a matter of months, perhaps a year or more, before he would have her risk a trip to San Francisco. In the meanwhile, he would find decent housing, get started in business, and send for her when he thought he could offer her something that would be more like a home in a settled community than this rough-and-tumble seaport for men bound to and from the mining country of the Sierra Nevada foothills.

5 William Bourn and George Chase sold the last of the cargo from the *Powhatan* then entered into the local shipping business, mainly through Captain Chase. By 1852, Bourn was a commercial banker at 68 Front Street. During these early days in San Francisco, the new banker took advantage of the many business opportunities that ranged from shipping to the acquisition of mining stock.[19]

Even though he missed Sarah, Bourn hesitated to have her come to San Francisco. Housing was poor, and the growing port city lacked law and order. The streets were dusty in the dry months and absolute mudholes during the wet seasons. Although Captain Chase's wife, with at least one of his six daughters, arrived in San Francisco in 1852, Bourn hesitated to send for Sarah until 1854.[20]

When he finally instructed Sarah to plan her trip to California, he advised her to take a Cornelius Vanderbilt steamer and come by way of Nicaragua. Even though the landmass was wider at Nicaragua, the route shortened the distance from New York to California by 375 miles; also, it was cooler and offered fewer opportunities to come down with a terrible fever.

Cornelius Vanderbilt's advertisements overlooked the difficulties encountered in the Nicaragua crossing, but Sarah Chase Bourn came from sturdy stock, and the trip to California by this route did not bother her. To the contrary, she found the trip was filled with wonder and excitement. She boarded a steamship in New York, and it made very good time as it sailed to San Juan del Norte at the mouth of the San Juan River. Here, the Vanderbilt company offered two means of passage to travelers bound up the San Juan River. Those with a minimum amount of money could hire *bongos* paddled and poled by natives. For more affluent passengers like Sarah Bourn, passage upstream was by small river steamers that puffed and paddled their way up the river to Lake Nicaragua's Virgin Bay.

From Virgin Bay, the voyage to the north end of Lake Nicaragua was almost a hundred miles by a lake steamer that afforded passengers a fine view of the large lake and of the high mountains to the north, as well as the heavy growth of trees that marked the shoreline. When the steamer reached the northern end of the lake, Sarah Bourn and the other passengers boarded wagons or rode mules on the plank road that crossed the mountains to the west. After a journey of some twelve to eighteen miles, they arrived at the Pacific seaport of San Juan del Sur. The town was no more than a cluster of ramshackle frame buildings posing as hotels, set among green foliage with a background of heavily forested hills.

If all the connections were made on time, this trip across Nicaragua was shorter than the Panama crossing. For Sarah Bourn, this was the case. She wrote to her brother, Philip Chase, on May 28, 1854, that her journey from New York to San Francisco took only twenty-nine days.[21]

As Sarah stood on the deck as her steamer sailed into San Francisco Bay and dropped anchor, her impressions of what she saw did not offer great promise. As she wrote to Philip, "the only conspicuous building . . . that presents itself to view, upon entering is the hospital, a large brick building several stories in height (naval hospital), and situated on a point named Rincon, the whole country is very undulated, and presents a barren appearance in regard to forests, shrubbery, etc., but a fine climate obviates much of that, not withstanding, 'tis very sandy."[22]

Still, Sarah had successfully made the journey from New York to San Francisco, and she was filled with joy at the sight of William who was waiting on the pier. No matter how disappointing the appearance of the city inside the Golden Gate, Sarah's joy at seeing the tall, handsome figure of William Bourn waiting for her more than made up for the rough, uninviting look of this harbor city. To Sarah, who had not seen her husband for almost four years, it all became more than worthwhile as she stepped onto the pier and felt Bourn's strong arms hold her close while he told her how much he had missed her.

4

San Francisco: A Rough City of Golden Dreams

William Bourn and Sarah made their first San Francisco home at Bay State House on Front Street, which would serve them until something better could be found or built. Although Sarah was happy to be with her husband, she seldom saw him during the day. Will was establishing himself as a banker and as a man willing to make investments in anything that showed promise of turning a profit.

As Sarah became acquainted with this Gold Rush city, she gave a good picture of living conditions in her letters to her brother Philip. In describing the weather, she stated, "the winds are severe, but . . . one can with comfort wear woolen dresses the year round." As for beauty, she saw nothing to please her eyes: ". . . there is not a tree or hardly a shrub to meet the eye, in this City [one sees] perfect sand hill and the streets are or have been in a perfect turmoil, occasioned by the grades, and you never saw a busier set of people than are now at work." [1]

Among the busy people at work, none could have been busier than William Bourn. He seemed to have an eye for good deals, and in his bank on Front Street he was privy to ventures that showed a promising future. In many of his business deals, Bourn was often the principal stockholder and the man behind the scenes, investing in a wide range of growing enterprises such as shipping, the mercantile trade, agriculture, the first gas company, which was in the process of putting up gas lights for the lower part of Market Street, and the purchase of mining stocks.

Bourn's investments in mines included what was to become the Empire

Mine on Ophir Hill in Grass Valley. When he made this investment, he had no thought of ultimately owning and running the mine; he saw it as only one of many speculative investments. He became one of the shrewd players who saw the possibilities of great wealth as California's Gold Rush mining country began to change from placer mining to deep hard-rock mines. These new mines required capital, men who were able to invest in all the necessary equipment, and labor. Mining engineers would be needed to locate rich quartz veins, bring the ore to the surface, and oversee men and machinery to crush the ore and get the gold from ton after ton of quartz.

Gold was only one path to riches for William Bourn. He also was aware of San Francisco's needs as the town began to grow from a rough-and-tumble Gold Rush port into a city that would need all the trappings of civilization. As he worked long hours laying the foundation for the family fortune, Sarah—who was expecting their first child—observed this growing city as she kept up a steady correspondence with her brother and other members of the family.

In a September 25, 1854, letter to Philip, she wrote of the clouds of dust the wind blew about during the middle of the day. Then she wrote, "many tell me the rainy season is the most delightful. I'll tell you when I have experienced it, the streets are planked instead of paved, and the lower part of the City is lighted by gas, and soon 'twill be the upper part." Yet even as she wrote about the coming of gas-lighted streets, she did not mention that William was involved with the San Francisco Gas Company, which was in the process of making San Francisco "the first city west of St. Louis to light its streets by gas which was made from imported coal."[2]

As Sarah awaited the birth of her child, she and William were happy about the growth of his business ventures. His partnership in the shipping business with her father continued to do well, as were his commercial banking business and his many investments in such diverse affairs as the San Francisco Gas Company and mining stocks. The Empire Mining Company of Grass Valley had yielded between 1852 and 1854 over $900,000 in gold.[3] So the birth of Mary (Maye) Champney Bourn on February 11, 1855, came as a delightful bonus to the Bourns.

Two years later, the Bourns moved to 15 Waverly Place, and while they adjusted to their new home, Sarah gave birth on May 31, 1857, to William Bowers Bourn II, who would be brought up in a much more civilized city than Sarah had seen upon her arrival by steamship in 1854. Two years after her arrival, San Francisco's Second Committee of Vigilance gathered a citizen-army of between five and six thousand men, built Fort Gunnybags on the present site of 243 Sacramento Street, and armed this sandbagged fort with thirty cannons, plenty of ammunition, and several thousand muskets. Here, these self-appointed guardians of the law tried and hanged the notorious politician-racketeer, James P. Casey, who in 1852 shot and killed James King of William, editor of the *Daily Evening Bulletin.* Another murderer, Charles Cora, also awaited trial in this fort. This act of vigilance—for the second time since the hanging of criminals by the First Committee of Vigilance in 1851—had a strong impact on the city's criminal element, which beat a hasty retreat out of San Francisco. So young William Bourn II was a baby in a city known throughout the country as one that would not tolerate acts of crime and violence.

2 Searching for a better home for their growing family, the Bourns moved to another house at Fremont Street near Folsom Street sometime in 1858. While they were living here, Sarah became pregnant again, and the family moved once more, during 1859, to Third and Brannan Street. On June 5, 1859, their third child was born and named Sarah Frances (Zaidee) Bourn.

That same month, another rich mining discovery took place in western Utah Territory, in what was to become Nevada, when two miners named Patrick McLaughlin and Peter O'Riley made rich silver strikes in Six-Mile Canyon. At once, Henry Paige Comstock and Emmanuel Penrod, who had been working in the canyon, claimed that the strike was in ground they had been mining. After some debate, the men reached an agreement that resulted in a four-way partnership. Then on June 22, John D. Winters Jr. and J. A. Osborne were given a one-third interest in what was to be known as the Comstock Lode for building two *arrastras* to crush the ore.[4]

Samples of the ore were sent to J. J. Ott's Assay Office in Nevada City, and tests showed that the ore was worth almost $4,000 in gold and silver per ton! This was at a time when silver ore that assayed for more than $100 per ton was thought to be a very good grade, well worth the expense of mining it.[5]

By July 1, 1859, this news was reported in the *Nevada Journal* of Nevada City. Shortly after, the news spread throughout California's gold country and became the talk of San Francisco's financial world, as miners, saloon keepers, merchants, and even drovers with herds of livestock headed for Washoe and the new bonanza.

The rush to the boomtowns of Gold Hill and Virginia City began with the hard trip through Placerville and over the Sierra Nevada before the snows of winter closed what passed for a road that climbed into the high granite country to cross what is today's Echo Pass. It then made the descent on a cliff-hanging road that gave a view of Lake Bigler (Tahoe) and Lake Valley. But long before a miner bound for Washoe ever reached this height, he had to wait in line at Placerville for many hours, and sometimes even days, until he could move ahead and enter the stream of traffic.

Beyond Placerville, during the Comstock boom, there were as many as ninety way stations on the mountain road. These places bore such names as Three, Five, Six, Nine and Ten Mile Houses. There was also Sportman's Hall at Pollock Pines, where as many as five hundred to a thousand head of horses and mules could be kept in the stables and corrals each night.

After Sportsman's Hall came such way-stops as Pacific House, Riverton House, Whitehall, Silver Fork, Kyburz, Strawberry, Slippery Ford House, George Swan's Upper Toll House, Snow Slide House, Audrian's Station, Sixty Mile House or Summit Station. "Here, above seven thousand feet, travelers saw a cliff-hanging road cut into the sheer granite face. In the distance they could see Lake Valley and had their first view of Lake Tahoe."[6]

In Lake Valley the popular stop for travelers headed for the Comstock country was Yank's Station. Here, the corrals held two hundred head of horses, mules, and oxen. There was also a fourteen-room hostelry, two saloons, a general merchandise store, a cooperage, and a blacksmith shop.[7]

Beyond Yank's Station, the road followed the Pioneer Trail, and travelers passed such stops as Hiram Barton's Milk Ranch, Fountain Place, Pine Grove House, Woodburn's Sawmill, Hawthorne House, Sierra House, Miller House, McCumber's, Lapham's Stateline Hotel, and Friday's Station, where the road swung up into the mountains and then dropped into the Carson Valley down the steep Kingsbury Grade.

Once a Washoe-bound traveler reached the foot of Kingsbury Grade, he was in the beautiful Carson Valley. Here, the road headed north along the foothills of the Sierra Nevada to Mormon Station (today's Genoa), and from there, north to Carson City. Many travelers stopped here overnight and heard the latest news about the Comstock Lode. The next day, miners and all the others bound for this big bonanza headed upgrade through the short sagebrush country, crossed in and out of Silver City and Gold Hill, then swung up the last grade to enter Virginia City.[8] There, crowds of prospectors, potential investors, ladies of the evening, saloon keepers, and faro dealers made their new home on the steep east side of Sun Peak (now called Mount Davidson) as dreams of big stakes and sudden riches danced in their minds. This was the kind of excitement that William Bourn heard about in San Francisco, as the Comstock Lode became the talk of the city's financial district. Stockbrokers, mining men, and merchants all yearned to be in on the action, because everything they heard promised that this new strike—in both gold and silver—was bound to be a Big Bonanza.

3 Two years after the discovery of silver and gold in western Utah Territory, William Bourn's family moved from their home at Third and Brannan Streets to a larger house at 1105 Taylor Street. On June 20, 1861, Sarah Bourn gave birth to her fourth child, who was named Frank Washington Bourn. By this time, William had become interested in two mines in Gold Hill in what had become Nevada Territory on March 2, 1861.[9] The Imperial and Empire Mines had both showed great promise and had stamp mills established in 1860. Now, Bourn awaited the incorporation of these mines and the first issues of stock. As he already knew, the San Francisco Stock and Exchange Board was to be established before the end of 1862, and with his connections in the financial world of San Francisco, he would hear of good investments in the Comstock Lode before such knowledge became common. When the Exchange was actually established in September, 1862, many of the Comstock mines put their stocks up for sale. Bourn purchased shares in two Gold Hill mines that eventually merged, the Imperial and the Empire.

Rich in both gold and silver, these mines paid a steady and handsome profit for a good number of years. Bourn crossed the Sierra Nevada many times to check his investments, and he became thoroughly acquainted with deep mines where the shafts took workers into the depths to work with pick, drill, shovel, and black powder in miles of subterranean galleries or drifts. Ore was brought to the surface where it was crushed in stamp mills and then dumped into metal pans to be subjected to a new extraction process invented by Almarin B. Paul—a friend of George Hearst. Almarin "dumped quicksilver, salt, and copper sulphate into his pans. After a trial of hot water, he shifted to steam as a method of providing heat. He soon adopted heavy iron mullers that would grind as well as mix the pulverized rock. Almost unconsciously, he then added another chemical. Iron filings worn off the muller and pan by friction proved to be an essential ingredient."[10]

Thus the "Washoe Pan Process" was born, which was to prove a major asset to hard-rock mines where gold or silver, or both, had to be coaxed out of the ore. One of the major developments in mining on the Comstock was the square sets of timbers devised by Philip Deidesheimer, which meant "that timbers were mortised and tenoned at the ends so that they could be fitted together to form hollow cubes, each cube interlocked with the next in endless series. In large underground chambers some of the hollow cubes could be filled with waste rock . . . to make a solid pillar of wood and rock from floor to roof."[11]

Major problems in the Comstock mines were the terrible heat and the lack of fresh air as the mines went deeper and deeper on either a straight or incline shaft as far down as three thousand feet below the surface. To solve these problems, mine owners cut air shafts that went into the mines, and alternated working crews at least every hour. Even then, they had to douse the men with ice water so they could stand temperatures that often reached over 100 degrees Fahrenheit.

There were other dangers as well—cave-ins that crushed workers or sent them plunging to their death at the bottom of the shaft, and mine fires that burned the timbers and trapped workers until their lungs starved for air. There were also run-of-the-mill accidents when tired men smashed drill-holders' hands with sledgehammers, or when men hit themselves or tapped into a stream of hot water that might be as much as 170 degrees Fahrenheit.

To keep subsurface water from scalding the workers or flooding the shaft and drifts, the mine owners installed large pumps. Still, despite the costs to mine owners and the constant danger to miners, who might number as many as five to seven hundred men per shift, the richness of the lodes kept both mine owners and miners willing to risk money and lives on the riches of the earth.

Bourn was one of these players in a game that promised either great riches or the loss of money that could have been used in a wiser fashion.

4 By 1864, William Bourn was making a considerable name for himself in the financial world of San Francisco. His commercial banking business prospered, his investments in mining stocks were bringing in good

dividends, as was the Empire Mine at Grass Valley, and the Imperial and the Empire mines at Gold Hill in the Comstock country of Nevada became bonanzas. Bourn also realized profits from his investments in the San Francisco Gas Company and the Fireman's Fund Insurance Company, which was formed in 1863. In addition, he continued to maintain an interest in commercial shipping, and he was purchasing real estate. It was a time when most of his business ventures were offering good returns, and this tall, handsome man became highly respected in the financial world of San Francisco. He was known as a man of sharp wit who possessed what was called the "Bourn Luck."

During the early part of 1864, Sarah Esther Chase Bourn decided to travel to Brooklyn and visit her relatives, even though she knew she was with child and no doubt would give birth in the East. She and William talked it over, and he investigated the new trip across Panama via the forty-seven miles of the Panama Railroad Company, which was the successful dream of Cornelius Vanderbilt when it was completed in 1855. The cost in 1864 for this half-day trip from Panama City on the Pacific to Aspinwall on the Atlantic was only $25 for adults, half that for children under twelve years old, and for children under six years, one-quarter of an adult's fare.[12] After his investigation, Will gave his consent for Sarah to make the trip East. True, he worried about not being with her when she gave birth to their fifth child, and he was also concerned about taking care of the other children while Sarah visited branches of the family living in the East, but he agreed to her wishes and saw to her travel arrangements.

After Sarah sailed to Panama City on a steamship, William threw himself into his many endeavors, but his working hours did not interfere with watching out for the four children. Though they had servants and a woman to see to their needs, William tried to spend most evenings at home, for he wanted his children to be assured that they had not been deserted by their parents.

Through letters from Sarah, he was informed about the family in Brooklyn, and in the latter part of April, he received a letter from Sarah telling him of the birth of their fifth child, Ida Hoxie Bourn, on April 2, 1864. At the same time, Sarah said she would come home as soon as the baby was able to make the voyage to Colón, the train crossing of Panama, and the voyage up the Pacific Coast to San Francisco. Meanwhile, she implored him to lighten his work so he would not get the terrible headaches that often bothered him.

However, to ask Bourn to slow down was almost like trying to stop a runaway team. By this time, in addition to his own businesses and his control of stocks in various mines and other investments, William was one of the nonfounding directors of the Fireman's Insurance Fund[13] that took a great amount of his time because he was new to the insurance business.

But the men who had the courage to start this company on May 6, 1863, after listening to Captain William Holdredge, made certain that their Board of Directors contained San Francisco businessmen noted for their ability to make sound investments and employ men who could fulfill the jobs they had been hired to do. This resulted in the replacement of Captain Holdredge himself, who was deemed incapable of leading the Fireman's Fund along a profitable trail through the hazards of the insurance business. Consequently, the Board of Directors replaced Holdredge with Samuel Parker as president of the company before the end of 1863.[14]

Even as Bourn worried over what had to be done, he had his other San Francisco enterprises to be concerned about, as well as the need to go over the 1864 reports he received as the president of the Imperial Mining Company of Gold Hill, Nevada.[15] Even for a dynamic man like Bourn, the burden was almost too great, yet as a man of wealth he was careful about money and responsibilities. Hence, what some people saw as a certain stiffness about him only reflected the concerns that he had to wrestle with on a daily basis. These worries detracted from his true personality as a warm family man of great wit and humor.

5 At the beginning of the fall of 1864, Will was happy to see Sarah and baby Ida return home after their stay in Brooklyn. She told him of their relatives and described the new and easy journey across Panama aboard the forty-seven-mile railroad that Vanderbilt had financed. As she described it, the hard journey that Will had made in his crossing seemed like something that belonged in a nightmare.

Sarah told her husband that his sister, Hannah Bourn Ingalls, and her son, William, would be coming to visit them in the fall of 1865. This was good news to Will, who missed his sister and other family members, and he suggested to Sarah that he take some time off so they could show his sister something of Northern California.

However, Bourn's business ventures continued to be very demanding. His position as president of the Imperial Mining Company and the Empire

Mine of Gold Hill, Nevada, took more of his time than he had envisioned. Just to get to the booming Comstock, Bourn had to travel by steamboat to Sacramento, by the Sacramento Valley Railroad to Folsom, and then by stagecoach to Placerville and up and across the Sierra Nevada every time he was needed at Gold Hill.

Even so, both mines paid fine dividends in this Civil War period when the Union needed the riches of the Comstock Lode to fuel its war machine against the Confederacy. The Imperial Mining Company was returning $23.40 per ton of crushed and treated ore, and the Empire was returning $22.74 per ton, treated in the Washoe pan process.[16]

But as Will told Sarah about his investments in the Comstock Lode, he also told her that he had been buying more stock in the gold mine at Grass Valley, California. When she asked what its future might be, he went over its early history when George D. Roberts located the Ophir Hill lode in 1850. He found that the "vein runs in greenstone in a northwesterly and southeasterly direction, dipping westerly with an incline of 30 degrees." Roberts' attempts to get gold from such a narrow vein of quartz were unsuccessful, and in 1851 he sold this claim to Woodbury, Parks, and Company, who named it the Ophir and consolidated it with other claims in order to enlarge the mine. "Ophir Hill yielded liberally, but was mismanaged, and the owners failed in 1852. The mine was sold at auction, John R. Rush buying one half and the Empire Mining Company the other half." Then in 1854 "Rush sold his half interest to the Empire Mining Company for $15,000. In the ten years between 1854 and 1864 the Empire Mining Company took out $1,056,234."[17] And as Will told Sarah, the stock he was buying in this mine was now giving a steady return and offered an even better future.

As Will went over the prospects of the Empire Mining Company, of Grass Valley, he told Sarah that the mine had been sold once again. During her trip to Brooklyn, the mine was purchased by Captain S. W. Lee and A. H. Houston.[18] Even so, Bourn continued to invest in its stock issues.

What he hated to tell Sarah was that his investments at Gold Hill, Nevada, might be nearing a dangerous situation. The only official at the Imperial-Empire mine that Bourn could rely upon was P. J. Buckminster, the superintendent. In his letters to Bourn, Buckminster expressed concern that officers of the mine were not paying much attention to the possibility that a drift from the Apple and Bates Mine, owned by William Sharon, appeared to be cutting into the west red vein of the Imperial Mine.[19]

Still, with the many businesses that Bourn had to keep in mind, he believed it would be good for him and the family to have his sister and her son come to San Francisco for a visit. Not only did he wish to see his sister and his nephew, who would be a good companion for his son, but he also believed that once they arrived he would be forced to take time off from his many interests. This time would give him relaxation and perhaps relieve him of the terrible bouts of biliousness and headaches that bothered him more and more. All things considered, Bourn's decision to invite Hannah and Willie to come for an extended stay in San Francisco was definitely not a passing thought but a firm and happy decision.

5

An Interlude of Family Happiness

In the fall of 1865, the Bourns awaited the arrival of Hannah and Willie, coming by steamship from the East via Panama. Suddenly, Will received distressing news from the Imperial Silver Mining Company that indicated its dealings were not what he expected from a well-run business. On September 24, 1865, Bourn wrote to the mine's president and trustees and tendered his resignation as a trustee.[1]

Meanwhile, Bourn was informed that the new owners of the Empire Mine in Grass Valley—Captain S. W. Lee and A. H. Houston—had purchased additional property and had pumped water from the mine for about two months. On September 1864, they began to operate the mine on a systematic basis. Along with this, the new owners built a new thirty-stamp mill, added other structures and equipment, and even painted the interior of the mill's ceiling and exterior. Overall, the new stamp mill was designed so it resembled a steamboat in some ways, and it was called the "Steamboat Mill."[2]

With one mining investment apparently under good hands and with most of his other investments and business interests doing well, Will relaxed, as much as he ever could, and looked forward to sister Hannah's arrival.

2 On October 5, 1865, Hannah Bourn Ingalls and her son, Willie, who would celebrate his twelfth birthday at sea, boarded the steamship *New York* in the harbor at New York to begin their voyage to Panama on

their way west to San Francisco. The *New York* was a wooden side-wheel steamer that had been built and launched in 1864 at Greenpoint, Long Island, for Cornelius Vanderbilt. The vessel had first entered the service between New York and Aspinwall in September 1865. This large steamer had three decks, two masts, and accommodated 870 passengers—200 first-cabin, 170 second-cabin, and 500 steerage.[3]

Two days after sailing from New York, Hannah wrote to her husband and mentioned that their ship had steamed past Cuba.[4] The next sign of land was when they sailed into the new dock at Aspinwall. Here, they regained their land legs and got aboard one of the passenger cars of the Panama Railroad for the four- to four-and-a-half hour journey to cross the forty-seven miles of track that took the train from Aspinwall to Panama City. During this trip through the exotic interior of Panama, Hannah was amazed at the quantity and variety of food she saw growing in profusion both in the wild and on large plantations.

The next view they had was the old Spanish adobe buildings, the great cathedral, and the harbor where the Pacific Mail Steamship Company's vessel *Colorado*—another large side-wheel steamer—was already building a head of steam as the captain awaited passengers from the Panama Railroad.

The *Colorado* was an imposing sight to all who first saw her, for the ship was over three hundred feet long and weighed over three thousand tons. She had three decks, three masts, fifty-two staterooms on the main deck, and berths for 1,500 passengers in the steerage. And when Hannah and Willie sailed for San Francisco in 1865, the *Colorado* was armed against any threat from potential attack. The vessel had two 20-pound field cannons on the quarters and two 30-pounders forward. She was also armed with an assortment of rifles, muskets, and revolvers. While the arms on this passenger ship might have seemed strange, the passengers soon learned that there was danger from pirates of the Confederacy. The Aspinwall ship *Ariel* had been attacked at sea by the C.S.S. *Alabama* on December 7, 1862, when the *Ariel* was southbound from New York on her run to Aspinwall. The ship was not sunk, but the Confederate vessel forced the *Ariel* to allow a boarding party to come aboard, which robbed the ship of $9,500. On the Pacific Coast run, there was concern about both the possibility of attack by Confederates and also attack by pirates who were rumored to be active in the area.[5]

But the only stop the *Colorado* made on its voyage to San Francisco was at Acapulco Bay, where the ship's anchor was dropped and permission to come ashore was asked by the captain. In Hannah's letter of October 16,

1865, she wrote that at first they were denied permission to land, for this "miserable looking place . . . is in possession of the French and we are not allowed to go a shore, neither can we get any fruit as we expected." After some exchange of words, the American consul managed to talk the French into allowing the passengers to come ashore to purchase food. As Hannah described it, she "bought bananas, oranges, limes, and a basket."[6]

The stop in Acapulco was only a short break in the voyage and allowed the travelers hardly enough time to get their land legs back before they were under way again. Soon, the *Colorado's* paddle wheels slapped into the sea with a steady beat as the ship eased out of the harbor and headed northward along the Pacific Coast on the final leg of its voyage to San Francisco.

On October 27, 1865, the *Colorado* sailed through the Golden Gate and made her way to the Pacific Mail Steamship Company's wharf at the foot of Folsom Street.[7] Here, the *Colorado*'s voyage ended as the engines were halted, and the lines were tossed to waiting dockhands to tie the ship against the pier.

From the deck of the ship, Hannah caught sight of her brother William with Sarah, Mary, and young Willie standing and waving as they waited for them to follow the line of first-class passengers being escorted down the gangplank.[8] Here, Hannah felt an overwhelming joy at seeing her brother again, and when she reached the dock, the greeting from Will and Sarah was a grand reward after the long journey from New York. As Will had their luggage put aboard a carriage, Hannah got her first glimpse of San Francisco. On the carriage ride to the Bourn home, Will and Sarah gave her a vivid description of how much San Francisco had changed and how it continued to grow into something far greater than a seaport for the mad rush to the Gold Country that it had been in the earlier years. Now, it was spreading out as landfills made room for expansion beside San Francisco Bay. The city of barren hills was moving in the direction of becoming much more than temporary tents and shack—it was becoming a city of beauty.

3 Hannah was fascinated by the quality and quantity of fresh fruits and vegetables available for the Bourns' kitchen. During the first week of her visit, Hannah feasted so much that she felt compelled to write to her husband and mention that she was getting fleshy and heavier. Yet while she enjoyed her visit, she was very concerned about her brother, and she wrote to her husband, "It really makes me feel sad to see him devoting all his en-

ergies to the accumulation of wealth, he is thinking and planning all the time and so industrious and prudent so far as he is concerned."[9]

Meanwhile, twelve-year-old Willie Ingalls and his cousin, eight-year-old Willie Bourn, were having a great time, for they not only got to know each other as cousins but also became close friends. The two Willies traveled everywhere that William and Sarah took Hannah sightseeing. On one of these trips, Will took the family on a buggy ride on the Point Lobos Toll Road to the Cliff House, which had been built in 1863 by Captain Junius B. Foster.[10] When they stepped down from the buggy, they felt the ocean breeze and heard the roar of the breakers and the barking of the many Steller's sea lions that rested on Seal Rocks. As Will guided the family into the Cliff House, the buggy driver took the horses and carriage to a long, single-story parking stable for carriages and horses. As he did this, the Bourn party took a great view table overlooking Seal Rocks and the southward stretch of Ocean Beach. It was a lunch that neither Hannah nor Willie Ingalls would ever forget.

After lunch, Bourn directed his driver to take a sightseeing trip back to their home. As Willie Ingalls remembered, this side trip took them to Mission San Francisco de Asís, called Mission Dolores, which was founded by Father Francisco Palóu in 1776.[11] From here, the buggy ride took them through the upper part of the city, and they had a grand view of San Francisco Bay, Yerba Buena Island, Alcatraz and Angel Islands, and the East Bay hills that stretched for miles in a south-to-north direction—convoluted hills mainly covered with dry grass and scattered outgrowths of brush, with few trees except for oaks and some hidden groves of redwoods in shaded canyons that served as gathering places for banks of coastal fog. On the lower hills and the flats that stretched westward toward San Francisco Bay, William Bourn pointed out the growing community of Oakland.

As the month of December 1865 began, Hannah was fascinated by all the friends who visited Will and Sarah during the holidays. On December 8, the Bourns had a festive holiday dinner for eighteen. Late that night, William had a terrible bilious attack that required treatment "from a doctor who came to the house." Bourn recovered quickly and mentioned that he would have to make a trip to Washoe to check on something that was causing trouble in the Imperial Silver Mine in which he had agreed to continue his role as a trustee. Before he left, he enrolled his son in "a new school called Union College. It is under the direction of Dr. R. Townsend Huddart who has taught for many years in New York." In the rest of her letter of December 10, 1865, Hannah wrote that her brother offered to pay for the enrollment of Willie Ingalls in the same school.[12]

On December 17, 1865, Hannah wrote: "My brother has gone to Washoe. He left Saturday and will not be home until after Christmas. We do not know what has called him there at this season unless it is the depreciation of stocks, and he wishes to see for himself if there is a cause. It is a journey of several days through a rough and disagreeable part of the country, very cold with snow several feet deep."[13]

4 After William Bourn returned from the Comstock Lode at the beginning of January 1866, Willie Bourn and Willie Ingalls were enrolled in Union College. Unknown to them, however, Bourn had lost nearly $100,000 in a loan to his brother-in-law, Henry Bashford of New York. Bourn had trusted him when he loaned this large amount of money to him, but there was no security for the loan, and Bashford's failure to live up to his word "came upon him like a thunderbolt."[14]

Discouraged by the loss of money and the betrayal of his faith in Bashford, Will decided to take a break from work and show Hannah, Sarah, Mary (Maye), and the two Willies something of the countryside close to San Francisco. On February 27, 1866, the family got into the buggy and headed south to the Santa Clara Valley. Here, they visited Mission Santa Clara de Asís, which was built in 1777. The original church and the one to replace it were destroyed by a flood, then by an earthquake, so the Mission Santa Clara that the Bourns visited was the third building to represent the Catholic Church in the Santa Clara Valley. That night, they stayed at Saratoga Springs, named after the Congress Springs at Saratoga, New York. During this period, wealthy San Franciscans often stopped at fashionable resorts that had grown up around warm-water springs.[15]

After the Bourn party left Saratoga Springs, they passed through San Jose and traveled into the foothills of the Coast Range some twelve miles southwest of San Jose. Here, they visited the New Almadén Quicksilver Mine. This mine, rich in cinnabar, was first owned by Andrés Castillero, who claimed it in 1845 when he was a captain of the Mexican Cavalry. By 1863, he had lost his claim through a decision of the United States Supreme Court. The mine was bought in 1863 by the Quicksilver Mining Company, whose president was Samuel F. Butterworth, and it became very prosperous. Two separate towns near the mine housed the Mexican workers and the Cornish workers, just as two separate cemeteries housed the dead of the Catholics and Protestants.[16]

To young Willie Ingalls, the visit into the depths of the mine was exciting enough to be recorded in his journal. As Willie wrote, "we went down into the mine. Mary [Maye] Bourn and another gentleman led the way and a Spanish boy took them down, another boy took Uncle William, Willie and myself, and I enjoyed it very much. Mother and Aunt Sarah did not go down into the mine but went into the tunnel . . . I went down to the bottom of the mine and I knocked some pieces off and the men said they were very rich and while we were down there, there were four or five blasts and Uncle William was told that it was the richest that they had ever struck."[17]

After visiting the New Almadén Quicksilver Mine, the Bourn party visited Mission San Jose, then stopped for the night at another watering place called Warm Springs, located on the road from San Jose to Oakland. The resort was situated on land that had formerly belonged to Rancho Agua Caliente, and its hot springs earlier had been a favorite of Ohlone (Costanoan) Indians, who liked to soak in the hot water. In 1850, part of the rancho and the springs were purchased by Clemente Columbet, who put up buildings for a resort that became one of the fashionable watering places in the Bay Region. In 1858, Columbet leased the resort to Alexander Beaty.[18]

It was March 4, 1866, and Hannah was fascinated by the blooming wild flowers and the variety of birds. To Hannah, the country was an Eden filled with fruits and vegetables. A warm breeze turned fields of grass into waves of green interspersed with wild flowers. She heard the songs of many types of birds gathering food and materials for their nests.[19]

A few days after this trip to the Santa Clara Valley, Samuel Parker, president of the Fireman's Fund Insurance Company and a close friend of William Bourn, died suddenly on March 14, 1866, as he entered the Lick House for lunch.[20] This loss saddened Will considerably, and as a director of the Fireman's Fund Insurance Company, he knew that it would be vital to find a replacement for Sam Parker. Bourn also knew that finding a man of Parker's quality would not be an easy task. The more he thought about it, the more he wanted to leave San Francisco for another family vacation that would give him time to relax and to think of what qualities the candidate for the office of president of the Fireman's Fund Insurance Company should possess.

5 On April 7, 1866, the Bourns and the Ingalls sailed aboard the steamer *Paul Pry* for Napa County. As they sailed up San Francisco Bay, Hannah wrote that "the absence of trees all about San Francisco is a very marked feature, but I feel the mountains make up for it in a great measure." William told the family that he needed to take a brief holiday as he thought over the offer from the Fireman's Fund Insurance Company to become its third president. When the *Paul Pry* reached the north end of San Francisco Bay, Will told the family that they still had a way to go before they reached White Sulphur Springs, a popular watering place for San Francisco tycoons of the mid-nineteenth century.[21]

The *Paul Pry* worked its way beyond San Francisco Bay and passed Mare Island, where there was a dry dock. When Hannah wrote to her husband, she described Mare Island as a place "where vessels are brought to be repaired . . . there was one upon the stocks, and a number of others waiting their turn. The *Monitor Camanche* lay there; also an old craft that was in the War of 1812."[22]

Beyond Mare Island, the *Paul Pry* entered the narrow Napa River and continued slowly until it reached Suscol Landing beside Suscol Creek's confluence with the Napa River. Here, at this landing and creek named after the Suscol or southwestern branch of the Patwin tribe, Bourn hired a wide wagon that had "three seats with a great deal of springs, and (was) covered." As Hannah wrote, the rental of a wagon with good springs allowed them to avoid riding a stage, for "stages on these routes have no springs, and are very low." The day was warm for early April, and Hannah found the Napa Valley beautiful. She was fascinated with the splendid oak trees, the green grass, and the large flock of sheep that she saw grazing on the Oak Knoll Ranch.[23]

Willie Ingalls described this trip in his journal and stated that "we did not arrive at the springs until about eight o'clock." In the morning, Willie wrote that "the hotel is situated right in the canyon on the side of a mountain, and there is a stream of water running right by the side of the house." But there was much that Willie did not know about White Sulphur Springs. "The resort . . . had a long history . . . back to 1853 when it was founded by the Alstrom family who also built Hotel St. Helena. Once the Del Monte of California, it was the watering place for San Francisco tycoons of the mid-19th century, who came here by train and stagecoach, then by carriages to the springs. A special Western Union telegraph office kept the wealthy visitors in touch with the San Francisco Stock Exchange."[24]

After an evening at White Sulphur Springs, the Bourn party drove back to the main road and then continued on to Calistoga Hot Springs, where the family saw the geysers and hot springs, which, as Willie Ingalls wrote, "will boil an egg in three minutes, and we boiled one and it tasted as well as though it had been boiled by the fires." Here, there were twelve cottages and a hotel. The cottages were all named, and as Willie wrote, "we spent the night at the Revere House."[25]

On the morning of April 9, Willie Ingalls wrote that he and the rest of the party were up early to watch the geysers blow steam and hot water into the air. He also mentioned a swimming pool, which was "warm, and Uncle William, Mary (Maye), Willie and myself all went in bathing. Uncle William and I swam out in the deep part and dove down and had some fun. I must tell you about Willie: he had been boasting of his swimming, saying that he could swim better than I, so I let him keep on, so when I got in I just swam out to see if he would follow me. But instead of following me he kept hold of the rope, standing there and looking at me, and he could not swim a stroke."[26]

The next day, William Bourn received word that he was needed at the Fireman's Fund Insurance Company as soon as possible. That morning, April 10, the family boarded a carriage that took them to Napa. Here, they "took steamer cars for Suscol Landing, about four miles from Napa. We took the boat which took us down to the City; on our way down we stopped at Mare Island and at Vallejo. At Mare Island there is a fine fort and it is where all the man-o-war men stay, and they have gas on the Island, and they have a Burial Ground. This is where they bury all the sailors that die on the Island."[27]

Upon the return of the Bourn party to San Francisco, William Bourn met with the directors of the Fireman's Fund Insurance Company. They wanted him to become and remain president of the company on a full-time basis, but he told them he was too involved in other affairs. He knew that he would have to devote a great amount of time to the company in order to become a president who was careful about money, because as chairman of the finance committee, he would have to possess greater knowledge of the firm's operation than anybody else in the company.[28] Still, Bourn was the first to admit that he did not know insurance, and he believed the firm should have somebody familiar with underwriting and all the various aspects of the insurance business. So he made it clear that he would remain as president only until the board of directors was able to find a man truly qualified for the post.

Knowing that Hannah's husband would be right for this position, he offered him the job if he would move to San Francisco. Hannah pointed out in a letter to her husband that their son Willie and Willie Bourn were good companions, especially in games and sports.[29] But Ingalls turned down the opportunity to come to California because he was doing very well in the East. Within Hannah's letters is an underlying sorrow that her husband would not consider the position, because she was happy to be near her brother and she was well aware of the friendship of the two young cousins, who by this time were playing baseball for the Rincon team and having a grand time as companions in school, sports, and travel.

Unable to convince his brother-in-law to come to San Francisco and accept the position of president of the Fireman's Fund Insurance Company, William Bourn stayed on as honorary president of the firm. But he also agreed with the board of directors that David Jackson Staples, who had crossed the Overland Trail in 1849 with the Boston-Newton Company in search of a fortune in Gold Rush California, would make a good president. Never finding his fortune in gold, David Staples had tried hauling goods from Stockton to the mines in the Mokelumne Hill area. Then in 1850 he bought a tract of rich farming land southwest of the Mokelumne River, which he ran until 1862, when he was appointed port warden of San Francisco. In 1866 he accepted the position of vice-president once the insurance company agreed that he could serve on a trial basis for the first year.[30]

6 Once Bourn was satisfied that the board of directors had selected a good officer to head the Fireman's Fund Insurance Company, he suggested that the family do more traveling and sightseeing before Hannah had to return to Brooklyn. He proposed a trip to the grove of Big Trees in Calaveras County.

Again, the two Willies were given leave from school, as was Maye. All the family boarded the river steamer *Julia* during the first week of May and sailed up the San Joaquin River to the inland port of Stockton. Here, they boarded a rough-riding stagecoach that bounced and swayed as it traveled along the dirt road that climbed out of the San Joaquin Valley into the foothill country of the Mother Lode.[31]

By May 8, 1866, the stagecoach had passed through Angels Camp and stopped for the night at Murphys, a Gold Rush town left over from the boom times. Here, the Bourn party stayed over for a short visit. The next day, they finished the twenty-mile journey from Murphys into the Sierra Nevada and the grove of Big Trees, where they stayed at James W. Sperry's hotel. During their visit, they saw the "stump upon which four quadrilles can be danced. It is covered by a very pretty octagon shaped building, painted white, with green blinds."[32]

Even though this dance hall on the stump of a tree intrigued Hannah Ingalls, the whole thing represented a tragedy. In the early 1850s, Captain H. W. Hanford, head of the Union Water Company that had built the flume into Murphys, decided to fell this great *Sequoia gigantea,* then strip it of its bark and send the remains to New York as an exhibit of a natural giant. The tree was over three hundred feet tall and at least thirty feet in diameter, and the loggers hired to fell it found that axes and saws were not the right tools for the job. They resorted to boring into the great tree with pump augers from opposite sides. Five men worked at this for twenty-two days. When they finished, they inserted wedges and drove them in with logs hung by ropes from the tree. Finally, when the workers took a lunch break on the last day, the great tree fell with a thunderous crash. The loggers then cut the bark off the fallen tree and numbered the pieces so they could be put together in San Francisco to give viewers an idea of the size of this giant. The tree's bark was freighted by wagon to the Port of Stockton, where it was loaded aboard a ship and brought to San Francisco. There, the numbered pieces of bark were reassembled, and the "tree" was exhibited. After this, it was sent around the Horn to New York for another display.[33]

The Bourn Family saw more than a dance hall on a stump. Close to this was a bowling alley on the flattened surface of another trunk. The surface was eighty-one feet, which gave enough space for two alley beds.[34] But the greatest sight was the magnificent Calaveras Grove of Big Trees with trails that wound beneath giant trees that dated back to before the birth of Christ and gave visitors a feeling of being in a natural cathedral.

On May 10, 1866, the Bourn party caught the stagecoach to Murphys, where they stayed overnight in the Murphys Hotel. During this part of their homeward trip, William was uncomfortable, because during his last night at Sperry's Big Trees Hotel he had broken his upper set of false teeth. The following morning, they caught the stagecoach to Stockton, which took them through Angels Camp then down the rough grade to Copperopolis—a copper mining town of about five thousand people. From there, the stagecoach rocked and swayed until it reached the floor of the San Joaquin Valley and traveled on to Stockton, where the Bourns caught a steamer bound downriver for San Francisco.

Upon their arrival in the city, Will went to the dentist at once. The dentist worked part of Saturday and all day Sunday, and when Bourn received his new set of teeth on Monday, Hannah wrote: "He is greatly pleased with the change, and they are an improvement upon the set he broke. He has ordered two more sets as he says no money would tempt him to be in that situation again." [35]

Will suggested that in Hannah's remaining time in San Francisco he take her to Yosemite. Although he had to leave for Nevada on May 16, 1866, he hoped to return early enough so that the Yosemite trip could take place. Realizing that her husband might not get back early enough, Sarah said "she would be willing to go without him under the circumstances if we could join a party, and it has occurred to me (the artist) Mr. Watkins will soon leave for that locality, and I am going down to see what arrangements can be made as soon as I post this letter." [36]

Unfortunately, Hannah never got to see Yosemite, because Will's trip to settle a problem of infringement upon the Imperial-Empire Mine at Gold Hill, Nevada, took more time than he expected. Although William Sharon's claim-jumping tunnel, which ran from the nearby Apple and Bates Mine, was taking tons of ore from their west vein, Bourn could not get the other officers of the Imperial-Empire to react against what amounted to outright theft.[37]

By the time Will returned from Nevada, Hannah was ready to sail for home. The remaining day and evening were spent at the Bourn home, and on Saturday, June 9, 1866, Hannah and Willie boarded the large wooden side-wheel steamer *Golden Age,* which was owned by the Pacific Mail Steamship Company and had three decks, three masts, and was almost 273 feet long. Once the farewells were said and all the passengers and baggage were aboard, the *Golden Age* moved away from the Pacific Mail pier at the foot of Folsom Street. As passengers stood on the decks and waved their last goodbyes, the *Golden Age* was guided out into the stream by the pilot boat as it made its way toward the Golden Gate. For Hannah and Willie, the next port they would see would be Manzanillo, Mexico, on June 15, 1866. Seven days after that, they would disembark at Panama City and catch the train across Panama to Aspinwall, where they would board the *Northern Light,* which would take them to New York.[38]

For the Bourns and the Ingallses, the days in San Francisco and in the areas of Northern California would always remain as a time of great joy, a time of getting to know each other again, and a time to savor in lifelong memories.

6

Bourn's Nevada Adventures

In the latter months of 1866 and the beginning of 1867, William Bourn held positions that would have been too much for an ordinary man. In his San Francisco office, he carried out the combined duties of president and director of the board of the Fireman's Fund Insurance Company. At the same time, he served as president of the combined Imperial-Empire Mine at Gold Hill, Nevada; found the energy to add more shares to his portfolio of mining stocks in the Comstock Lode and the Empire and North Star mines in Grass Valley, California; and continued to investigate other gold mines in the Grass Valley area as well as other silver strikes in Nevada.

At this same time, Bourn was becoming interested in other money-making ventures, such as the purchase of city lots and buildings in San Francisco and timber land in Michigan and Washington Territory, and possible investments in ranches as far south as San Bernardino and north of San Francisco in Napa County. He was always searching for investments that might promise a healthy return on his money.[1]

Even as Bourn's fortune grew, a new problem developed in the latter part of December, 1866. A union, called the Miners' League, was formed in Gold Hill, and it threatened to close most of the rich mines of the Comstock Lode. The superintendent of the Imperial-Empire, J. D. Greentree, refused even to listen to the union's complaints. Instead, this former sea captain told the union's inspection committee to "go to hell and keep to their own business."[2]

During the weeks at the end of December 1866, and the beginning of

January 1867, as the temperature dropped toward zero and stinging blizzards swooped down from the peaks of the Sierra Nevada, the Miners' League debated the course of action to take in the face of such an unmovable force as Greentree. The union members agreed that all underground miners were to receive $4 per day. If this demand was not met, the miners were prepared to go out in full force and shut down the Imperial, as a beginning of what could become a general strike throughout all the mines of the Comstock Lode. Cummings, Hay, and White, the union leaders, gathered about two hundred union miners just before noon on February 11, 1867, at the hoisting works of the Imperial. They called the men out of the mine and managed to persuade them that the miners had to go along together if they were to receive a fair wage for their work in the shafts and drifts of these deep mines.[3]

Greentree was away at the time, so the union members left him a note warning him against putting miners underground for wages less than $4. Instead, the superintendent immediately fired three union men and convinced the superintendents of three other mines—the Yellow Jacket, Kentuck, and Crown Point—to fire Cummings and Hay as well as two other union members. He did all this without consulting the officers of the company in San Francisco. Soon, telegrams announcing the closing of the mine created a flurry of movement on the San Francisco Stock Exchange, and stock in the Imperial dropped $10 per share. With this bad news, Bourn had to depart for Gold Hill at once.[4]

Bourn's difficult journey began when he boarded a river steamboat at the San Francisco waterfront. Cold winds swept in from the Pacific and made the northeast voyage to the Carquinez Strait very unpleasant. When it entered the fast-moving current of the Sacramento River, the steamboat slowly moved upstream with its paddle blades slapping the rushing water. As the steamboat encountered thick, damp tule fog, it carefully worked its way upriver until it reached Sacramento in the early morning of the next day.

At this river port, Bourn and many other passengers had their luggage transferred to the depot of the Sacramento Valley Railroad for the twenty-two-mile journey to Folsom. Here, Bourn boarded a stagecoach headed northeast to Placerville. After leaving this Mother Lode town, the stagecoach continued on the Bonanza Road through the foothills until it began its climb into the snow-covered Sierra Nevada. As the team tired, the coach made a stop for the night at one of the stations—such as Sportsman's Hall twelve miles above Placerville. Or if the team was up to it, the next stop might have been higher up at Strawberry Valley House just below the high granite outcropping known as Lover's Leap. The fare at Mr. Berry's stage and wagon stop was rough and crude, and he was noted for having little more than straw to feed the teams, but it was a place to halt for the night before the next day's steep climb through the granite country to Echo Pass.

On the next day of travel, the stagecoach crossed Slippery Ford and began the slow passage upward to Echo Pass and an elevation of 7,382 feet. From here, the stagecoach waited until uphill traffic passed it, then began the downward grade on a road that had been carved and blasted from the face of a sheer granite wall. Between snow flurries, Bourn and the other passengers had a view of Lake Tahoe in the distance and of the mountains surrounding the great lake. Under the guidance of the stagecoach driver, the six-horse team moved down-grade at a slow pace as the driver set and released the brakes. At the bottom of the grade, the stagecoach pulled into Yank's Station, where the travelers were greeted by Ephraim "Yank" Clement, "the owner of a three-story, 14 room hostelry. His corrals held 200 head of horses, mules and oxen. He provided barns, a horse-change stable for the Pioneer Stage Company, a general merchandise store, a cooperage, a blacksmith shop and two saloons for his thirsty guests."[5]

After a night at Yank's Station, Bourn boarded the stagecoach as it began its journey toward Lake Tahoe over a snow-covered road cleared of deep drifts. Along the route now known as the Pioneer Trail, Bourn's ride aboard the rocking, swaying stagecoach took him past all the famous stops that lined the road. The stagecoach stopped at Friday's Station to take a rest and to ask about road conditions up Daggett's Pass and down the Kingsbury Grade on the eastern crossing of the Sierra Nevada to the Carson Valley.

At Friday's Station, the passengers got out and waited inside. The horses were watered and given hay before it was time to hitch them up again and begin the hard climb up Daggett's Pass to the summit of the Carson Range. Here, passengers had a clear view of the Carson Valley and the Pinenut Range to the east. Although the weather was cold, there were only a few clouds, but the possibility of an incoming storm from the west made the driver anxious to make the drop from the 7,375-foot summit down the steep switchbacks of the Kingsbury Grade that followed Haines's Canyon to the floor of the valley. Here, the driver brought his team to a halt to give them a rest and let the passengers stretch their legs on level ground.

Once the horses and passengers were rested, the stagecoach turned north and followed the road along the base of the Carson Range as they passed

Peter Van Sickle's wayside station. About two miles beyond this point, the stagecoach pulled into Genoa (old Mormon Station). After stopping here for another break, the driver got his passengers back into the coach and cracked his whip in the air to start the team for the last thirteen and a half miles northeast to Carson City. From here, if passengers wanted to go into the Washoe Mountains and the towns of the Comstock Lode, they had to make arrangements to catch Langton's Pioneer Express, a four-horse stagecoach that made daily runs from Carson City to Silver City, Gold Hill, and Virginia City.[6]

The stage for Gold Hill did not leave Carson City until two o'clock the next afternoon, so William Bourn and other passengers bound for the Comstock stayed overnight at the Ormsby House at the southwest corner of Carson and Second Street. This hotel was run by G. L. Gibson and R. H. Vancell, who had become the proprietors after the founder, Major William Ormsby, was killed in 1860 during the war between the white settlers and the Paiutes of Pyramid Lake.[7]

After breakfast on February 17, 1867, Bourn purchased his ticket to be certain he would have a seat on Langton's stage and checked his suitcase to be loaded aboard the coach. Then, even though the weather was cold and storm clouds were gathering in the Sierra Nevada, Bourn walked through the town and noticed the growth of the community. The location of Carson City in its beautiful valley not far from the base of the Carson Range of the Sierra Nevada was ideal—trees for lumber were not too far away, water was plentiful, and its location was good for people and freight bound to or from California.

When Bourn finished his stroll around Carson City, he returned to the Ormsby House for lunch. Between one and two o'clock, he boarded the stagecoach. The wind had turned cold and seemed to blow in from the sagebrush-covered hills to the north as it whipped the grass of the meadow and blew dust clouds from the dirt road. Bourn and the other passengers wore heavy coats and spread a robe over themselves to keep warm. In the eighteen miles the driver had to go from Carson City to Virginia City, the stagecoach worked its way up the road that cut into the Washoe Mountains in a series of switchbacks and over a toll road from Half-Way House on the Carson Road to Gold Hill. On the way up the grade, the four-horse team pulled the coach and the load of passengers and luggage into Silver City. At the next stop, Gold Hill, Bourn got off the stage in the late afternoon. As he picked up his suitcase and walked across Main Street to the What Cheer Hotel[8] to rent a room, Langton's stage pulled out of town and entered the toll road that separated Gold Hill and Virginia City.

2 The day after Bourn's arrival in Gold Hill, all the towns in the area were blanketed by the snows of a windblown blizzard. Still, Bourn met with attorney Charles De Long, who handled legal matters for the Imperial-Empire Mine. It was an extremely cold day, and De Long told Bourn that the cost of firewood had jumped from its usual price to $50 a cord and might even go higher if the blizzard kept up. The Chinese wood merchants had already sold off their supply and had begun to dig beneath the snow to cut roots, which they sold on the streets as fast as they were gathered for $60 a cord.[9]

Bourn learned from De Long that the Miner's Union was very strong and that no other miners would cross the picket line in the face of demands that the union considered fair. The miners justified their position by reminding owners that they daily risked their lives underground where the ventilation was inadequate and there was always the danger of swinging a pick and puncturing an underground channel of hot water. Air temperature increased about 3 degrees for every hundred feet of depth, and at depths of three thousand feet the water in the mines reached temperatures of 170 degrees Fahrenheit. Crews in the deepest shafts were able to work only in alternate hours, so they could rest from the heat and shower themselves with ice water.[10]

After hearing this from De Long, Bourn let the union know that he would meet with its representatives, Cummings and Hay, on February 27. This would give him time to talk to Greentree at the Imperial and to examine working conditions in the mine.

When the meeting between Bourn and the union took place, Bourn first asked why the Imperial had been struck. He pointed out that there were other mines paying less than $4 a day and the union had not gone out on strike against them. Cummings replied that the union had nothing against him or the Imperial—although Greentree was another matter—and that there were probably not six men in the union who even knew Bourn's name, adding that he himself had not known it until that day.[11]

Then, as a way of bypassing Greentree, Bourn requested that future grievances be presented to the mine's attorney, De Long, who would communicate them to the owners. If the union's demands were reasonable, they would be granted. The owners would pay wages as high as any of the other mines, but no more.[12]

Cummings replied that the union would be fair but requested a daily wage of $4 for men who worked underground on an eight-hour shift. Bourn asked if the union thought it fair where one man could put in a good day's work, while a weak man might pick only half as much. Cummings's answer was that such a man had no place in the mine. Furthermore, he made it clear that $4 per day was for men working underground; men shoveling on top or working at some other job that did not require the ability of an underground miner were not represented by the union. He also assured Bourn that the union would watch out for members who had a sick mother, wife, or sister to support. Finally, he summarized the union's position when he told Bourn that they wanted $4 per day for men working underground, but they did not intend to make any distinction between union and nonunion men. Then Cummings promised that Greentree would not be harmed and that the fire companies of Gold Hill and vicinity, which were made up of miners, would be ready to protect all property and officials of mines that paid $4 per day. Bourn agreed to the union demands.[13]

With the end of the strike, Bourn was ready to travel back to San Francisco, but a violent snowstorm continued until the third of March. It was not until March 7, 1867, that he was able to catch a large sleigh headed west across the Sierra Nevada by way of Dutch Flat and the Donner Pass Toll Road, because the Placerville route remained closed.[14]

Bourn rode the Pioneer Line Sleigh (purchased by Wells, Fargo in 1864) down the thirteen miles of switchbacks on the Geiger Grade. At the bottom, they traveled some eleven miles to the site of present-day Reno. The sleigh continued west along the north bank of the Truckee River. As the snow grew deeper, the horses pulling the sleigh floundered but managed to force their way as stinging whips popped across their rear quarters. The most difficult part of the journey came after they passed Donner Lake and climbed upward between the great granite peaks that had been cut, drilled, and blown apart by Chinese workers for the tracks of the Central Pacific Railroad. Even after the sleigh topped Donner Pass, it still had a hard journey along the Dutch Flat and Donner Lake Toll Road.

During that winter season of 1867, forty-four storms struck the Sierra Nevada and passed on into the Great Basin. The wind came out of the west and pushed great banks of storm clouds ahead of it. When Bourn and his fellow passengers began this journey, the temperature was around 20 degrees above zero. During the course of the storm, the temperature slowly climbed to about 32 degrees.[15] As a storm passed, the snow let up, but then men and animals were pelted with both hail and a freezing rain.

The sleigh driver had men who broke a path in front of his team, but even that effort was hardly enough as the storms continued without let-up. The major force that allowed them to continue their journey was the help of teamsters from the Central Pacific Railroad Company, who continued to bring sleds loaded with supplies from the end-of-track for some fifteen thousand Chinese workers driving tunnels into the great granite cliffs. The diet of these workers included dried oysters, abalone, squid, dried bamboo sprouts and mushrooms, assorted vegetables, pork, chicken, noodles, rice, salted cabbage, dried seaweed, rice crackers, sugar, various kinds of dried fruit, Chinese barbecued pork, peanut oil, and tea.[16]

Even with snowshoes, the teamsters floundered up to their shoulders in fresh snow. Later, they traveled on skis that they called "Norwegian snowshoes."[17] Still, they kept moving, and with great effort they broke a path for the horses pulling the sleigh beyond the summit and down through the snow drifts in the canyon of the South Fork of the Yuba River to the bridge that crossed it. Finally, after a journey that seemed impossible most of the time, they reached Cisco, where the sleigh passengers were able to board the train at the end-of-track.

From Cisco to Sacramento it was a ninety-two-mile ride on the Central Pacific Railroad.[18] During this part of his trip, Bourn saw Gold Run, Cape Horn, and the Mother Lode town of Auburn. From here, the train went downgrade into the Sacramento Valley. As the trackbed leveled off on the floor of the Great Valley, the train picked up speed, and in a short time, compared to the rest of Bourn's Sierra Nevada crossing, the train pulled into the Sacramento depot. It had been an incredible journey, and Bourn was happy to escape the epic snows of 1867, which almost matched the storms that had trapped the Donner Party in the deadly winter of 1846.

At the Sacramento waterfront, Bourn booked passage on one of the fine river steamers headed for San Francisco. During this voyage down the turbulent Sacramento River to its confluence with the San Joaquin River downstream from Rio Vista, he got his first chance for a decent night's sleep since he left Gold Hill.

The voyage from Sacramento ended at the Broadway Wharf on San Francisco's waterfront. Here, deckhands tossed landing lines to men waiting on the wharf. At last, William Bourn was back in San Francisco.

3 Will was exhausted by his winter trip from Gold Hill and the rugged crossing of Donner Summit that he described to Sarah and the children.

When he returned to his office, he reported the settlement of the strike at Gold Hill. Then he learned of a new silver discovery far to the east of Virginia City and Gold Hill, in the newly named White Pine Mining District about 120 miles east of Austin and about 110 miles south of Elko. Although there was still a lack of sound information, the boom on the Comstock Lode seemed to be slowing, and farther to the east at Austin, Nevada, the Reese River mines were beginning to become part of mining history. A new dream began to take shape, and seasoned prospectors talked about going to White Pine.[19] By September, news from White Pine was sparse but promising to Will and others willing to risk investing in mining stock.

Then an event in the Nevada desert took place that would create a new bonanza for prospectors, investors, and mining men of the American West. In late 1867, a prospecting party guided by a Shoshone Indian called "Napias Jim" (*Napias* was the Shoshone word for silver) arrived at what came to be known as Treasure Hill. On the top of this bare, windy mountain, nine thousand feet above sea level, Napias Jim pointed out areas where there was plenty of silver. But this was not ordinary silver, as James D. Hague later pointed out. This was horn silver, a soft silver chloride mineral found only in arid regions like the Great Basin.[20]

The first lode discovery was made by prospectors Murphy and A. J. Leathers, who staked out the claim to the Hidden Treasure Mine on the crest of windblown, treeless Treasure Hill. When news of this discovery reached San Francisco, newspaper reports featured the boom, and the editors went along with San Francisco businessmen in stressing the importance to the city of this new silver strike. Financial houses like the Bank of California considered the White Pine discovery as possibly another Comstock Lode. William Bourn took a gamble and bought as much stock in the Hidden Treasure Mine as he could obtain, because this mine was extremely rich for about one thousand feet in length and two to eight feet in width, producing horn silver that ran in value from $1,000 to $5,000 per ton. For early claim holders and those who bought stock in the Hidden Treasure Mine, the profit was substantial.[21]

Having already endured the incredible winter trip from Gold Hill and over Donner Summit, Bourn had no desire to return to the wilds of the Great Basin. He wanted to be home with Sarah, who was expecting their last child, who came into the world as Maud Eloise Chase Bourn on November 15, 1867. So while Will rejoiced in the birth of another child, the agent who represented him and the Bank of California made the long journey—over 500 miles—from San Francisco to Elko, Nevada. The 110-mile trip from the overland train depot in Elko to the White Pine mines was made by stagecoach.[22]

The earliest miners to reach the new silver strike in the White Pine country found their first winter tough to endure. At first, men lived in caves—even calling the first settlement Cave City—and if they were lucky they had either brought tents with them or rented them from merchants who arrived in White Pine to sell goods to miners. By May, 1868, Cave City became Hamilton, and one of the first buildings was a saloon for thirsty customers. Icy winds blew one storm after another across this barren country all winter, and the temperature at the top of Treasure Hill, where a small town was thrown together, was often near zero or somewhere below. During the summer of 1868, as the town of Hamilton was built, the miners took time to construct a graded road that wound up Treasure Hill to Treasure City, built just below the crest of the mountain.[23]

The mile-and-a-half uphill hike from Hamilton was replaced by a two-and-a-half-mile toll road. Although the road made it easier to haul loads up to Treasure City, it did not change the nature of this place, which was wide open to the winds that blew across the summit. Water had to be brought up the grade from Hamilton, and it sold for eight cents per gallon. Still, Treasure City was close to the richest deposits of silver in White Pine, and between eight hundred and one thousand miners lived here during the first season of the strike.[24]

Back in San Francisco, Bourn received dispatches from his agent regarding the activities of the Hidden Treasure Mine and the other mines of the White Pine District. He was impressed with the richness of the strike. But news of more towns being built—such as Shermantown, two miles southwest of Treasure Hill, and Swansea, a milling town, three-fourths of a mile north of Shermantown—made Bourn wonder how long the boom in the White Pine Mining District might last. During the spring of 1869, the population of the area grew to some twelve thousand people willing to endure the winds and snows of winter and the heat of summer, along with a shortage of both wood and water.

On the southern side of Treasure Hill, another town called Eberhardt sprang up and proposed to be a milling center. On the top of Treasure Hill, hopeful men built White Pine City, but this attempt at town building was doomed to failure, as it never got beyond the stage of tents and crude shanties. It was Hamilton that gradually took over as the major city in the mining district, becoming the area's headquarters for business, government, and the travel center as the best roads came to a halt at Hamilton. It was the one mining-camp town in the White Pine Mining District that offered the amenities that appealed to miners, engineers, and investors, for Hamilton had the Withington Hotel, a main street with buildings of some substance, and two newspapers. By September of 1869, it had become the county seat of White Pine County, which had been created out of Lander County, Nevada.[25]

Even with the growth of White Pine County, news began to spread in 1870 that some of the early silver strikes were beginning to peter out. Still, other strikes were made. But in the early part of 1870 another major problem struck this mining area—a shortage of water. Bourn's agent, F. A. Benjamin, sent word to Bourn's San Francisco office that the White Pine Water Works had managed to reach the Hidden Treasure Mine with a pipeline, but final construction was delayed while the builders awaited the arrival of pipes from San Francisco. In March 1870 the White Pine Water Company decided to shut off the water supply for Hamilton and Treasure City. When word reached Bourn, he knew that the water company had to be sold to pay off a claim against it by the Bank of California. He sent word to Benjamin to buy the water company and saw to it that he had enough money to outbid anybody else. The agent paid $43,000 in gold coins for the water company.[26]

However, Bourn's expenses for the purchase and repair of the White Pine Water Company were high, which meant that water was not going to be cheap for any customers. Bourn's principal interest was to have enough water to keep the mills operating, and his agent leased the Treasure City part of the operation to another contractor, who agreed to run it and see to its maintenance and repair.[27] The result was that water doubled in price from two cents to four cents per gallon. Although citizens of Hamilton and Treasure City were furious about this development, the company's hard bargain resulted in a regular water supply. Short of putting in their own water system at a tremendous price, even if they located a good supply of water, Hamilton and Treasure City finally had to rely upon the White Pine Water Company. The company completed a twelve-inch pipeline from Illipah Springs, some three miles to the east. The water came just in time, because during that summer of 1870 Hamilton had a fire when a bakery burned. Thanks to the new water system, the town was saved.

While Bourn received word of this from his agent, he also was notified that silver production was coming to a close. This was almost the end of William Bourn's Nevada adventures. He was no longer associated with the Imperial-Empire Mine at Gold Hill, and as the horn silver of the Hidden Treasure Mine began to run out, Bourn looked toward Grass Valley, California, where he now had the controlling shares of stock in the Empire Mine. He was making new plans to exploit the riches of this great gold mine, which had much more promise than the Hidden Treasure Mine atop a barren mountain in the vastness of eastern Nevada's White Pine County.

7

Bourn's Luck

As William Bourn profited from both the Comstock Lode and the silver strike in Nevada's White Pine County, so too did the city of San Francisco, for it was silver and not gold that turned San Francisco into a major city on the Pacific Coast. During these boom times, the old wooden and canvas buildings of the City of Hills gave way to buildings of brick and stone. Gas lights became much better than they had been, and rough wooden sidewalks changed to substantial plank sidewalks, though during windy days dust from the many unpaved streets continued to be a nuisance. Still, San Francisco was California's major city, and it was the hub of financial dealings for the western states.

In 1862, the steady increase of mining properties resulted in the formation of the San Francisco Stock and Exchange Board. But within ten years "business had so increased that the eighty members, to which the first exchange was limited, were not considered sufficient to properly conduct all the daily transfer of stock, and a second board was organized, called the California Stock and Exchange Board."[1] By June 7, 1875, the Pacific Stock Exchange opened for business in the Halleck Building on the corner of Sansome and Halleck Streets. No longer was the Pacific Coast dependent upon the New York Stock Exchange.

During the late 1860s and the early 1870s, the Bourns continued to live in their big house at 1105 Taylor Street. Although it had a large yard and was protected from the outside world by a fairly high wall, Sarah Bourn was not content with city life and yearned for a country home in the Napa Valley.

Sarah might well have pointed out that the journey to Napa Valley had become much easier after the completion of the Napa Valley Railroad all the way to Calistoga in October 1868.[2] Trips for the Bourns to this beautiful area became more frequent as they looked over possible sites for a second home. Although the journey still required a trip by steamboat to the railhead at Vallejo, it eliminated the Napa River journey to Suscol Landing and the buggy or stagecoach ride from there to St. Helena. Also, the stop at Vallejo gave them the opportunity to visit young Willie, who was attending the College of St. Augustine in Benicia.

The College of St. Augustine, an Episcopal military school, was founded in Benicia in 1867. Under the leadership of Bishops William Kip and John Wingfield, the sixty-acre campus surrounded a large parade ground used for drilling and physical recreation. "Classrooms and dormitories were comfortable. But the stress was on strict *discipline* as the essential element in military instruction. Every day of every session 'each cadet from babyish 13-year old grammar school boys of Form VI to razored seniors near graduation from Form I—was obliged to drill in infantry tactics and to attend divine services in the chapel.'"[3]

Regulations for the cadets were designed to make them into officers and gentlemen. "From tattoo, 8:30–8:45 P.M., till reveille, 6 A.M. the cadet was required to maintain 'PERFECT SILENCE' (the cap's are the College's)." Cadets wore uniforms of red-trimmed gray jackets and pantaloons, which could be obtained from Julius Opperman of Benicia. "On weekdays, students had an hour of drill, 8 hours of sleep, one and a half hours for meals, and five and a half hours for recreation and special duties. On Saturdays and Sundays, the schedule was changed but all duties were still performed with a strict regard to punctuality. Every Sunday, the Commandant led the entire cadet corps to the Cathedral of St. Paul's for service, after which the students were urged to spend at least part of the afternoon in reading Scripture."[4]

While military training was compulsory, students could join the baseball, football, gymnastic, and rowing teams on a voluntary basis. "A full eight hours of each day was assigned to 'mental culture,' largely classroom study. Courses were broken into four categories, classical, literary (including history), scientific, and commercial. Courses were tailored for graduates' entrance into the University of California."[5] However, a great amount of emphasis was devoted to Bible reading, for it was the Bible that gave the college its standards for truth and duty.

Although many of the students at St. Augustine's came from California and Nevada, others came from "Honolulu, Mazatlán and Manzanillo, Mexico; Kentucky; Washington Territory; Auckland, New Zealand; New York; Utah; Chambery, France; Idaho; and London, England."[6]

Young Willie Bourn was ten years old when he was enrolled in this strict institution in 1867. However, one hopes that his first years were spent in St. Augustine's grammar school, which "taught besides the usual subject, bookkeeping and practical English, thus fitting the students who completed only the preparatory course for the business world."[7]

The years that young William Bourn spent at St. Augustine's were not easy, but they did give him a solid background for his next challenge when he was enrolled in the University School in San Francisco. This institution was started in late 1865 by George Bates, an Oxford graduate.[8] And when young Willie entered here after his stint at St. Augustine's, he was well prepared for the course load at this college preparatory school.

3 By the latter part of 1869, William Bourn had acquired controlling interest in the Empire Mine at Grass Valley. Unlike many stockholders who were content to read reports and receive dividend checks, Bourn's interest in mining went way beyond that of a typical investor. After his experiences at the Imperial-Empire silver mines at Gold Hill, Nevada, and the Hidden Treasure Mine in White Pine County, Bourn gave his full attention to the operations at the Empire and frequently made the tiring trip from San Francisco to Grass Valley.[9]

But as Bourn took full control of the Empire Mine, the miners were in the midst of a strike that successfully closed the mine, for the workers went along with the vote of the Miners' League. As a result, both the Empire and the nearby North Star were shut down, and 350 men were out of work. As at Gold Hill, Bourn once again had to deal with a strike. This time, though, the quarrel was not over daily wages. Instead, the men struck over the idea of replacing black powder, which they had used for years, with dynamite, a newly developed explosive.[10]

Bourn was well aware of the need to treat his workers fairly. He listened to their worries about the change from black powder to dynamite, and he realized it would take time for the miners to accept the use of what they called "giant powder." Realizing this, Bourn allowed the continued use of black powder for almost a year, until local experiences in other mines proved that dynamite was no more hazardous than black powder in blasting walls of quartz.

As he did in any business in which he became involved, Bourn took the time to learn the history and the potential problems of the Empire Mine.

The Empire Mine was formed by pulling together many smaller mines and mining claims. Mines such as the Ophir, Rush and Laton, Keefe and Judd, Magenta, Osborne Hill, Pennsylvania, Gold Hill, Golden Treasure, Granite Hill, Houston Hill, Sultana, Central North Star, W.Y.O.D. (Work Your Own Diggings), and others came together as a result of an idea developed by a young miner named Charles A. Brockington. Brockington, two of his brothers, four or five friends, and about twenty-five or thirty other miners formed the W.Y.O.D. and in a cooperative mining venture worked this rich area successfully for many years. After people who formed the Work Your Own Diggings Association began to die, the W.Y.O.D. was sold to the Empire Mine.[11]

The beginning of the Empire Mine was on Ophir Hill, one mile southeast of Grass Valley. Here, in October 1850, George D. Roberts located a gold-bearing ledge.[12] He worked it for several months but became discouraged with the hard work of separating the gold from the quartz.

The gold-bearing veins of the Empire Mine, as well as those of the other Grass Valley mines, were difficult for the first miners to work. These men had been accustomed to working larger quartz veins near the surface, where the ore could be shoveled into a sluice box or rocker that allowed them to flush out non-gold-bearing soil and rocks while the heavier gold and gold-bearing quartz sank down in the open trough to be captured by obstructions, such as cleats or blocks of wood. This form of placer mining was the early method used in the Mother Lode country south of Nevada County. In that area, the veins were much wider, and access to the gold was easier as it did not—in the beginning—require the digging of shafts and tunnels. However, one other thing that helped these miners capture gold from the ore was the use of quicksilver, which had the characteristic of amalgamating with gold. Then the gold was separated from the amalgam once the mercury was vaporized inside a retort.[13] Fortunately for these first gold seekers, the New Almadén quicksilver mine had been discovered in 1845 just south of San Jose, and it was able to supply all the mercury needed by miners. So as the miners began to develop the northern mines of Grass Valley and Nevada City, mercury was easily available.

The gold-bearing veins of quartz in these northern mines tended to be from only sixteen inches to a maximum of two feet in width, and they usually had an average dip of 30 degrees to the 3,000-foot level. However, this dip grew steeper as the depth of the mine increased, and at the levels between 3,800 and 4,200 feet the dip could be as much as 55 degrees. Getting to this gold-bearing quartz required a new method of mining that differed considerably from the early days of the California Gold Rush.

Mines in the northern area, such as the Empire and the North Star, required a new set of techniques. Shafts had to be dug, as well as drift tunnels off these shafts that followed the course of the veins. In the Grass Valley area, most of the miners who knew the craft of hard-rock mining far underground were Cornishmen from England, often humorously called "Cousin Jacks" because it was said they always knew of a cousin who was a good miner. These miners, who took pasties in their lunch pails and called these folded meat pies "letters from home," were masters of deep underground mining. They knew all the aspects of mining, including the art of shoring up underground excavations, setting an explosive charge, operating heavy machinery and Cornish pumps.[14] These underground operations required considerable capital from owners and investors, and there were risks, both for the miners working deep in the depths of the earth and for owners and investors who could lose their money.

New techniques were required for deep hard-rock mines like the Empire. Steam engines, fueled by local timber, became the first source of power for the Empire and continued in use until Lester Allen Pelton of Camptonville, California, invented the Pelton Water Wheel in 1878. This device replaced the steam engine at the Empire Mine and remained the major source of power until it became possible to use an electric-powered engine. To handle the continual problem of underground water, Cornish pumps, which were developed in Cornwall to pump water from the tin mines, were installed at the Empire Mine to pump water to the surface at a rate of some 18,000 gallons per hour. The pump rod, which worked at eight to nine strokes per minute, shot the excess water into drain tunnels.

The Empire Mine had a headframe ninety-four feet tall. Using cables to hold the man-cars that shot down the incline shaft on tracks at speeds of 600 to 1,200 feet per minute, the miners were given a wild ride to the levels at which they were working. This same headframe and cable hoist also brought up large ore bins filled with quartz to be crushed in the stamp mill and lowered supplies into the depths of the mine by using the ore bins on their return journeys down the shaft.

All the underground work was done in the darkness, and at first the only light miners had came from the candle each man wore on his hat. By 1906, carbide lamps replaced the candles, and later both the shaft and tunnels were made brighter by the introduction of electric lights. In the beginning, the Cornish miners used double-jack drilling methods—one man holding the drill and the other man hitting the head of the drill with a sledgehammer—to drill a hole into promising-looking walls of quartz. Once the hole was deep enough, the miners put black powder into the hole around a fuse long enough to give them time to get away from the blast. Then, with the call of "fire in the hole," the fuse was lit and the miners retreated to a safe area until the sound of the blast and the cloud of smoke blew past them in the drift tunnel and passed out into the main shaft.

By the early 1900s, hand drills had been replaced by pneumatic drills and black powder gave way to dynamite. Still, many aspects of mining remained the same. Once things were clear after a blast, the open hole of the stope was checked to make sure that things were safe. Then the miners loaded the ore cars at the foot of the stope. The cars ran on level tracks on the floor of the tunnel, and a mule pulled each car of ore, which weighed about 1,200 pounds, to the junction of the tunnel and the shaft. Here, the ore cars dumped their loads into bins at the shaft, "from which the skips, each holding 3,500 pounds, are loaded." Then the miners signaled the hoist, and the load of ore was pulled to the surface and dumped on the grizzlies, or screens, at the top of the headgear. Here, the finer particles fell directly into the lower bins while the coarse pieces fell into a separate bin that held 150 tons. In front and below this bin was the No. 5 Gates crusher, which was fed with a steady stream of quartz when the gates leading from the bin were opened. All waste rock—except for that left in the depths of the mine—was loaded into skips from a compartment of the shaft bins, then hoisted and dumped into another bin and carried by cars to a circular waste dump where it was deposited.[15]

Next, the gold-rich ore was moved into the crusher of the thirty-stamp mill built by Captain S. W. Lee—always called "the steamboat mill" because its painted ceiling and superstructure had a resemblance to a steamboat. Each stamp weighed eight hundred pounds and dropped at a rate of fifty-eight to sixty-five times per minute, echoing like thunder throughout Grass Valley. The mill had a capacity to crush forty tons of quartz per day.

The powder from the crushed ore was spread over plates of copper that had been silver-plated and coated with a thin layer of mercury. This was then scraped clean, and the amalgam of silver, gold, and quicksilver was taken to the retort furnaces. There, the amalgam was heated in the furnaces to boil off the silver and mercury for re-use. After this process, the remaining gold was cast into bars and shipped to government mints.[16] The Empire Mine was very rich, and during the period from May 1, 1854, to December 31, 1863, it produced $1,056,234.40 in gold, without counting the value extracted from the sulphurets.[17]

But luck does not continue without its opposite in loss. Fire, a dreaded word in the mines, swept through the Empire Mine's mill on September 20, 1870, destroying the mill, the pumping and hoisting equipment, and the winter supplies. The total damage amounted to $140,000.[18] Five months prior to this fire, Bourn had hired a Mr. Nesmith as the Empire's new superintendent. He now headed the rebuilding of the structures destroyed by the fire. During Nesmith's time, the mine was reopened, and another gold-bearing ledge that produced ore valued at $35 to $40 per ton was discovered.[19]

In early 1871, Bourn had a new twenty-stamp mill constructed. It was steam-powered, and its nine-hundred-pound stamps dropped nine inches at a rate of seventy-two times per minute. Within a year of the completion of the mill and the reopening of the mine, eighty miners were employed at $3.00 per day, sending eight thousand tons of quartz from the depths of the mine to the new mill at a cost of $12.50 per ton for the mining. Meanwhile, the eleven men employed in the mill crushed the quartz at a cost of $1.50 per ton.

Bourn's trips to the mine eased off during this period, and he had the Wells Fargo Bank make the payroll delivery to Grass Valley. With the mine turning out a considerable profit and his other investments doing well, Bourn became known on San Francisco's Montgomery Street as a man who had what his fellow businessmen referred to as "Bourn's Luck." Everything he became involved in seemed to add more money to his fortune and gave added proof that he possessed a golden touch.

4 But good fortune also possesses the reverse side in bad fortune, and "Bourn's Luck" took a tragic downward turn on January 24, 1872, when

eleven-year-old Frank Washington Bourn fell off the high wall that surrounded their family home in San Francisco.[20]

Crushed by the death of her younger son, Sarah Bourn felt more than ever the need for a country home where she could escape not only the sad memory of Frank's death, but also everything she had never liked about life in San Francisco. First, there had been the rough frontier city she had known when she had first arrived, then there was the combination of the fog and city life in general that she disliked. Most of all, there were those periods when Will was absent from home when his various mining investments required his presence either in Nevada or at the Empire Mine in Grass Valley. While trips to such places as the Santa Clara Valley or the Calaveras Big Trees were joyful, there were not many of these escapes from the city. The closest journey into the countryside were trips the family made to Napa County, where they stayed either at White Sulphur Springs or north of St. Helena at Calistoga. These trips took Sarah away from San Francisco to a rural setting where grass and oaks covered the low rolling hills and the beauty of vineyards caught her eye. In addition, spring, summer, and even autumn were warm and not chilled by the constant presence of either fog or a cold wind blowing in from the Pacific.

In the spring and summer of 1872, Will and Sarah made frequent trips away from San Francisco to the lovely countryside of the Napa Valley. During these trips, they began to look for some property where they could build a country home.

On August 8, 1872, the Bourns bought a ranch that appealed to them from the widow Mrs. Cornelia Baldwin Stanley, who agreed to sell the ranch to Sarah Esther Bourn for $15,000. Located near St. Helena, the property included sixty acres of vineyard and a house called the Red Cottage—also called The Pines—on the northern end of its boundaries, and another called the White Cottage or the Manzanita Cottage and another sixty acres of vineyard toward the southern boundary. There was also the Baldwin family home, a two-story Victorian structure with two major wings and two porches, built about 1854. Although it was more than a modest house, the Bourns thought they might replace it so their country estate would have a view of all the natural beauty of the hills and the valley. This land, which the Bourns called Madroño, offered the privacy of country living, and it was only a short trip into St. Helena two miles to the northeast. The location of Madroño also placed it within a short buggy ride up Sulphur Springs Road to the turn-off to White Sulphur Springs Resort.[21]

In order to have more room for the family and guests, the Bourns had the original house carefully torn down. Then, in a better location that would take advantage of the grand views, they began to build another home using lumber from the original. But this structure was to have stone walls to support the wooden siding and was to be much larger than the Baldwin home. While the new house began to take shape among the pines and oaks, the Bourns made their temporary quarters at the White Cottage. But even as the carpenters and stonemasons were still working on this new home for Madroño, travelers noticed it because of its tall wooden tower.

To young Willie Bourn, the room near the tower became a favorite place when he was home from school. Here, he entertained his sisters with his ability to manipulate a full deck of cards with great dexterity. But just as often, Willie was put to work on the farm, where he fed more than a hundred chickens and gathered eggs, fed his mother's Chinese pheasants, and often watched his mother's silkworms eating mulberry leaves. At times, he worked in the barn where he helped curry the carriage horses known throughout the Napa Valley for their quality. To other people in the valley, it became a matter of pride to own a Madroño-bred carriage horse descended from a proven line of quality breeding.

During this time, Sarah's sisters, Charlotte Starr and Caroline Chase Bowers came to live at Madroño. Charlotte, whose husband, William Starr, had deserted her and only sent money on an irregular basis, lived in the Red Cottage with her young son, George Starr, while Caroline and her daughters, Manzanita and Edith, lived in the White Cottage, where they took care of elderly Captain George Chase.[22]

While the Bourns enjoyed their country home, they kept the Taylor Street house in San Francisco, for the family lived in the city during most of the year, even though Sarah made frequent trips to Madroño. Will's many business enterprises required his presence in the city. Furthermore, during the school year the girls attended school in San Francisco, and by 1873 young Will, who was sixteen years old, was almost through his secondary education at the University School.

With a steady supply of wealth coming in from the rich veins of the Empire Mine in Grass Valley and from Bourn's other investments, William Bourn's reputation as one of San Francisco's business giants continued to grow among other financial tycoons of Montgomery Street.

8

Tragedy and Responsibility

While William Bourn continued to spend most of his time in San Francisco watching over the many aspects of his business empire, Sarah threw her energy into making Madroño an ideal country estate as well as a working ranch. At the beginning of 1873, she was learning all she could about tending her vineyards. She questioned local vintners about the proper care of the vineyards and about the best grapes to plant if she planned on making changes or if she acquired more land for new plantings.

As Sarah watched over the final touches on the new family home, Will and Willie came often to visit the ranch. Upon arriving at St. Helena aboard the train, they were picked up at Crane Station by one of the Italian workers who met them with a buggy. From here to Madroño it was no more than a two-mile journey. At the ranch, Sarah and the girls—if they were not in school—would be standing on the porch awaiting their arrival.

During these visits, Willie Bourn got to know his younger cousin George Starr, who was between ten and eleven years old. At this time in the lives of the boys, the difference in age between them stood in the way of their forming a close friendship.

During holidays and especially in the summertime, Sarah and Will had great times with the family gathered together at Madroño. Family dinners were a time of lively conversations ranging from the world of literature and music to the quality of wines made from the grapes of Madroño's vineyards. There were also trips up the canyon to visit White Sulphur Springs, where they enjoyed the hot waters and where the swimming pool was a special treat for both adults and children.

Such days got Will's mind off his business activities, and Sarah loved to see him relax and enjoy himself. But even at Madroño business intruded when Will talked to Sarah about increasing the size of their ranch. While she agreed to consider the possibility of adding to their holdings, she made it clear that she was not ready at that moment to take on the responsibility of caring for additional land. She did agree that it was a possibility to consider for the future.

Sometime during one of his summer visits in 1873, Will suggested to Sarah that it would be good for their son if they invited his cousin Willie Ingalls to come to San Francisco again for a prolonged visit. As he explained it, the young man could stay with Willie and him at the Taylor Street home in the city. Even if such a visit were only for a summer, as he put it, the boys would be good company for each other, and he would take them on his trips to the Empire Mine in Grass Valley. Furthermore, they would all come to Madroño as often as possible. All this appealed to Sarah, and it only remained for them to contact Hannah and Willie and offer the invitation.

2

In 1873, Bourn's business office in San Francisco was at 401 California Street. Here, he kept a keen eye on the daily fluctuations of the stock market, reviewed reports from the Empire Mine, and watched over real estate investments, such as the house and lot at the northeast corner of Third and Brannan Streets, the lot and house at the northwest corner of Guy Place and First Streets, the property at the southwest corner of Front and Merchant Streets, the improved property on the corner of Davis and Commercial Streets, and three bay-front water lots that had to be filled with earth before they could be used. Away from San Francisco, Bourn owned a 10,000-acre ranch outside San Bernardino, 660 acres of timberland in Washington Territory, and 1,760 acres in Michigan. In addition to the Empire Mine in Grass Valley, Bourn still owned the mill and mill site in Dayton, Nevada, and the water supply and springs in Treasure Hill.

During the years 1873–1874, Bourn added to the property around Madroño by purchasing an upper ranch of 276 acres and a lower ranch of 376 acres. Other than the main house at Madroño and the Red Cottage and White Cottage, there were no other homes east of Sulphur Springs Avenue, and the land was used for a wheat field and a small walnut orchard, while to the west of Sulphur Springs Avenue was vineyard land. Within the boundaries of the Madroño estate there were quite a number of bull pines, which the family used as an ongoing firewood supply.[1]

Besides San Francisco real estate, out-of-California timberland and mining land, Bourn now found that he was becoming more of a rancher than he had ever dreamed he would be. Although he enjoyed Madroño and all that it offered to the family, he sometimes wondered about the wisdom of keeping the other ranches, which offered only a minimum return on the original investment costs and presented additional yearly expenses in upkeep and taxes. Madroño, on the other hand, not only served the family well as a second home but held the promise of future profits in the annual production of a saleable crop of wine grapes from its vineyards.

Meanwhile, the greatest money-maker for Bourn was the Empire Mine. Since his acquisition of the controlling stock in 1869, the production of bullion showed a dollar value of $123,000 from October 1869 to October 1870; $64,000 (the year the mill burned) from October 1870 to October 1871; $110,000 from October 1871 to October 1872; and $168,000 from October 1872 to October 1873.[2]

All things considered, by the beginning of 1874 William Bourn was on his way to developing a gold mine of note. Yet this tall, handsome man with the well-trimmed beard and mustache had many irons in his financial fire, and the future for this hardworking man with a gambler's passion for making financial decisions—which seldom were anything other than winning moves—showed an even brighter tomorrow just over the horizon.

3 In January of 1874, Will and Sarah welcomed the return of Willie Ingalls to California. It had been nine years since he had come west with his mother, Hannah. Then, he had been a bright, talkative twelve-year-old who wrote with a flair and constantly added observations to his journal and the letters he sent home to his father and other family members in Brooklyn, and though he was four years older than his cousin Willie Bourn, they had hit it off in a grand manner. Now, young Ingalls was twenty-one and Willie Bourn was seventeen, but the age difference mattered even less than it had during their first meeting. It was as though the two young men had been separated for only a matter of a few weeks, not nine years.

The house at 1105 Taylor Street in San Francisco became a livelier place with the addition of Willie Ingalls, and when Sarah and the girls were at Madroño, Ingalls and young Bourn assisted William Bourn Sr. with any task he assigned to them. One such job was to travel with him to Grass Valley with the payroll for the Empire Mine, for at this time Wells Fargo's charges for performing such a service had gone up again. To Bourn, this constant fluctuation of prices was not only annoying but an added expense that he saw no reason to pay. After all, trips to the mine were a chance to get away from San Francisco and an opportunity to keep in touch with the operation of the mine. The only flaw about taking the payroll to the mine was the need to carry a Colt revolver. To Bourn, this was a confounded nuisance because he was not accustomed to handling a pistol. Still, a large payroll made up of cash required some means of protection. A careless word about the movement of such a sum of money—say, even the mention of it by a bank employee to a friend during lunch at one of San Francisco's restaurants—offered the opportunity for a waiter or some other diner to hear and accidentally pass it on to another who might let such information leak out to a stranger who might well be a stagecoach robber or at the very least be a friend of such a highwayman.

During the first months of 1874, Bourn and the two Willies often made the long trip from San Francisco to Grass Valley to deliver the payroll. There was talk about these trips among Bourn's fellow financiers, but most of this talk centered around one theme: William Bourn's carelessness in handling a pistol.

As winter moved toward spring, the happy life of the Bourn family and their relatives at Madroño was shattered by the unexpected death of Sarah's sister, Charlotte Chase Starr, on April 11, 1874. Forty-three-year-old Charlotte had lived less than two years in the Red Cottage at Madroño with her young son, George. After her burial in what came to be the Bourn Family plot in the cemetery alongside Sulphur Springs Avenue, twelve-year-old George Starr went to live with Aunt Sarah at Madroño.[3]

Sarah saw to it that young George was sent to the College of St. Augustine, the Episcopal military school in Benicia where Willie Bourn had endured the required silence, daily military drills, and daily chapel attendance. Sarah reared young Starr as though he were her own child, and when he was not attending school he learned the work ethic at Madroño doing required chores that ranged from working in the vineyards to cleaning out the barn and painting the elaborate wooden fence that ran the length of the northern border of the Madroño property along Sulphur Springs Avenue.[4]

While cousin George Starr worked full-time at Madroño as the summer of 1874 began, Willie Bourn and Willie Ingalls lived in the Taylor Street home in San Francisco. Not only were they good company for William Bourn Sr., they were quick learners as Bourn introduced them to the world of business and investments that included stock transactions, real estate, farm and ranch land speculations, and the complicated science of removing gold from quartz brought up from the depths of the Empire Mine, which was then being worked on twelve underground levels at a depth of 1,250 feet. These drifts were reached through the main incline shaft, and altogether there were 7,900 feet of drifts. On their trips to the Empire Mine with Bourn, the young Willies also learned that such deep underground mining was very expensive. At this time, the cost of sinking a shaft was $12 per foot. Added to this were the $8 per foot cost of the drifts, $8 per ton cost of removing the gold quartz, and the expense of $1.75 per ton to mill it. Though these costs were high for this time, the mine had a bullion production of $12,000 per month.[5] With frequent trips from San Francisco to the Empire Mine, Bourn was able to expose his son and nephew to the art and craft of deep underground mining. Both young men were eager to learn, and it was a pleasure for Bourn to give them the opportunity.

These trips to the mine became an adventure to the two Willies, and as the summer of 1874 moved into July, the cousins were eager and ready for the next trip to Grass Valley. And they knew that in the latter part of the month, they would once again join Bourn on his payroll delivery to the mine.

4 In the first few weeks of July 1874, William Bourn complained of severe headaches, but he did not go to a physician to see if anything could be done to relieve the pain. Instead, he carried on with his business. On the evening of July 23, as he strolled with his son and nephew, he stopped to talk to a friend on the corner of California and Montgomery Streets. As the conversation continued, Bourn told the young men to get their supper, and that he "would be up to the house presently."[6]

Young Bourn and Ingalls waited for him to return, for they knew the next day was going to be a long and hard one because they were going to take the mine payroll to Grass Valley. But Willie Bourn decided to go out for awhile and told his cousin to come and join him after his father got home.

Bourn returned home around 8:30 P.M. He asked about his son, and young Ingalls said that he had gone out and that he was going to join him.

Ingalls noticed that his uncle was tired, so he was not surprised that he went directly to bed.

When the young men returned from a short evening on the town, about eleven o'clock, they did not want to disturb the elder Bourn so they went to bed right away.

On the morning of July 24, Bourn was still in his bedroom. Willie Bourn went into his father's room and came back with some money his father had given him for breakfast. "We left the house at 9 o'clock and after breakfast went to the office."[7] As the work day got into full swing, it was necessary at about 11:30 A.M. for Ingalls to take a message from the office to Taylor Street so Bourn could read it and send back any reply he might wish to make.

When Ingalls reached the home, he bounded up the stairs to his uncle's bedroom on the second floor. This was a large room with windows that offered a view of San Francisco Bay, and just off the bedroom was an alcove with a luxuriously furnished bathroom. Ingalls knocked on the bedroom door, and when he received no answer, he opened the door and looked in and saw nobody in bed. He hurried toward the bathroom door and stepped inside. "To his horror and surprise, he saw lying on the floor . . . the body of his uncle dressed only in a night-shirt, which was saturated with blood. The head lay toward the bathroom door, and the body was lying partially on the face, with one arm encircling the head, at the feet lay a large-sized navy revolver."[8]

Ingalls bounded down the stairs, pausing only to tell the housekeeper, Miss Thomas, who was so deaf that she had to use an ear-trumpet, not to let anyone disturb Mr. Bourn's body until the coroner examined it. Then he hurried to the California Street office where he haltingly told his cousin and the others about the death of the man they all admired and loved. The coroner was then notified, and the son and nephew met him at the house.[9]

As the coroner examined the body, it became evident to him that William Bourn had been standing when the fatal shot was fired. "The night-shirt was blackened and burnt where the bullet entered which was about an inch to the left of and above the navel. The wound was a terrible one, the bullet having gone clear through the body, in an upper direction, passing through the heart, and just pushing out the skin near the spine."[10]

After the coroner's initial examination of William Bourn's body, he determined that he had taken his own life. But as he did so, he announced that he was going to summon a jury to determine whether this had been a suicide or an accident. Then he turned to William Bourn Jr. and William

Ingalls and asked where Mrs. Bourn was. When they told him that she was at the country home near St. Helena, he said that it was necessary to inform her at once, but that the news of this tragedy had to be broken to her as delicately as possible.

After conferring with each other, Willie Bourn asked his cousin to contact his mother. Willie Ingalls agreed, and told his cousin that he would telegraph his aunt at once and then catch a steamer to Vallejo to meet her and the girls and accompany them back to San Francisco.

Ingalls left the Taylor Street home to travel to Vallejo to meet Sarah and the girls. At four o'clock on the afternoon of the tragedy, the coroner's inquest began with nine prominent businessmen serving as jurors to determine the final ruling in the death of William Bourn.[11] It was just four days after the Bourns had celebrated their twenty-fifth wedding anniversary and barely a month since Will's sixty-first birthday.

5 When Willie Ingalls met Sarah and his cousins in Vallejo, he broke the news as gently as he could. But news such as he carried could only be a terrible shock, since it came without warning and followed hard on the earlier tragedy in April when Sarah's sister Charlotte Chase Starr had died.

Even as young Ingalls and the grief-stricken Sarah and her daughters sailed from Vallejo, the news of William Bourn's death was a front-page item in the late afternoon newspapers of San Francisco. Headings on such stories ran from "A Millionaire's Death: Shocking Suicide of a Noted Capitalist" to one-word headings of "SUICIDE" followed by variations of "Wm. B. Bourn Shoots Himself Through the Heart—His Body Found in His Bath-Room—A Sad Spectacle in a Home of Luxury."[12]

By the time Willie Ingalls escorted his aunt Sarah and his cousins off the steamboat and hired a carriage for the sad ride to their home, it was after eight o'clock in the evening of July 24, 1874. William Bourn's body had been removed from the house, and the coroner's inquest had adjourned with the understanding that they would meet again the next day to interview William Bourn Jr. and his cousin, William Ingalls. At the end of this terrible day, the members of the coroner's inquest had not reached an agreement as to ruling William Bourn's death a suicide or an accident.

When Sarah, the girls, and William Ingalls arrived at the Taylor Street home, Sarah quickly took charge, once she heard what had happened from her son.

The day after her husband's death, Sarah waited for the results of the second meeting of the coroner's inquest. First, the jury interviewed William Ingalls. When asked about William Bourn's health and state of mind, Ingalls explained that for "some weeks past he had complained of pains in the head." [13] When asked if there were any other problems, young Ingalls indicated that though his uncle frequently complained of feeling badly, he had not seen his physician and had insisted on tending to his business.

As the coroner pressed on with his questions, he asked about the empty vial of chloroform that had been found in the bathroom. Ingalls reply was: "I think that was used by Mrs. Bourn, who was greatly troubled with neuralgia." [14]

Next, the coroner had William B. Bourn Jr. sworn in. But Willie was unable to shed any more light except to agree with what his cousin had said. Beyond that, he said that "his father was strictly temperate always, and was a kind, indulgent and affectionate parent." [15]

After Willie's testimony was finished, the coroner presented young Bourn with the effects found in his father's room. The items he handed to him were "a handsome watch and chain, a lot of private letters, a bunch of keys and $22 in money." [16]

The jury then deliberated and decided that William Bourn had died from ". . . a wound from a pistol bullet inflicted by his own hand while laboring under great nervous excitement and mental prostration, superinducing temporary aberration of mind." [17]

Later, another meeting of a new coroner's jury, composed of prominent businessmen who had known William Bourn for most of the years of his career, met to go over all the evidence of Bourn's death. Their finding came down to their knowledge of William Bourn's careless handling of firearms and their agreement that he was a man of sound mind who certainly had not indicated any signs of depression or despair. To them, the cause of William Bourn's tragic death was an accident, for no man would try to commit suicide by shooting himself in the stomach. Without doubt, Bourn had been trying to load his Colt revolver and did not realize that he had a bullet in a firing position as he fumbled with the pistol and dropped it, causing the weapon to go off and fire a shot upward into his stomach and through his body. This was the last of any official investigation into this great tragedy, but it did not erase the rumor fed by newspaper headlines that William Bourn had taken his own life.

William Bourn's last will and testament, written on August 27, 1872, and filed in the office of the clerk of the Probate Court, City and County of San Francisco, on July 28, 1874, was a document that clearly indicated the wishes of a man who was sound of mind and kept his house in order at all times. The house and lot at 1105 Taylor Street were listed as Sarah Bourn's separate estate, as was the Madroño property. Within this will, Bourn bequeathed to "my beloved wife, Sarah Esther Bourn, all horses, carriages, household furniture, farm stock and farming utensils."[18] The same terms of the will applied to such items as pictures, engravings, and plates.

Sarah Esther Bourn was named executrix of the will, and Bourn's close friends Alpheus Bull of San Francisco, Seth Pinkham of Oakland, and Charles Langley of Napa were named executors. These men "as Trustees and in trust to covert [*sic*] the same (estate) into money as speedily as good management will permit, and to invest the same in interest paying bonds of the State of California, of the City and County of San Francisco, of the United States of America, each or either, at their discretion, to hold such Bonds in trust for the following purposes: To pay $^{6}/_{12}$ six twelfths of the income thereof during her life to my said wife, and the other six twelfths ($^{6}/_{12}$) of the income to the guardian (William H. Patterson) of my children for their support, maintenance and education, until each shall arrive at majority, it being my intention that when each child shall arrive at age, he or she shall receive one twelfth ($^{1}/_{12}$) of such Bonds, and on the death of my wife to divide the remaining six twelfths ($^{6}/_{12}$) among my then surviving children as fast as they become of age, it being understood and it is my will that the children of any deceased child shall take the same proportion that its parent would have taken if living."[19]

In the materials filed in probate court in 1874, the final appraisal amounted to $579,771.88, and the liabilities came to $275,960.11, leaving a total net of $303,811.77.[20] Of course, this final figure did not include the property, nor did it include the Empire Mine at Grass Valley, which was to add even more to the family fortune as it continued to operate as one of California's richest gold mines.

The family grief would ease in time, even though it would never truly vanish for Sarah Esther Chase Bourn. But for William Bourn II, the future promise of greatness was simply passed on to him from his father as a relay runner might have handed a baton to the next sprinter or long-distance runner on the team. Young Willie was the runner for the completion of the race and the receiver of the final gold medal once he crossed the finish line.

9

The Cambridge Years

After the death of her husband, Sarah Bourn insisted that her son return to the University School in the fall term to complete his studies. During this period, cousin William Ingalls agreed to stay with him at the family home; while young Bourn finished his courses, Ingalls worked in the Bourn office. Sarah was in and out of San Francisco as she settled her late husband's affairs and tried to learn as much as possible about his investments and his key business ventures.

For Sarah, the months after her husband's death until the end of 1874 were crucial for her future and those of her son and daughters as well as young George Starr. After conversations with her husband's close friends, and especially after listening to Horace F. Cutter, Sarah decided to send her son to Cambridge University at the beginning of 1875.

With these decisions made, Sarah concentrated on the many aspects of her late husband's business affairs. The Empire Mine operations continued to provide a major source of income for the Bourn family, but wide-ranging investments in other mines—such as the Hidden Treasure Mine in White Pine County, Nevada—and Bourn's many other investments convinced Sarah that she needed somebody to assist her in the varied aspects of the family business. She was cautious about moving too quickly, and in the months immediately after her husband's death she relied upon men who had worked for her late husband and upon close friends in the San Francisco business community.

As Sarah began to understand more about the Bourn holdings, she relaxed somewhat and found time to spend at Madroño, where she caught up on the operation of her ranch and vineyards. During this short period toward the end of 1874, Sarah got her son ready to travel to England. The holidays of the fall and winter of 1874 saw Willie Bourn, Willie Ingalls, young George Starr, and the Bourn girls fill Madroño with joy and long-needed laughter. Still, for Sarah there was a lingering sadness during her quiet hours; and as the time for the departure of her son to England and his cousin to Brooklyn to rejoin the Ingalls family drew closer, Sarah dreaded the void that would occur once the two Willies were gone.

As the tragic year of 1874 came to an end, her son and his cousin caught the overland train and headed east. For young Bourn, this was only a momentary stop as he was booked aboard a ship to sail to England; but for Ingalls, it was a journey home. During the first week of January 1875, Sarah received a letter from Zebediah Ingalls in which he told her of his son's safe arrival home. He thanked Sarah for her care of Willie and expressed his sorrow, once again, over the loss of her husband.[1] This letter from Brooklyn put a kind of closure to a year of sadness in the Bourn family, and Sarah looked toward a new beginning in 1875.

2 In the latter part of January 1875, William Bourn II began a new phase in his life. After his arrival in London, he traveled by train to Cambridge to begin his studies at this university noted for its long history of scholarship. Cambridge University had its beginning in 1209 A.D., when some Oxford scholars were forced to leave that university after trouble with the local townspeople. They came to Cambridge, the site of a Roman camp dating back to 43 A.D. The work of archeologists and historians indicates that this Roman camp was called Durolipons and that it was established as a fortified stronghold and served as an administrative center. It appears to have been prosperous, with substantial villas on both sides of the River Cam. Here, at this crossroads of English history, the Romans, then the Saxons and the Danish armies passed by during their respective invasions of England. At this site, the former Oxford scholars established a community, and by 1284 A.D., they opened the doors of Cambridge University's first college, which supported and housed a few scholars.[2]

When young Bourn arrived at Cambridge, he discovered that he was too late to enroll in the Lent Term, which had started in the middle of January.

His tutor told Bourn that he was not expected until the fall of the year and that it was doubtful that he would be able to enter the university until then. However, Bourn had a letter, probably from Horace F. Cutter, who had attended Cambridge, for a Mr. Perkins, a tutor at Cambridge's Sidney Sussex College. Upon receiving this letter, Perkins informed William that he could get him into Sidney Sussex College as a pensioner—an undergraduate obliged to pay his own expenses.

By the time of the Easter Break, young Bourn was beginning to feel at home at Cambridge. While he prepared for his entrance into Sidney Sussex College—where Oliver Cromwell had once been a student—Bourn decided to take a walking tour during the Easter Break. At this time of the year, the daffodils were in bloom, and many shallow-draft punts were gliding along the waters of the River Cam.

After the Easter Break, Will began the Easter Term of 1875 and worked hard at his studies. In a short time, he proved that he was an excellent scholar, one able to pick up difficult concepts with relative ease. By the time of the usual lull for preparing for the term exams in May, Bourn did not have to study with desperation. Instead, he found time to get away from the campus and look over the town and some of the countryside. When the exams took place, he was refreshed and passed easily.

During the long period from the end of examinations in June until the beginning of the Michaelmas Term during the first week of October, young Bourn appears to have traveled the nearby countryside exploring the natural beauty of the land and stopping at villages for a day or two and then continuing his tour. For him, this period between terms was a time of healing, a time to resolve the horrible death of his father in his own mind, and a time to focus on good memories and upon the responsibilities he would have to face once his years at Cambridge came to an end.

3 While her son began the Michaelmas Term at Cambridge, Sarah Bourn was busy in the fall of 1875 as she supervised the harvest of the grapes from the vineyards at Madroño. After this was finished, she traveled to San Francisco to confer with the Bourn office. The first news she heard concerned the output of the Empire Mine from October 1874 to October 1875, and she was pleased to learn that the mine showed a bullion production of $201,000 for the year.[3]

This report from Frank Nesmith, superintendent of the Empire Mine, was encouraging to Sarah. But there were other mining investments that bothered her, for she saw no income from them. Worst of all, the Hidden Treasure Mine in White Pine County, Nevada, was still costing money in salaries. Sarah received word that there was a possibility that the mine might strike another lode if it went deeper, for as she understood things, T. E. Eberhardt, a miner from Austin, had joined forces with a British company to become the Eberhardt and Aurora Mining Company, Limited, in February 1870, and that company had obtained the right to buy lands, mines, and minerals in Nevada, and to purchase shares in other mining companies operating in the state. This venture showed a profit in 1871 and in 1875, before it began to sink a tunnel into Treasure Hill with great expectations of striking another vein of rich silver chloride ore.[4] Sarah wanted no part of any such scheme that might be proposed for the Hidden Treasure Mine.

Fortunately, Sarah's common sense caused her to insist upon more information about White Pine County and Treasure Hill before she agreed to invest additional money into what she perceived as a short-lived mining boom. Indeed, Sarah's wait-and-see attitude was correct, for though the British investors were speculating in White Pine County, most California mining people that Sarah knew were convinced that the boom was over for all the mines, including the Hidden Treasure Mine.

For the Bourn mine on Treasure Hill, the year 1870 was the high mark in production, showing an income of $2,137,801. After that, it was all downhill, and Sarah would ultimately learn that production for 1876 was down to only $38,268.[5] So her move in holding back with regard to the White Pine mines in 1875 was wiser than some of the advice she received from people on the scene.

In addition to her late husband's business ventures and her vineyards, horses, and chickens at Madroño, forty-six-year-old Sarah had a large family to house, feed, clothe, and educate. Her eldest daughter, Maye, at twenty was able to watch out for her younger sisters. Zaidee was sixteen, Ida eleven, and Maud only eight years old. William was now eighteen, and his letters from Cambridge indicated that he was becoming a responsible young man. And her late sister's son, George Starr, was doing exceedingly well at the College of St. Augustine in Benicia. All things considered, Sarah was very satisfied. Even so, with so many responsibilities, she had very little time for relaxation.

4 As his mother kept the various business affairs in order, young William Bourn entered the Lent Term at Cambridge University in the middle of January 1876. During his second year, he became a fellow commoner—a student paying his own expenses—at Downing College. Unlike the rest of Cambridge University with its traditional pattern of courts, Downing College had avoided the Gothic appearance at the request of King George III. Instead, under the guidance of architect William Wilkins, enclosed courts gave way to buildings designed in the classical Greek style and to wide-open lawns that were to become a model for future college and university campuses. The college was named after Sir George Downing, whose will provided that if his relatives died childless all of his estate was to be used for the founding of a new Cambridge college.[6] But it was only after a long legal battle that Cambridge obtained possession of the estate from other members of the Downing family.

As the Easter Break of 1876 began, the young Californian stopped at a local barber shop to get a haircut. Here, he knew that the barber—along with other men in the trade—had a side business as a bookie. The big betting at this time was on the annual Easter Break rowing race between Cambridge and Oxford on the Thames River from Putney to Northlake. When young Bourn was told the odds of the race, he did not think them great enough, so he asked the barber what odds he might offer if he placed a wager on a dead heat for the race. Laughing at this Yankee brashness, the barber replied that such a bet was foolish, but if Bourn wished to place one, he would offer odds of one thousand-to-one.

Bourn replied that the odds were just fine and placed a ten-pound wager that the race would end in a tie. On the day of the race, the barber was caught by an event that no one had anticipated, because the race, for the only time in its history, ended in a dead heat. This caused economic failure for the unfortunate barber as he paid off Bourn's bet. However, Will put the barber back to work for him when he became the new owner of the shop.

After the Lent Term examinations, Will took a short vacation from the campus to see more of the countryside around Cambridge. The natural beauty of the area, with its trees, shrubbery, carefully groomed lawns, and neatly laid-out formal gardens, caught his fancy. At this stage of his life, he knew that one day he would like to have a country estate with such gardens and trees trimmed to fit into a formal design.

Young Bourn also saw the farms and villages of the nearby countryside. He thoroughly enjoyed these walking tours. One wonders if he ever traveled thirteen kilometers southwest of Cambridge to visit a place called Bourn, which to this day has the oldest recorded windmill in the country.[7] In addition to his country tours, the period between Lent Term and the summer break gave Will time to catch the train to London, where he attended the theater and went to concerts. He also took advantage of his time in London to visit historical sites, tour the museums, and savor the flavor of this great international city with its districts and citizens that reflected so much of the other nations that had played an important role in the history of England.

While Will toured the English countryside and visited London in the spring and summer of 1876, events in the United States were capturing the attention of the English. In the summer of 1876, the United States held its Centennial Celebration at Philadelphia, only to be upstaged by news of the stunning defeat of the flamboyant George Armstrong Custer and the 7th Cavalry at the Battle of Little Big Horn, where Sioux and Cheyenne warriors under the leadership of Crazy Horse and Sitting Bull defeated Custer and his troopers. This event produced front-page headlines in the English newspapers. Other stories from the United States that year included a report on the invention of the telephone and reviews of Mark Twain's *The Adventures of Tom Sawyer.*

In the fall, Will began the Michaelmas Term, and he looked forward to renewing his studies. As he became engrossed in his classwork, the fall months seemed to pass very quickly, but as October and November passed and December began, Bourn received a letter from his mother asking him to come home and help her with family affairs. However, she indicated that she would be able to send him back to Cambridge once she had a firm grip on things at home. So even before the end of 1876 Will sailed for New York, and as he did, he wondered if he would ever return and complete his studies and receive a degree from Cambridge University.

5 Upon his arrival home, Will enjoyed the last week of the holiday season. Then at the beginning of 1877, he worked with his mother as she conferred with Alpheus Bull about the distribution of her late husband's estate, which was to begin on March 20, 1877. At that time, Sarah was to receive one half of the estate. For the other half, Alpheus Bull—a good businessman and a close friend of the late William Bourn—was to act as guardian. In this position, he was to see that the estate was divided among

the children as they reached their majority. Maye, the eldest, was to receive her share in 1877, and William was to receive his share in 1878. After that, Zaidee's share was due in 1880, Ida's in 1885, and Maud, the youngest child, was to receive her share in 1888.

With the settlement of the late William Bourn's estate underway, Sarah was able to inform her son about the various family businesses. She told William, or Willie, as she continued to call him, that she had hired D. Z. Parkhurst as a cashier and bookkeeper to handle many aspects of the business affairs, both in the 401 California Street office and as far away as the mining properties in Grass Valley, where the output of the Empire Mine was not as good as it had been, and in the distant mining venture in White Pine County, Nevada, where the Hidden Treasure Mine appeared to be about exhausted.

In the spring of 1877, Sarah felt that she had time—especially with her son to help her—to ease up on keeping such a close watch on the daily budget for the family. For the first time since she had lost her husband, Sarah realized that her burden was lighter. Now, she found time to talk to her son about planning a trip abroad to refresh her soul. As she explained to him, she would travel to the East first and visit relatives, then with his help she would book passage on a steamer sailing for Europe. But even as she made these tentative plans in 1877, she knew she would have to make arrangements for the care of Madroño as well as the California Street office and the San Francisco home. Furthermore, the ages of her younger children meant that she would have to take them along on her European excursion. Though she would have Willie's help as far as England, from that point on she knew she could count on Maye, who was twenty-two years old, and Zaidee, who was seventeen, to assist her in taking care of twelve-year-old Ida and ten-year-old Maud.

As for business, the October 1877 report of bullion production from the Empire Mine showed a closing figure of $171,000.[8] Although this represented a gain of $49,000 over 1876, reports from Superintendent Frank Nesmith indicated that while the mine was showing a fair profit, the veins at lower depths seemed less and less promising. Most of all, he feared that his crew of Cornish miners might be entering a barren zone that would be void of gold if they continued to increase the depth of the mine.

Sarah shared all this information with her son, and she took it into consideration before she completed her plans for a European holiday. She informed D. Z. Parkhurst of her plans and told him that she expected to be kept well informed of the progress of the Empire Mine. Furthermore, she told him to find out if any Bourn money was being spent on the Hidden Treasure Mine. If that were the case, she wanted any cash flow to that operation stopped until information about Treasure Hill showed more promise than the British investments in that desolate country, because the last dividend declared by the Eberhardt and Aurora Mining Company in January 1877 amounted to only three shillings per share.[9] If that was the extent of promise at Treasure Hill, Sarah wished no part of any more mining ventures in that region.

As the holiday season of November and December came and passed, and as they celebrated the coming New Year of 1878, Captain George Chase's health took a downward spiral. Even though he had suffered from paralysis for some time, Sarah's father had managed to show "a happy and buoyant temperament, roaring out jolly sailor songs and spinning yarns of sealife to his friends."[10]

Sarah spent more and more time with her father at the White Cottage where her sister Caroline had watched over him until her marriage to John Brayton Bowers. Now the death watch became Sarah's duty. During January and February she listened as her father recalled events of his early life at sea, for he had been a sailor since he went to sea at fourteen from the family home at Martha's Vineyard, Massachusetts. Even after his marriage to eighteen-year-old Mary Elmes of Wiscasset, Maine, he continued to follow the life of a seaman and then the life of a master of his own vessel. For thirty-four years, Sarah's father had been involved in the merchant service. To Sarah, even in the last weeks of his life her father was a man of the sea, just as Will Bourn had been in the early years of his life.

Now, as she watched her father slip away, she realized that this was better than the sudden shock of her husband's death while he had many good years to live. With her father, she knew it was coming, and she had been ready for his last days for some time. But even as he wrestled with the pull of final darkness, she wondered if he still lived with the nightmare of her mother's sudden death as she sailed to New York aboard the U.S.S. *Constitution* in August 1867.[11]

Finally, as the last of February vanished, Captain George Chase died in the White Cottage at seven o'clock on Wednesday morning. At the time of his death, he was seventy-six years, seven months, and twenty-one days old. But as Sarah sat with her father during his last moments of life, it must have seemed ironic to her that her father had lived so much longer than her husband.

6 In May 1878, Will returned to Cambridge with the intention of finishing his degree. Although he was too late to enroll for the Easter Term, he remained at Cambridge and continued to read and prepare for the so-called "Long Vac Term," which began in the middle of July and ran for four weeks.

Meanwhile, he heard from his mother and sisters, who had arrived in Paris. His mother wrote that she planned to stay in Paris until she felt rested, then she and his sisters would travel to other countries and cities in Europe. By October, they planned to be at Villa Dubochel, Clarens, Switzerland.

Even as Cambridge began its summer vacation period, Will remained on the campus, attended the City Festival in the middle of July, and then began the "Long Vac Term." He sensed that he might not be able to finish his third year at Cambridge and obtain his degree, so consequently he thought that he should take advantage of the time he had left.

Upon completing the short summer term, Will had a break from his studies that lasted from the middle of August to the first week of October, when the Michaelmas Term was to begin. During part of this time, he traveled to London to see as much as he could of the great city, for he believed that this might be the last time he would be able to indulge himself as a free and easy tourist, and he thought that his stay in England should result in his coming to know London in the way that he knew San Francisco.

While in London, Will began to run short of funds, and before he returned to Cambridge, he sent a telegram to his mother at Villa Dubochel asking for additional money to see him through the Michaelmas Term at Cambridge. When he did not receive an immediate answer, he sent another telegram which read: "Money not arrived. Can you send me two hundred fifty pounds with answer." Although Sarah had already telegraphed the money to him, Will quickly sent another telegram in which he stated: "Send cheque immediately. Cannot draw on telegraphic order." This second telegram was followed by a third stating, "Money arrived do not need cheque at present. Cambridge tomorrow."[12]

What Will did not know at this time was that his mother was concerned about what was happening at home. In a letter to D. Z. Parkhurst on October 7, 1878, she made it clear that she was not pleased with the way he had been handling her affairs during her absence. She instructed him again to stop all payments of money to the operation of the Hidden Treasure Mine in Nevada, then she told him that she was not happy that the Empire Mine had not been able to pay any dividend to its stockholders. Finally, she wrote: "Inform me of the prospects of the Empire Mine, and I will patiently await results of this letter, admitting it is a scolding one. All expenses to be stopped that do not pay for keeping alive."[13]

Even as Will prepared to resume his studies at Cambridge, his mother informed him that he had to return home at once, for his father's estate was nearly exhausted and she needed him to assume the responsibility of the estate and of all the family affairs. Most of all, she wanted him to see what was happening at the Empire Mine so he could make a decision about any future operations at Grass Valley.[14]

Will notified his mother that he would follow her instructions and leave Cambridge at once. However, as he stated in later years, "I begged my people who were in Switzerland to return."[15] He considered this an emergency that required the full backing of all members of the family.

None of this news came as a surprise to young Bourn, for he had been expecting it for the past year after he returned home in 1877 and saw the tenuous nature of the family's investments. His only sorrow was that he knew he would never return to Cambridge as a student. He presented the university with a set of sterling silver candlestick holders in thanks for the wonderful years he had spent there. Now it was time for him to put to practical use all that he had learned, for ahead of him was the full responsibility of trying to follow in his father's footsteps.

10

Young Bourn and the Empire Mine

Upon William Bourn's return home in the latter part of 1878, he was no longer a growing young man. His face was much fuller, and he had long, dark sideburns and a well-trimmed, full mustache. His dark eyes appeared to be even deeper than his sisters had remembered, but his quick wit and sense of humor were as delightful as ever. The major difference that his mother noticed was his serious side, for he had matured greatly during his years at Cambridge. Now that he was home at Madroño, he had long talks with his mother about the various family businesses. Then, after a conference with the employees at the San Francisco office, he left no doubt as to who would be in charge.

Sarah was more than happy to see that her boy had become a man with a deeply serious side, and that he was anxious to grasp all aspects of his father's enterprises. When the twenty-one-year-old learned that three outside mining engineers had examined the Empire Mine for his mother and had reported that there was no longer a future for this famous Grass Valley mine, he refused to believe it until he had examined the site himself. He was astounded to learn that by November of 1878 all mining operations had ceased "when all pay ore in sight was extracted, pumping was suspended, and the main incline, which had reached a depth of 1,200 feet, on the dip of the ledge, was allowed to fill with water." [1]

At the end of the holiday season, young William Bourn went to Grass Valley. At first, he was distressed to find a drop in population in what was now being described as "a worked out, dying camp, with but three mines in active operation—the Idaho, New York Hill and Empire—the first in bonanza and the other two in borrasca."[2] As for the Empire Mine being in borrasca, or no longer producing pay ore, Bourn refused to accept this idea. After all, the Empire had been one of the richest deep mines in California, and there was a long way to go before the mine became too deep to operate at a profit. In his mind, the great gold-producing days were not over. Even if many of the mines around Grass Valley were shut down, Bourn believed there was much more gold to be found below the 1,200-foot level of the Empire's incline shaft.

While many mining men scoffed at young Bourn's ideas, he forged ahead after he had examined as much of the underground levels of the Empire as he could. When he was finished, he was satisfied that somewhere below the 1,200-foot level it would be possible to locate either the rich Ophir vein or possibly other gold-producing veins.

Satisfied that the gamble was worthwhile, Bourn formed a new company and named it the Original Empire Mill and Mining Company. Shareholders of the Empire were invited to join him in this new venture, but except for Charles F. Fargo of the Wells, Fargo Express Company, all the other shareholders passed up Bourn's offer. He was not discouraged by their lack of faith, and after close study and much preparation, he acted with determination. "The reconstructed company took possession in 1879, shortly afterwards commencing pumping operations and soon resuming shaft-sinking."[3] By July 18, 1879, Will Bourn was satisfied that things were once again moving as they should at the Empire, and he sent a telegram to Sarah at Madroño informing her that things were settled to his satisfaction. He also thanked her for taking out a mortgage on Madroño to help him open the Empire Mine.[4]

Still, things were not done without added trouble. "Operations were conducted under the greatest difficulties, financial and otherwise, for this was a period when belief in California quartz-mining was at its lowest ebb."[5]

2 Even as Will forged ahead on reopening the Empire Mine, he made a long, arduous trip to visit White Pine County, Nevada, in late May 1880. Accompanied by Joseph Fulton of San Francisco and M. Provine of Grass Valley, Bourn examined the family holdings in the Treasure Hill region. After looking over the Ward Beecher, Hidden Treasure, and Mammoth mines, he decided that prospects of getting more silver seemed good only in the Ward Beecher. To carry on work in this mine, he assigned Joseph

Fulton the task of superintending the mining. He assigned Provine, a good mill man, to remain at Treasure Hill and to put the Manhattan and Big Smokey mills into good working order.

Even as Will traveled by stagecoach to Elko, Nevada, where he caught the train to California, he was dubious about the long-term prospects for this venture. Still, he was willing to take a last gamble in the high desert country of eastern Nevada, for almost in a romantic way, he hoped he might be extremely lucky and hit the kind of rich strike that had brought so much money to his father from the Hidden Treasure Mine.

But as work continued throughout 1880 and into 1881, Bourn had to give up on this lost hope in the desert wilderness. Though some silver was found, it hardly warranted the expense of mining it. So by forging ahead on the reopening of the Empire Mine in Grass Valley, he gave his life a definite focus for the immediate future, and he made two moves that were to influence his personal and business life.

In the summer of 1881, he hired his cousin, nineteen-year-old George Starr, and put him to work as an apprentice. As such, Starr began his career as a gold miner by working as a mucker alongside the Cornish miners in the depths of the Empire Mine. Then in the fall of 1881, Bourn traveled east and married Agnes Moody in Yonkers, New York. On October 12, 1881, Will launched his married life by sending a telegram to his mother at Madroño in which he wrote: "Agnes and I are married. Your telegram received. Our only regret is your absence. Our love to all. Will and Agnes."[6]

Upon Bourn's return to California, he once again resumed his control of the search for new, rich veins in the depths of the Empire Mine. However, the next two years were difficult ones for him. In 1882, personal tragedy struck when his first child, a son, died in infancy on August 24, 1882.

As though he were driven by the death of his child, Will watched over the daily progress of the underground work at the mine as the incline shaft cut through barren ground and neared the 1,700-foot level. While he studied daily reports and waited for some indication of relocating the Ophir vein or the possibility of some new vein or veins, he made plans for changes in the mining methods being used.

Among things that he wished to do at the Empire were the replacement of steam power with water power; the addition of more stamps to the twenty-stamp mill; and the improvement of the hoisting works, machine shops, carpenter shop, and the other buildings associated with the daily process of extracting gold from the depths of the earth. Yet Will knew that such changes could not take place until he could raise the considerable amount of money to accomplish his vision.

With an underground crew of 100 to 160 men working shifts around the clock at $3.00 per man per shift; and with 8 to 10 men working above ground at $2.50 per shift, the cost of going deeper with the incline shaft and of cutting drift tunnels off the shaft to explore the walls of the tunnels—even as they timbered them—for signs of a rich vein or veins in the quartz added to the mounting expenses for the daily operation of the mine.

Then in 1883, the same year that Bourn's daughter Maud was born, the Empire Mine passed through barren ground and the drift tunnels off the main shaft began to show rich veins once again. Mules were sent to these tunnels, where they were used to pull the ore carts along the track line to the edge of the junction of the tunnel mouth and the incline shaft. Here, the ore carts were tipped, and their loads fell into skip carts that were pulled by the hoist to the surface, where the ore was transferred to the stamp mill for crushing. In this manner, ore was carried to the surface from this newly uncovered vein that ran in a northerly direction and dipped west at a thirty-degree angle and remained about fifteen inches wide.

This new discovery was extremely rich. The vein and its nearby fissures had a mixture of gold that was almost of specimen quality, and the greenish-white quartz in which the vein was found was also very rich in gold. In addition, the ore uncovered by the Cornish miners, who mucked this heavy ore into iron carts, contained a mixture of mineral concentrates called sulphurets. These sulphurets contained a mixture of iron sulphides or pyrites as well as lead sulphides or galena. The yellow-colored pyrites, often called "fool's gold," and the gray-black galena had somewhere between three to seven ounces of gold per ton of ore. But these minerals were extremely hard, and at this time the Empire Mine did not possess the technology to extract gold from them. Consequently, these mineral concentrates accumulated in piles called tailings.

By 1884 another rich vein was discovered, and like the other veins in the Empire Mine it also ran in a northern direction and dipped to the west at a thirty-degree angle. Will was delighted with this new discovery, and he decided that it was time to shift from steam power to water power. This was a major move in the history of the Empire Mine, and it required two years of work and expense before the completion of the water line allowed water to run through a twenty-two-inch pipeline all the way from the Grass Valley Water Company reservoir at Loma Rica to the Empire Mine.[7]

During this time, Sarah Bourn and Will's sisters moved to New York, where Sarah enrolled the girls in Miss Webb's finishing school. In this period, Sarah and her daughters ultimately made their home-away-from-home at the Dakota Arms, where they had a large flat in this famous building. While she lived here, she received letters from Will and George Starr that kept her up to date on what was taking place at the Empire Mine.

In 1884, Will became interested in the nearby North Star Mine, which had been idle for nearly ten years. The possibilities of working both mines struck him as something worth considering if the property and mineral rights could be purchased for the right amount of money. But first he wanted an examination by a first-rate mining engineer; and he hired John Hays Hammond, who had examined the Empire Mine for him.

After Hammond examined the North Star at its deepest levels, he was certain that once the mine was pumped out and timbering replaced wherever needed, it would be possible to locate the faulted vein and develop other promising ore shoots. With such information in hand, Will and a group of Grass Valley businessmen purchased the mining property for $16,000. Then with a total working capital of $40,000 and an additional assessment of $20,000, the new owners of the North Star were able to rehabilitate old mining equipment and buy new machinery. By 1885 they had put together one of the most modern mining plants in California. Between 1884 and 1886, the North Star was pumped out, the lost vein was located, a modern thirty-stamp mill was constructed, and like the Empire, the North Star came to life and showed new profits for all who invested in it.[8]

3 During the period from 1884 to 1887, Will kept his mother well informed about the progress of both the Empire and the North Star mines. On May 8th, he wrote: "The water company has finished the pipeline to the Empire and will now proceed to the North Star. It has been an immense undertaking, but it will be a success in a short time. All machinery at the Empire will be running with water power." In addition, he informed Sarah about the forthcoming fall wedding of cousin George to Elizabeth Crocker, known as Libby.[9]

In 1887, Bourn sold the North Star to John Hays Hammond and James D. Hague. All three men became friends, and as John Hays Hammond stated in his *Autobiography,* they spent their time with "quartz by day and pints by night."[10]

During this period, the Bourn and Hammond families vacationed together in Yosemite Valley. Even here, they could not escape the mining business, for they received a telegram from James Hague at the North Star, which Hammond recalled stated: "Pipeline supplying power bust. Mill shut down. What do you advise?"[11]

After they finished laughing about Hague's distress, Bourn and Hammond composed and sent a telegram to Hague: "Advise mending pipeline and restarting mill."[12]

After the Yosemite trip, Will received a letter from his mother in which she wrote that she and his sisters were going to travel abroad once more. She informed him that he could reach her in Naples, Italy, by the latter part of February. Concerned by this sudden move, Will wrote to his mother to be certain that she and his sisters had enough funds to cover their expenses.

By April, Will added to his business holdings by entering the banking business as one of the directors of the First National Bank of Grass Valley, which opened for business in the Holbrooke Hotel block. The bank's president was David McKay Jr.; the vice president was Charles P. Clinch; and the cashier was H. D. Andrews. All these men, as well as John Hays Hammond, were listed as directors of the new bank in the *Grass Valley Union* of April 19, 1887. By moving in this direction, Bourn, who was forty-one days short of his thirtieth birthday, was following in his father's footsteps once again.

During this same spring, V. M. Clement, superintendent of the Empire Mine, resigned. Bourn temporarily appointed George Starr as acting superintendent, but by the summer, he wisely gave him the full title of superintendent of the Empire Mine. His cousin had served six years of apprenticeship in the mine, and twenty-five-year-old Starr had been much more than an average worker as he moved from mucker to shift boss to foreman.

Along the way, Starr had learned much about the craft of mining from the Cornish miners, who were key figures in working the deep hard-rock mines. In the mines around Grass Valley and Nevada City, the "Cousin Jacks" carried on their craft and honed it to a fine edge. As young Starr worked beside them, he listened to them and absorbed their knowledge of underground mining. He watched the way they did things, and as they paused for lunch, they told him what they knew as they brought out their folded meat and potato pies, called pasties.

Working in the darkness of the mine, Starr learned enough from these miners to have earned a degree from a first-rate mining college. Even as he picked at loosened walls of gold-bearing quartz that had been blown open by dynamite into an excavation called a *stope,* and as he shoveled the heavy quartz into an ore cart, Starr got a continual lesson in the craft of gold mining. The Cornish miners talked of the danger from unsuspected pockets of gas; of the hazard of striking an unaccounted and unexploded charge of dynamite; and of the terror of a sudden roar of falling earth, rocks, and broken and splintered timbers during a cave-in.

In addition to learning from the "Cousin Jacks," George Starr used his free hours above ground to read key books on geology and gold mining, and he listened closely to his cousin Will and to such mining engineers as John Hays Hammond and James D. Hague. This combination of experience and Starr's drive to learn as much as he could about mining made him the correct choice to fill the position of superintendent of the mine. In a letter that Bourn wrote to his mother, who was staying in Venice, Italy, in July 1887, Will stated: "George Starr is a jewel—he is the new Superintendent of the Empire and a fine one!"[13]

4 By the beginning of 1888, Bourn was ready to move on to new ventures. His faith in both the Empire and the North Star had been correct, for both mines were showing a steady profit. James Hague was running the North Star since Bourn's sale of the mine to him and a group of eastern investors in 1887. Now, in 1888, Will was ready to sell his major interest in the Empire Mine. Yet even as he considered this move, he realized that he was about to part with a business that he had pulled from the edge of extinction and had made into a mine that was a working example of how to search the depths of the earth for elusive veins of gold.

The Empire Mine's shaft had reached 1,700 feet on the incline, or approximately 750 feet vertically. Miners descended into the depths on so-called "man-cars" that shot downward from the headframe into the darkness until they reached the mouth of a drift tunnel. In such a tunnel, miners carried on their work in the early years with only the light from their candles held in a miner's iron candlestick holder. This had a loop on one end, and next to it a round twist in the metal to hold the candle; opposite the twist for the candle was an iron hook that looked like a hay hook, followed by an iron rod that ended in a sharp point. A miner could hang his candlestick holder by its hook or he could shove its sharp end into any nearby support.

As mining equipment changes took place, the miner's candlestick gave way to the carbide lamp and the hand drill was replaced by the pneumatic drill. But it wasn't until the turn of the century that the mine had electric lights underground. Even then, men working at the far end of a drift tunnel—following a vein as they worked in a stope—might not have electric lights if the distance to an electrical outlet at the main shaft station would be too far.

In general, working conditions at the Empire Mine were a model of what mining conditions should be as 1888 began. The large Cornish pump raised 18,000 gallons of water per hour to the surface. Both the hoisting works and the stamp mill were run by water power; and in the forty-stamp mill, each 850-pound stamp dropped seven inches at a rate of ninety times per minute. With a steady thunder that echoed throughout Grass Valley, the mill crushed as much as two tons of ore during a twenty-four-hour shift, and in this same time it used as much as 1½ cubic feet of water per minute.[14]

Despite his accomplishments with the Empire Mine, Bourn was anxious to move on to other business activities. He consulted with Hague and agreed to sell controlling interest in the mine to him. However, Will did not let all control go, because he held on to considerable stock and retained his position on the board. In addition, he was happy that Hague retained George Starr as the Empire's superintendent.

On February 1, 1888, a terrible disaster occurred in Napa Valley. Sarah, who had returned from Italy, had hired roofers to put new sheet roofing on Madroño. As they were working, the roofers accidentally dropped some hot coals. The new roofing served as kindling, and the roof caught fire, which spread quickly. The roofers tried to stomp out the first flames, then they got off the roof and ran for the garden hoses. But the water pressure was so low that the hoses were useless.

Seeing the smoke and fire, six carpenters and their foreman drove their wagon to the home, jumped off, and began to help save whatever they could from the fire that was beginning to engulf all of Madroño. But all they could save were some pieces of furniture, 150 shutters, and the home's hardwood doors. Other than these few items, all that remained of Madroño after the fire were the home's massive stone arches and walls. All the rest was gone. Countless family pictures, personal belongings, art works, business papers, diaries, and letters had gone up in smoke. With this loss, all that remained of the grand years at Madroño when Sarah and her late husband built it as their country retreat were memories.

For Will, the loss of Madroño was a terrible shock, and he quickly made his way to St. Helena, only to discover that his mother had taken up temporary residence at the Hotel Rafael in San Rafael. As he moved into the White Cottage, he wrote to his mother on February 7, 1888, "there is so much of Madroño beyond the reach of fire. I do hope that all your little treasures will be found."[15]

Even as Will tried his best to hold hope for the rescue of some of his mother's "little treasures," he was shocked by what he saw as he walked around the scene of disaster. The charred ruins and the ghostly stone arches and walls were daily reminders of all the good years the family had enjoyed in their country retreat, where daily walks through the vineyards, grand country dinners for the family and guests, and lively conversations that ranged from business to politics to history, to the arts, and most of all, to nature were carried on every evening.

Now, as the cooling ashes left only the aroma of a blackened dream, Will looked upon the charred ruins as one of his next projects, and he contemplated where to begin again.

William Bowers Bourn I was born in Somerset, Massachusetts, on June 21, 1813. He was a man of means when he emigrated to San Francisco in 1850. He made a fortune in gold and silver mines before his untimely death on July 24, 1874. *Courtesy, A.W. B. Vincent Collection, San Francisco.*

William Bowers Bourn II was born on May 31, 1857, in San Francisco. He was the second child of William B. Bourn I and Sarah Esther Chase Bourn. He took over the Empire Mine after his father's death and went on to become one of the great builder-sons of San Francisco. He died at Filoli on July 5, 1936. *Courtesy, A.W. B. Vincent Collection, San Francisco.*

The Empire Mine's tall headframe looked like a long drop on a roller coaster. The picture shows other buildings used in the mining operation. The stacked logs were for use as mine timbers in the many miles of drift tunnels that followed gold veins beyond the main shaft station levels. *Courtesy, A. W. B. Vincent Collection.*

The Empire Cottage was designed by Bourn's friend Willis Polk. He used quartz rocks from the mine for the walls and trimmed the doors and windows with bricks. Both the living and dining rooms were paneled with redwood. The house included four bedrooms, a kitchen, and quarters for the servants. Surrounding the house were twelve acres of landscaped grounds containing lawns, gardens, fountains, and pools. *Courtesy, A. W. B. Vincent Collection, San Francisco.*

Two man-cars were lined together for this picture taken below ground at one of the Empire Mine's stations. Each miner carried a candlestick holder and a candle. This holder with its sharp end and side hook could be thrust into a mine timber or hung by its hook from a timber or an outcropping of rock. Electricity was available at the station level, but at the time of this photo there were no electric lights in the drifts where the miners worked. *Courtesy, A. W. B. Vincent Collection, San Francisco.*

The Greystone Cellar as it appeared in the early fall of 1889. By this time, partners William Bourn II and E. Everett Wise were crushing seventy tons of grapes per day, and they were storing 250,000 gallons of wine for aging. *Courtesy, A.W. B. Vincent Collection, San Francisco.*

Sarah Bourn's country home, Madroño, was near St. Helena in the Napa Valley. In 1888, it caught fire and burned. This was a great loss to the Bourns, because the house had been for many years the family gathering place. *Courtesy, A.W. B. Vincent Collection, San Francisco.*

In 1915 William and Agnes Bourn began the building of Filoli, their country estate near the Crystal Springs Reservoir in San Mateo County. By 1919, Willis Polk had completed the construction of the main house. This photograph shows the courtyard and entrance to Filoli. *Courtesy, A. W. B. Vincent Collection, San Francisco.*

The ballroom at Filoli continues to fascinate visitors. The large Ernest Peixotto mural shows a boat on the surface of Lake Killarney, and the man standing in the boat represents Arthur Rose Vincent. In the distance is Muckross House. The small mural near the doorway depicts the Bourn grandchildren, Elizabeth Rose and Arthur William Bourn Vincent, at play in the garden of Muckross House. The painting over the fireplace is of Muckross Abbey. *Courtesy, A. W. B. Vincent Collection, San Francisco.*

Standing outside the entrance to Filoli's carriage house is Sidney Woods, head butler for many years. In the background is the clock tower designed by Arthur Brown Jr. *Courtesy, A. W. B. Vincent Collection, San Francisco.*

Sarah Esther Chase Bourn, matriarch of the Bourn family, posed for this picture in 1899. *Courtesy, A. W. B. Vincent Collection, San Francisco.*

George Starr was William Bourn II's cousin. After the death of his mother, he was raised by his aunt, Sarah Esther Chase Bourn. He became one of the top mining engineers in the gold-mining areas of California's northern mines and in South Africa. He began his mining career as a mucker at the Empire Mine and went on to help young Bourn develop the Empire after other mining engineers had proclaimed its demise. At the time of Bourn's sale of the Empire Mine to the Newmont Mining Company in 1929, Starr was the managing director of mines for the Empire Mines and Investment Company. *Courtesy, A. W. B. Vincent Collection, San Francisco.*

Sky Farm in San Mateo County was built for Prince André Poniatowski, who later sold it to his brother-in-law, William Crocker. At the time of this photograph, Will and Agnes Bourn were renting the house. The flags and bunting were in celebration of the March 30, 1910, wedding of their daughter, Maud, to Arthur Rose Vincent of Ireland. The scene shows tables set for the wedding reception. *Courtesy, A. W. B. Vincent Collection, San Francisco.*

This Bourn family portrait was taken at 2030 Broadway, San Francisco, in March 1919. First row, left to right: Maud Bourn Vincent, Elizabeth Rose Vincent, Sarah Esther Chase Bourn, and Ida Hoxie Bourn. Second row, left to right: Arthur Rose Vincent, Agnes Moody Bourn, Maye Bourn Tucker, William Bowers Bourn II, and Maud Bourn Hayne. *Courtesy, A. W. B. Vincent Collection, San Francisco.*

Although William and Agnes Bourn were confined to their bedrooms because of declining health, they held a "Drunk's Dinner" to celebrate the repeal of the Eighteenth Amendment on November 24, 1933. As the invitation stated, "Mr. and Mrs. Bourn Being Sober Will Not Be Present." The hostess for this dinner was Will's sister Ida Bourn (right foreground). Surrounding the table (clockwise from her left) were Edward Eyre, Mrs. Ansel Easton, Maud Bourn Hayne, Gerald Rathbone, Mrs. Samuel Eastman, Robert Hooker, Marjorie Josselyn, (unknown), (unknown), George Starr, Mrs. Gerald Rathbone, Arthur Brown, Samuel Eastman, Maye Bourn Tucker, (unknown), Mrs. Arthur Brown, Thomas Barbour, Mrs. Osgood Hooker, and Louis F. Monteagle. *Courtesy, A. W. B. Vincent Collection, San Francisco.*

(*left*) Muckross House in County Kerry, Ireland, was purchased by William Bowers Bourn II in 1910 for his daughter, Maud, and her husband, Arthur Vincent. This Elizabethan-style house of one hundred rooms and sixty-two chimneys overlooks the Lower and Middle Killarney Lakes. In 1932, Mr. and Mrs. William B. Bourn and Arthur Vincent gave Muckross and its eleven thousand acres to Ireland for a national park and as a memorial to Maud Bourn Vincent. *Courtesy, The Office of Public Works, Dublin, Ireland.*

Agnes Moody Bourn and William Bowers Bourn II in the late 1920s at one of Will's favorite spots in the gardens of Filoli. *Courtesy, A. W. B. Vincent Collection, San Francisco.*

11

The Napa Valley Years

As the Bourns knew from the original property deeds, the site of Madroño once had been part of the Bale Ranch. In 1841, after his marriage to María Ignacia Soberanes, General Mariano Vallejo's niece, Dr. Edward Turner Bale—a former English surgeon—called his land grant Rancho Carne Humana. This large ranch stretched from just south of the future site of the town of St. Helena to the country around Calistoga in the northern portion of the Napa Valley.[1]

In late February 1888, Will's driving interest was to rebuild the family home. The first steps included removing the remains of the terrible fire and drawing up plans for a new house. The next step was to incorporate the surviving stone arches and walls into the plans, for these were reminders of the blaze and symbols of endurance. To combine the new with remains of the old struck Will as a vital step in recapturing the spirit of Madroño.

During this time of planning and building, Will's mother and sisters Ida and Maud lived in the Hotel Rafael in San Rafael.[2] Sarah saw this as a good location, because San Rafael was not too far from St. Helena, so it was easier to visit Madroño to see how the new house was progressing. On such visits, she stayed with Will and Agnes in the White Cottage. Sarah watched the progress of the new house and looked over the vineyards, the chickens, and the horses stabled in the barn. Sometimes Maud came with her mother, and at other times Ida came. The only members of the family who did not have any say as the work on a new Madroño began were Zaidee, who was in New York, and Maye, who was in Dresden, Germany, as part of her tour of Europe.

No expense was to be spared in rebuilding the Bourn country estate, even though the insurance policy had returned only $41,300 for a loss estimated at over $75,000.[3] But Will and his mother were not people who hesitated about cost. To them, if something was worth doing, it had to be done correctly. With a steady income from many investments, including stock in the Empire Mine, the Bourns were not short of money.

As work proceeded, they decided that the new house would have a very large living room, a formal dining room that would accommodate the whole family as well as guests, a much larger kitchen, plenty of bedrooms and bathrooms to serve the needs of a large family, and a water supply system with enough water pressure for any emergency. A major consideration in rebuilding Madroño was to recapture the atmosphere of the original home, for it was this special feeling that had made Madroño a unifying gathering place for all members of the Bourn family.

2 Rebuilding the house was not the only thing on Will's mind in the spring of 1888, for he also began to give attention to the vineyards. There were some sixty acres of vineyards when Bourn took charge of the business in early 1888. Among the first things he did was to make arrangements with Charles Krug to have the grapes from the Bourn ranch processed into wine at the Charles Krug Winery just northeast of St. Helena. In this operation, Bourn and E. Everett Wise formed a partnership, for Bourn considered Wise a knowledgeable vineyard owner and a sharp businessman. Krug, a young German who had once been winemaker for General Vallejo at Sonoma, had the knowledge and facilities to convert Bourn's and Wise's grape tonnage into wine, then to age and bottle it so that neither man would be at the mercy of the San Francisco wine monopoly.

For most Napa Valley vintners, the San Francisco wine dealers represented a yearly threat to their income. The dealers had the cooperage to store and age young wines, and they knew that most of the growers lacked such facilities. As a result, ranchers were forced to sell to San Francisco wine merchants at prices that ran as low as fifteen to eighteen cents per gallon. Such prices were keeping Napa Valley vintners on the edge of bankruptcy.

Deeply concerned about such unjust business practices, Bourn suggested to Wise the idea of constructing a large wine cellar in the area with a storage capacity of at least two million gallons. Wise agreed that while such a venture would be expensive, over a period of time it would more than pay for its cost. Most of all, it would break the stranglehold the San Francisco wine merchants had on the growers of Napa Valley. In addition, the plan called for something that none of the banks were willing to do, because they refused to look upon wine as collateral. Bourn and Wise offered local growers an opportunity to obtain loans for ten cents on every gallon that they placed in storage, and the interest rate would be 10 percent per year.[4]

During the first weeks of March 1888, Bourn held meetings with local growers and presented his plan. He stated that the proposed wine cellar would have a storage capacity of two million gallons. Added to this, there would be at least thirteen tunnels cut into the hillside behind the winery to serve as storage for another million gallons of wine.

The construction cost for such a project, Bourn estimated, would run between $250,000 and $500,000, but he was not asking growers to help with direct financing. He and Everett Wise and other investors would finance the building of this cellar, but Bourn asked for an agreement from the Napa Valley growers that would commit them to store the wine from five hundred tons of grapes per year for five years. This required tonnage would amount to less than 5 percent of the valley's annual crop, and storage for wine would cost 2½ cents per gallon per year. Altogether, this was a small cost when compared to the money that growers would save by not being at the mercy of the San Francisco wine dealers.[5]

All this sounded good to the Napa Valley growers, and Bourn went ahead with his plan. By April 6, 1888, the first drawings and plans for the wine cellar were displayed in the office of the *St. Helena Star.* The cellar was to be built of stone, and the main building would have a frontage of four hundred feet, a depth of seventy-six feet, and a height of sixty-six feet. The cellar design called for concrete ceilings, iron beams and pillars, and cement floors. Furthermore, the building was designed to be fireproof.

Bourn and Wise included three floors and a basement in their plans for the cellar. The first floor was to be a storage area for some 576,000 gallons of dry wines; sweet wines, at least 600,000 gallons, were to be stored on the second floor.[6] At this stage of planning, no definite idea was presented for the use of the third floor, except that it could be used for either storage or manufacturing purposes.

The basement design included an engine room and an electric plant. As Bourn saw it, wires could be run from the basement to the other floors of the cellar as well as into the tunnels for lighting and power. The different departments of the completed wine cellar were to be arranged to provide for a uniform temperature at all times.

An arched driveway was to run in back of the cellar and in front of the mountainside. This was to be the area of the storage tunnels.

The plans for the cellar also called for the construction of a large distillery behind the main building. Meanwhile, the interior of the main building saw the use of a new form of concrete construction developed by Ernest L. Ransome of San Francisco, which united twisted iron rods into the concrete to combine the tensile strength of iron and the compressive strength of concrete into what is now known as prestressed concrete. In his work on the great wine cellar, Ransome's final plan called for using concrete and twisted iron rods in the second floor of the building. In this way, the final form of the floor was to be constructed with concrete beams and arches that included four twisted iron rods 1¼ inches by 1¼ inches in each beam. These beams were to be protected from leakage "by a strip of lead embedded in each half of the beam."[7]

Every other iron pillar used to support the ceiling was to be hollow to carry spilled wine off to the distillery. As Bourn and Wise pointed out, no cost would be spared in the construction of the winery. All stones for the cellar, as well as gravel and sand for concrete, were to be purchased locally. A large force of men was to be hired, and local workers were to be given preference in hiring. In this manner, the construction would add money to the local economy. Local Italian stonemasons would be key workers as the walls for the building were put into place. The concrete work was to be handled by the Ernest L. Ransome firm of San Francisco, and the firm of Percy and Hamilton of San Francisco was to provide the supervising architect.

Upon hearing about Bourn's plan to build this large winery, the San Francisco wine merchants reacted quickly. Ten of the largest firms formed the Wine Dealers Association, and they notified the grape growers of the Napa and Sonoma valleys that they had to sell their grapes to the association or the San Francisco Wine Dealers would not buy any grapes or wine from them. When this news reached the growers, many of them grew fearful and withdrew their commitments.

Will reacted quickly. He called for a meeting of the Napa Valley grape growers on April 7, 1888. Even though he had purchased twenty-five acres of land from Charles Krug just above the Beringer Brothers' land a mile north of St. Helena, he let the local growers know that if they did not support him by bringing in at least five hundred tons of grapes each year, he would not build a wine cellar.

When the crowd heard this possible turn of events, the meeting turned into a noisy affair. Speaker after speaker had his say. Then Bourn addressed the meeting again. He told the assembled gathering that he was willing to drop his demand for 500 tons to 350, but that was as low as he would go. Gradually, the growers began to swing toward Bourn's position until they were only 50 tons short of his demand. Then when it appeared that this request was not going to be met, Charles Krug told the crowd that he and eight other vintners would provide the additional 50 tons.

News of the commitment to construct this mammoth wine cellar quickly spread throughout the Napa and Sonoma Valleys. Its location was printed in the *St. Helena Star,* and it was reported that the winery would occupy the northern thirteen acres of the section of land purchased from Charles Krug, while the lower twelve acres would serve as the site of the large home that Everett Wise planned to build.

The building of the wine cellar captured the attention of Napa Valley residents, and a feature column titled "The Cellar" ran in the *St. Helena Star.* In the April 20, 1888, issue of the newspaper, the construction superintendent Judge Allison noted that he had thirty-nine men at work. Most were digging and drilling, and seven were running scrapers. It was done in this manner to allow the Italian stonemasons to begin their work, and to bring in other workers to excavate on the hillside and construct the thirteen tunnels, which were to be 16 feet wide, 11 feet high to the spring of the arch, and 14 feet 8 inches apart.

Many of the workers camped out on the grounds beside the site of their daily labor. Here they had tents, bedrolls, and cooking utensils. After a day of hard work, they built campfires, cooked their own meals, and sat around the fires, smoking and talking before turning in for the night. In a way, the building of the wine cellar had the atmosphere of a battlefield about it. Men, campfires, tents, the evening smells of cooking food and boiling coffee, and the sounds of men conversing about their work, their dreams, their families, and the need for money that had brought Napa Valley men and laborers from other cities and towns to work for a small sum of money on the building of the cellar. The total payroll for all the men hired came to ninety-eight dollars per day.

By the beginning of the second week of June 1888, the Ransome firm of San Francisco was making steady progress on the concrete work for the foundation of the front and back walls of the building. Bourn insisted that the gray stones be used in the front wall, and stones that were darker or of another color be used in the walls for the back and sides of the building. Meanwhile, work was started on six of the thirteen tunnels, while to the south of the wine cellar, Everett Wise's home was nearing completion.

On June 15, 1888, the cornerstone for the great wine cellar was laid. Wise and a few invited friends—William Bourn was not present—"gathered around a space about two feet square and twelve inches deep prepared in the southeast corner of the building for the reception of different articles, and after they had been placed, Mr. Wise, as master of ceremonies, passed a glass of old wine to each of the guests, while all took up a position near the corner while Mr. Parott took a photograph with his instantaneous photographing apparatus. . . . The health of Messrs. Bourn and Wise was drunk, while Mr. Williams and Mr. Delucchi carefully laid the cornerstone . . . assisted by Mr. Wise, who placed a trowel of mortar on it. As it was then quitting time for the men employed, they were all invited to come forward and take a glass of wine."[8]

In addition to the ceremony for the laying of the cornerstone, the following items were placed beneath it: "Bourn & Wise, one bottle of 1887 Sauvignon Vert, one bottle of 1886 Carrignan . . . an old ten-cent piece; Beringer Bros., one bottle of 1884 Brandy, and one bottle of 1884 Burger; Charles Krug, 1885 Riesling; Mrs. Weinberger, one bottle 1887 Riesling; Louis Zierngibl, one bottle of 1886 Johannisberg Riesling; Dungan & Mackinder, a copy of the *Star,* of April 13th, 1888, the date when it was announced to the public that the new cellar was to be built; a copy of the San Francisco *Chronicle* and *Examiner;* also several foreign and rare coins, mostly, contributed by the men at work."[9]

Throughout the summer of 1888, the crew of workmen, who ranged from laborers to professional cement workers from the Ransome Company of San Francisco, forged ahead with the help of the Italian stonemasons and some men who worked on the storage tunnels. Bourn and Wise watched as the back wall was completed in the third week of June 1888. At the same time, Wise's home was almost ready for occupancy. The three-story mansion had three steep pitched roof lines on the north, south, and east-west sides. The home had a wide covered veranda that ran across the east and south walls; the view to the north from the knoll site was of the rising walls of the great wine cellar under construction.

As the summer of 1888 ended, construction of the wine cellar forged ahead despite a slow-down caused by a delay in getting enough stones from the quarry. Then a cave-in on the back wall nearly trapped ten men and three horses, but all escaped without injury. In the second week of September, fifteen concrete arches, or one-half of the first wing, were completed, and they stood without any indication of weakness when the wooden braces were removed. In this same period, half of the arches over the first driveway were finished. Then to indicate the rapid progress of the project, new oak cooperage arrived from the David Woerner Cooperage Company of San Francisco. These wine storage tanks, which held as much as two thousand gallons each, stood outside the winery until it was time to place them inside.

As fall approached and the harvest moon of October rose in the sky to shine over the vineyards and the growing walls of the wine cellar, carpenters worked at a steady pace to build stands for the tanks and for smaller casks. In the October moonlight, the outline of the foundation for the tower and over half of the wine cellar stood out like great monuments under construction.

3 As 1888 eased into 1889, William Bourn traveled back and forth between his home in San Francisco and the White Cottage at Madroño. At home, he had time to be with Agnes and their daughter Maud, who had her fifth birthday in November 1888.

In San Francisco, Will looked over his business ventures in his California Street office, where he caught the cable car that dropped him off near his place of business. Whenever he boarded the cable car, he never had the needed change to pay his fare, but friends from the Montgomery Street world of finance were always aboard, and Bourn borrowed his fare from one of them. This became a running joke among these men, and one of them sent Bourn a bill at the end of a year. Upon receiving the bill, Will promptly paid his friend.

Along with his concerns over rebuilding Madroño and the construction of what he was now calling the Greystone Cellar, Bourn continued to watch the progress of the Empire Mine. Under George Starr's supervision, the mine had reached an incline depth of 1,700 feet by October 1, 1888. During this period, the total expenses for ore mined and milled came to $11.15 per ton. The mine continued to produce a high level of gold from its rich veins, and returns were excellent for both owners and investors.

At this time, Bourn became interested in two major utilities that he considered as potential investments. In his mind, both would play key roles in San Francisco's future. The first to catch his fancy was the San Francisco Gas Light Company. In 1888 this company received a two-year contract from the City of San Francisco "to erect and maintain 21 masts 150 feet tall each with 16,000 candlepower and 102 masts 40 feet high with lamps of 2,000 candlepower. Rates for the lighting service were fixed at $4.40 per night for each of the 150 foot masts and 55 cents per night for each of the 2,000 candlepower installations."[10]

The San Francisco Gas Light Company traced its origin to the work of the Donahue brothers' San Francisco Gas Company, which followed a firm that as early as 1853 had tried a few experimental gas lamps on Montgomery Street. Will was also interested in a new firm, the California Electric Light Company, which by 1888 operated the "first dynamo for incandescent lighting service."[11] Bourn believed that it was only a matter of time—and not too much time—before the electric and gas companies of San Francisco would have to unite. Consequently, he kept a close watch on the pioneer San Francisco Gas Company and the growing California Electric Light Company, because the future power source for San Francisco, it appeared, would be in the hands of either one or in a uniting of the two firms.

In addition to his interest in the future of gas and electricity, Will realized that water for San Francisco and other Bay Area communities was vital if economic growth was to continue. Knowing this, he became interested in the Spring Valley Water Company. Even though this company had its start in 1857–58 as the San Francisco Water Works, it soon changed its name to the Spring Valley Water Company as it moved down the Peninsula. Here it built the Pilarcitos Dam in the coastal hills and carried water from there to San Francisco in a thirty-two-mile redwood flume by 1862–63. Now, as Bourn watched the company's progress—a company that William Ralston had tried to control until his financial collapse ended all his dreams—the Crystal Springs Dam, the key part of Herman Schussler's catchment system, was only a year away from completion. Will realized that this water system held the future for San Francisco and the Peninsula, and he began to buy its stock.

But even with his many business interests in and around San Francisco, even with the social life that he and Agnes were enjoying as they met artists, writers, musicians, architects, and other creative San Franciscans in a society that was shedding its rough Gold Rush exterior for the subtle garments of civilization, Will heard the call of projects left unfinished in the Napa

Valley. By the beginning of the spring of 1889, he returned to the White Cottage on the Madroño estate, where he resumed the tasks at hand.

4 During the middle of April 1889, Bourn and Wise started construction of the winery's distillery, and they began to purchase such grapes as the Mission, Malvosie, and Zinfandel from ranches near the Napa River. At this time, they also began to vacate part of Charles Krug's cellar, which they had been using for winemaking since 1886–87. The upper story of their own wine cellar was almost ready for winemaking.

By the fifth day of May 1889, most of the work on the massive wine cellar had been completed, except for the tower. At this time, contracts were awarded for the installation of elevators, presses, and crushers, and Wise reported to the *St. Helena Star* that the tunnels soon would be open.

As the month of June neared a close, the north wing of the wine cellar was almost filled with oak cooperage holding about 100,000 gallons of wine. Storage tanks were put into place in the south wing, and workers were putting tanks together in the fermenting room. During this period, the stone tower was completed; a two-story stone distillery was under construction; and the offices for the winery were paneled in oak and mahogany, completed, and opened for use.

As of September 13, 1889, it was announced that the new wine cellar would be able to make up to 500,000 gallons of first-class wine, and there would be storage for about 200,000 gallons. This wine showed the first indication of income for Bourn and Wise, because some of this stored wine had been borrowed against by the grape growers, and all of the stored wine brought in two and one-half cents per gallon, per year.

Two weeks later, on the last day of September, it was reported that the two elevators, two crushers, and two massive hydraulic presses were crushing 70 tons of grapes per day. Bourn and Wise thought that the total crush would be about 3,500 tons. Of this tonnage, 1,200 would come from purchased grapes and 2,300 tons from Bourn's own vineyards. In addition, the firm purchased about 50,000 gallons of wine for brandy production, and 250,000 gallons of wine belonging to other vintners was in storage in the great cellar.

During this time, Everett Wise became ill and sold his half of the winery to William Bourn. Between the time of the sale and the fall of 1890, Bourn named his winery the Greystone Cellar, a name he also used on his own brandy and wine labels. The total costs for construction of the wine cellar vary according to which figures are added, but it is not out of range to estimate its final construction costs as somewhere around one-half million dollars. But mere figures do not do it justice. When finished, the Greystone Cellar stood out like a monument to the giants of the wine industry. The carefully selected stone gave the building the color of great age, and the size of the cellar, with its use of the very best in construction methods, made it a perfect home for wine and all the mythology of wine, which has its roots in the Old World but found a home to match that history in the grandeur of the Greystone Cellar. Idwal Jones compared the structure to some massive Colossus built to stable war horses—a massive building of heroic stature that gave it the appearance of a centuries-old monument.[12]

12

San Francisco: City of Promise

As the decade of the 1890s began, William Bourn felt the call of a changing San Francisco. No longer was the city anchored in its rough-and-tumble beginnings. While its heritage from the California Gold Rush and the boom years of Nevada's Comstock Lode lingered in the building of individual fortunes, San Francisco was becoming a city of promise. As Will wrote: "No stranger could come here without encountering habits of life and thought in which she differs not only from his own home but from every other American city."[1]

Business interests were a major part of Will's bonding with San Francisco, for he saw a great future in its unlimited growth. Here was the beginning of a new kind of American city, one that held boundless opportunities. As Bourn envisioned it, the City of the Golden Gate would become *the* city of the Far West.

Although Will's interests in the wine business of the Napa Valley and in the gold production of the Empire Mine in Grass Valley were vital to him, he also had the vision to see San Francisco as an international city. He realized that new foundations for San Francisco's future would require an organized system of gas and electricity as well as a modern, reliable water system. By 1890, Will began to invest heavily in the late Peter Donahue's pioneer firm, the San Francisco Gas Light Company, which had its origin on April 1, 1873, when Donahue merged his San Francisco Gas Company with the City Gas Company and the Metropolitan Gas Company. Even though this was the beginning of the kind of system needed for San Francisco's future growth, there were other companies competing for the market, and Will saw all this as a waste that resulted in rate wars, a hodgepodge of different electric lines and gas pipes, and needless, inefficient duplication. The only way out of this mess was quite apparent to Will—the ultimate consolidation of all these utility companies into one major firm that would supply San Francisco with the needed utilities and maintain a steady program of modernization as well as keep rates within reason for all customers. As he bought more and more stock in the San Francisco Gas Light Company, Will saw the time for a merger as a quest, not a quixotic dream.

The other key ingredient for San Francisco's future was a steady supply of water; for this, San Francisco was dependent upon the Spring Valley Water Company. This firm had its beginning as the San Francisco City Water Works and was incorporated in 1850–51. Commonly, it was called the Bentsley Company after the name of its original owner. However, this company was not able to supply the water needs of a growing San Francisco, and by 1858 George H. Ensign and his associates bought out the San Francisco Water Works. Although they were limited at first to such sources of water as Mountain Lake and Lobos Creek within the Presidio and to the water from Lake Merced, the new firm changed the name to the Spring Valley Water Company and began to look for other sources of water. By 1862–63, the company had tapped the Coast Range watershed in San Mateo County by building Pilarcitos Dam. This was followed by the construction of the San Andreas Dam in 1868 under the engineering guidance of Herman Schussler.[2]

During this early period of the Spring Valley Water Company and into the 1870s, the company was controlled by such dominant men as Charles Crocker, Leland Stanford, Mark Hopkins, Collis P. Huntington, Darius Ogden Mills, William Ralston, James Ben Ali Haggin, Lloyd Tevis, and John Parrott. Under the influence of such powerful money men, the company bought all the farms in the area where San Mateo Creek cuts through the valley. During this same period, the company acquired the Crystal Springs Hotel, a noted old resort. To make way for the construction of a new dam that would form a man-made lake, the company tore down the hotel as well as the farm buildings it had acquired when it bought out the local farmers. They cleared the land of brush and trees and began work on the Crystal Springs Dam, which Schussler's workers completed by 1890. Upon its completion, the dam was considered the world's largest cement dam, and it drew engineers and other visitors who wanted to see this marvel of modern engineering.[3]

Will Bourn, in his usual scholarly fashion, studied the history of the Spring Valley Water Company thoroughly, because he wanted to know what had been done to develop a water system as well as what could be done to improve the existing facilities for storing and delivering water and to locate new sources to accommodate San Francisco's growth (in 1890 the population of San Francisco was over 298,000, compared to 56,000 in 1860 when the company was known as the San Francisco Water Works).[4] Bourn was aware of both advantages and dangers in any future acquisition of water company stock. The long-term possibilities of the company showed great promise. The one possible danger of acquiring too much stock was the City of San Francisco, because there was no way of knowing what its policy about water might be in the short run, much less in the long run.

As 1890 began, Will pursued his goals of acquiring more stock in the Spring Valley Water Company and the San Francisco Gas Light Company. Although he did this with his usual caution, he did have in mind a definite goal becoming one of the key players in the major utilities, for such utilities would be determining factors in the future growth and development of San Francisco. As a native San Franciscan, he loved the city, and he saw it as a very special place with the potential to become one of the major cities of the world.

2 The winter of 1889–90 was one that Northern Californians would never forget. The rainy season saw one downpour after another, and by April 18, 1890, San Francisco had received almost 43 inches of rain, while the Delta in the San Joaquin Valley was flooded by 115 inches of rain. "Bridges and roads were washed away, railroads blockaded for days or weeks at a time,"[5] and outdoor activity in San Francisco was limited by overflowing drainage systems that turned streets and sidewalks into rushing streams.

During this wet winter, Will spent much of his time in his office, where he kept up with the wide range of personal and family holdings. Among his concerns was the family property in the Napa Valley. Though the early work of rebuilding Madroño had been delayed by the steady rainfall, Will was concerned that neither he nor his mother had hired an architect to draw up proper plans for the new house. He was convinced that once the tremendous rainfall ceased, it would be necessary to have a plan drawn for Madroño rather than rely upon local contractors for suggestions. Meanwhile, the steady downpour flooded the vineyards, and farmhands were unable to tend the vines.

However, the wet winter did not prevent Will and Agnes from venturing out to visit friends who lived on Nob Hill and in the Pacific Heights area. They dined at such favorite places as the Poodle Dog and the Palace Hotel. Evenings on the town were also spent at the California Theater and the Tivoli Opera House.

As the Bourns moved into San Francisco social life, they became close friends of the William H. Crocker family and met and associated with other families who were among the city's most affluent and influential citizens. Yet even as they moved with ease among the richest elements of local society, Will found time to meet a group of highly talented, creative young people who were part of the Bohemian Club, which dated back to 1872. These young men were noted for their lively, diverse approaches to all forms of art from architecture to painting and sculpture and to poetry and prose. Among these talented artists were such figures as twenty-five-year-old Bruce Porter, a muralist, creator of stained-glass windows, and landscape designer. Young Porter's ideas for garden designs captured Will's imagination, because he loved gardens.

Through Porter, Will met the diminutive Willis Jefferson Polk, a talented young architect who was born in Jacksonville, Illinois, in 1867, the third of seven children. His father, Willis Webb Polk, was an itinerant carpenter-designer who traveled throughout the Midwest and the South. By the time young Polk was six years old, his father went to work as a carpenter-designer in St. Louis. Here, the senior Polk became prominent in local trade organizations and known as a man who advocated temperance. Young Willis at age eight went to work for a local builder, and by the time he was thirteen, he had become an office boy for Jerome B. Legg's architectural firm.[6]

As Will learned from Polk, the likable young man had left Legg's office to join his father's growing practice. In 1882, his father's rheumatism forced the family to move to Hot Springs, Arkansas, for his health, and it was here that fifteen-year-old Willis won a competitive contest for a schoolhouse design for Hope, Arkansas. Will also learned from Willis that in 1888 he had worked for Ernest Coxhead in Los Angeles for a brief time, then traveled to New York to work for Henry Van Brunt. Although he stayed only six months with him, he managed to attend Columbia College to take classes in architecture taught by William Robert Ware, who had been Van Brunt's partner. After this, Polk went to work as a draftsman for A. Page Brown and came to San Francisco with him in 1889. When Will met him, Polk and Fritz Maurice Gamble of Oakland had formed a partnership.[7]

As Will talked to young Polk, he found that he liked him and agreed with many of his ideas of what a house should be. For the moment, Will and Agnes were comfortable in the family home on Taylor Street, although in Will's mind the house was associated with tragic memories of his father's accidental death and the death of his younger brother, Frank, whose fall from the high wall surrounding the backyard had cut short his life at age eleven. Haunted by these memories, Will knew that the time would come when he might want to build a new home in San Francisco. And as he talked to Polk, he realized that he would want to consider him as a possible architect.

Meanwhile, Will knew that uncompleted tasks awaited him in the Napa Valley. His mother and his sister Ida were unable to live in the family home while carpenters and other craftsmen continued with the first phases of rebuilding Madroño. Considering this, Will talked to Polk in 1890 or 1891 about presenting a design for a new Madroño, but when his mother saw the drawing and floor plan, she did not like what Polk had in mind, and turned down the project. After this brief possibility of a Polk design, work on Madroño continued with local builders.

3

Throughout the wet spring of 1890, work continued on the Bourn and Wise wine cellar just north of St. Helena. All the great storage tanks were in place in the main building, and oak casks for aging wine rested on stands in the north wing of the cellar. During the spring and summer months, the crushing machinery remained quiet, but as the warm sun of late spring and early summer brought out the green leaves and the first sign of grapes on the vines, field workers moved through the vineyards to check the condition of the vines and do whatever was needed to ensure a good crop for the coming fall harvest.

While work in the vineyards went ahead, Will became busy in one of the two oak-and-mahogany-paneled offices, where he checked the records of the winery's first year of operation and planned the final work for the two-story distillery tower. He also went over the figures for the costs of the last projects at the winery, including the eight-foot-high stone wall that was to run along the front of the winery as well as some three hundred feet up the hillside on each end of the cellar.

But work was limited in the Napa Valley during that summer of 1890, because Will traveled back and forth from St. Helena to San Francisco. In the city, he kept in touch with his business interests through reports compiled by his office staff. News from the Empire Mine that summer was a mixture of good and bad. The good news was that cousin George Starr continued to improve mining operations by introducing compressed-air drills that increased the rate of speed for work on drifts, shafts, and other excavation.[8] The bad news was that the weeks of heavy rainfall in 1889–90 had slowed and then halted work in the mine until the excess water could be pumped out. Even then, the steady rain and the run-off water from melting snowpacks caused many delays in the operation of the mine. Finally, the warm summer of the foothill country helped the men to get the mine back into normal operation. The great pumps returned to their regular operation of pumping the usual flow of underground water from the drifts and shaft; the delivery of ore to the surface began again; and the stamp mill resumed its loud pace.

During this time, Will considered the direction of his business affairs. Two things were clear to him. San Francisco was going to need a controlled and reliable source of gas and electricity, and it needed a supply of water that would meet present and future needs. It was obvious to him that he should continue to invest in the San Francisco Gas Light Company and the Spring Valley Water Company.

One person he consulted about the San Francisco Gas Light Company was Joseph B. Crockett, who had been the company's president since 1885. Both men agreed that eventually it might become necessary to merge the company with George H. Roe's Edison Light and Power Company to eliminate rate wars and service duplication. However, they recognized that it was still too early to make such a move.

As the fall season began, Will was excited by a development outside his business affairs. On October 1, 1890, a bill passed in Congress making Yosemite a national park, and a troop of U.S. Cavalry was sent to the new park to guard the area and begin the tasks of making trails, preparing maps, and seeing to the administration of the new Yosemite National Park. Yosemite Valley remained a California state park within the national park. Although Will saw this as something that would have to be changed, the important thing was that one of his favorite places in the Sierra Nevada had been saved from the eventual harm that would have been the result of private interests controlling Yosemite.

That same fall, Will watched a successful grape harvest at Madroño and the other vineyards around St. Helena, then he watched the first major crushing in the Greystone Cellar on November 11, 1890. Three days later, he signed a contract for construction of the stone wall that would mark the cellar's front and side boundaries.

4 Through the first years of the 1890s, most of Will's business affairs moved along at a sure and profitable pace. Yet even as they did, he saw two things happen that were to affect his future. First, news from the Napa Valley was not all good. The deadly phylloxera, a genus of aphids commonly called the "grape louse," was beginning to spread among the vineyards of the Napa Valley, and the root stock of many vines was falling victim to this terrible killer. Second, news from the Empire Mine at Grass Valley indicated a marked decrease in the amount of gold-producing ore coming from the depths of the mine.

By the beginning of 1893, news from Grass Valley was discouraging. Even though Will no longer controlled the Empire Mine, he owned a considerable amount of stock, and his past association with the problems of the mine made him much more than a stockholder. To Will, the Empire was a key part of his family's history, so when a barren zone was encountered, Will was anxious not only because of the mine's inability to return dividends to stockholders but also because he had been through such a barren zone in the past and had proved that it was only a setback to be endured until another rich zone was uncovered at a lower depth. However, the worst news coming from the mine was that George Starr was leaving the Empire to join John Hays Hammond's staff of mining engineers in South Africa to work for Barney Barnato in the rich gold mines of South Africa's Transvaal region.[9]

Will also had immediate financial problems to worry about. At this time, he was short of cash as a result of the construction of the Greystone Cellar and the on-going rebuilding of Madroño. Along with these expenses, income on his investments dropped as a severe depression hit businesses across the United States.

The Panic of 1893 was beginning as President-elect Grover Cleveland got ready to take the oath of office in March 1893. Ever since the passage of the Sherman Silver Purchase Act of 1890, which authorized the U.S. Treasury to purchase almost double the amount of silver it had been buying for conversion into silver dollars, the nation's gold reserve had been dropping. Finally, the gold reserve reached a mark below the so-called safety line of $100 million. This caused fear among the nation's financiers, and businesses began to fail. The stock market fell, and the Treasury seemed unable to redeem either greenbacks or its 1890–issue treasury notes in gold. At the same time, the prospect of a silver standard meant that the federal government's debts would be repaid in silver dollars worth only sixty cents per dollar.

The combination of Will's out-of-pocket expenses, lack of returns from his Empire Mine stock, and minimal income from his stock in the San Francisco Gas Light Company added to his financial difficulties. Compounding this shortage of money was a sharp drop in income from other stocks affected by the Panic. As far as Will could assess his own position, his major sources of income at this time came from minimal first profits from the Greystone Cellar, minimal returns from other stock holdings, and stock dividends from the Spring Valley Water Company, which showed a 6 percent return.

Another drain on his bank account came from expenses related to the purchase on March 25, 1892, of a San Francisco lot at 2030 Broadway for his mother. Added to this were payments he and his mother had made to the San Francisco architectural firm of George Washington Percy and F. F. Hamilton for the design and construction of the home at 2030 Broadway during 1892–93, which came to $16,345.41, plus taxes on this house, the house at 1105 Taylor Street, the office at 401 California Street, the Madroño property, and the Greystone Cellar in Napa Valley.[10]

An indication of just how bad things were for Will came in two letters that he wrote on January 19, 1893. In a letter to his sister Maud, he described his various business losses, then he indicated that he was deep in debt. He ended this letter by asking Maud to refrain from telling their mother that he was almost broke. The same day, he wrote to his mother to inform her that her checking account was overdrawn by more than $7,000. He ended this letter by asking her to be more careful or to turn the task of balancing her checkbook over to him.[11]

Even as Will worried about his finances, his greatest concern was for what was happening in the Napa Valley. Phylloxera was spreading through the vineyards. Between 1889 and 1892, some ten thousand acres of vines between Napa and St. Helena had been destroyed.[12] Though the vineyards at Madroño had not yet been struck by the blight, there was no reason to think that these vines would be spared. Meanwhile, many growers who had planned to bring their 1892 crop into the Greystone Cellar had been wiped out, and this had cut down the tonnage expected for the wine cellar. For Will, this was another loss to add to his failing fortunes as 1893 moved along.

Throughout the rest of 1893, a few of Will's investments began to show some signs of recovery, but other holdings continued to diminish in worth as the nation's economy showed no immediate changes for the good. Banks failed, and thousands of businesses folded.

As the summer began, Will's mother and his sister Ida seemed unaware of the failing economy. By June 15, 1893, they had packed their best dresses, the family silver, and even rolled some rugs to take with them as they prepared to move from 2030 Broadway in San Francisco to Madroño. Although the house was not totally rebuilt, some rooms were finished, and they also had the White Cottage as a back-up place to live. They planned to remain at Madroño until the middle of September.[13] During this time, they would oversee the progress of rebuilding the family home, stroll through the vineyards, eat fresh ranch eggs, take carriage rides with a team of their fine horses pulling the carriage, and invite guests to come and visit them in the country, even if they had to "rough it" just a bit.

For Will, the remaining months of 1893 became a curious mixture of watching the depressed economy regain some strength, seeing his own finances show signs of recovery, wondering whether he would be able to maintain the Greystone Cellar, and watching a strange shift in San Francisco's political winds. As a staunch Republican, Will found himself applauding the local hero, Adolph Sutro, who was taking on Collis P. Huntington and the powerful Southern Pacific Railroad Company.

A local issue made strange bedfellows of such diverse interests as the People's Party—a populist movement—and William Randolph Hearst and the San Francisco *Examiner.* This battle began when the Southern Pacific bought the Market Street Railroad and doubled the trolley fare from five cents to ten cents. This aroused Adolph Sutro, who was building the Sutro Baths near the Cliff House. He quickly let it be known that he was building a tall fence around Sutro Heights and that in the future anybody who rode the cars of the Southern Pacific would be charged an admission fee of twenty-five cents, but those who walked or found another way to get to Sutro Heights or the Cliff House would be allowed to enter free.

Meanwhile, the battle between Sutro and Huntington assumed even greater proportions as Sutro, the wily tunnel builder of the Comstock Lode, obtained a franchise to build an electric railroad to Presidio Avenue with a branch line to Eighth Avenue to serve the park. Going beyond that, he decided to arrange free transfers from the Sutter Street line—an independent line free of the Southern Pacific—to his own. What amazed San Franciscans most of all was that Sutro attacked Collis P. Huntington and the Southern Pacific over the Funding Bill then before Congress. If this bill passed, it would allow the Central Pacific Railroad—the first unit in Southern Pacific's system—to put off repaying the $27 million plus interest that it owed the U.S. government for ninety-nine years and six months, at which time it would repay the loan at one-half of 1 percent interest. In this cause, Will found that despite his Republican loyalty he was cheering for Sutro in his monumental fight against the "Octopus."

As 1893 neared its end, Will watched with admiration as Sutro's fight against the giant Southern Pacific managed to swing the tide in Congress against such an outright gift of a huge sum of money to the railroad giant. Like many San Franciscans, Will cheered as Adolph Sutro's cause proved to be too much even for the powerful Southern Pacific and the hard-fighting Collis P. Huntington.

To William Bourn, Sutro's willingness to carry on the good fight was what he expected of himself as he faced his own financial problems. The year 1893 had not been a good one, but he was determined to improve his financial interests and the direction of his life during the coming year.

5 As 1894 began, Bourn saw an intrusion into one of his favorite places in San Francisco as two hundred acres of Golden Gate Park were torn up to make room for the Midwinter Fair. The idea had been presented to the City of San Francisco by Michael de Young, publisher of the San Francisco *Chronicle.* De Young had been a vice president of the World's Columbian Exposition in Chicago in 1893, and the success of this fair gave him the idea of showing off the advantages of San Francisco's mild winter climate by having a midwinter fair. The superintendent of Golden Gate Park, John McLaren, who was to do the landscaping for the fair, quit in dis-

gust when he learned that he would have to abide by de Young's wishes. McLaren was incensed as he watched the destruction of trees, shrubs, and grass as four-horse teams pulled scrapers to level an area for the construction of the fair.

Will Bourn agreed with Willis Polk that the Midwinter Fair suggested a frightful nightmare. The Grand Court had a carnival-like atmosphere as concession stands crowded in on it. Worse yet, the combination of pavilions with architectural themes that ranged from Near Eastern to pseudo-Egyptian to a Japanese tea garden to California mission-style made the fair a strange jumble of ideas that did not work well together. Added to these ill-conceived ideas, the fair's grounds were laid out in geometric patterns with different plants arranged to give individual definition to each section. Here and there in these gardens arose large mechanical structures that ranged from a curious electric fountain to a small replica of the Eiffel Tower.[14]

The overall plan, if one could call it a plan, was the object of harsh critical abuse. Boston's *Architectural Review* stated that the fair showed what happened when first-rate designers were not employed. Willis Polk blamed the shortcomings of the fair on the overall chaotic state of San Francisco's architectural scene.[15]

Not only did Bourn agree with Polk and other critics of the Midwinter Fair, he also deplored the destruction of one-fifth of Golden Gate Park's hard-won land in the long battle since 1871 against the dunes of the Great Sand Banks. It struck Will as ironic that the hard-won natural beauty of the park had been destroyed to advertise San Francisco's mild climate and natural beauty, because once the fair ended, this advertisement for San Francisco would be only a memory for family picture albums and historical records.

6 By the spring of 1894, it became obvious to Will that the impact of phylloxera upon the vineyards of the Napa Valley was ending his hope to realize a continuing profit from the wine cellar. Even though he had to buy out his partner in 1889 when Wise became too ill to carry on with work, Will now owned a winery with no foreseeable future, because the grape growers were unable to look toward a fall harvest sufficient to keep the winery busy enough to show any profit. Considering all the possible factors involved—including his other investments, which were just beginning to recover from the Panic of 1893—Will decided to let it be known that the

Greystone Cellar, the former Wise residence, all other buildings, and thirty-four acres of land were for sale.

By the first of June, the *St. Helena Star* reported the sale of the Greystone Cellar and adjacent buildings and property to Charles Carpy of the Napa Valley and San Francisco. One other bidder for the great wine cellar was Jacob Jacobi, a San Francisco wine dealer. Folklore states that the men offered identical bids for the winery and that they flipped a coin to determine who was to be the buyer. Jacobi won the coin toss, but on the train ride back from St. Helena to the ferry dock at the north end of San Francisco Bay the two men played a high-stakes crap game that saw Carpy become the new owner of the Greystone Cellar.

No doubt the romantic flavor of folklore regarding the transfer of the ownership of the Greystone Cellar will be appreciated by those who enjoy a good yarn. However, the dull truth is that the winery was sold to Charles Carpy in a business-like deal. The actual selling price remains unknown, because the papers regarding the sale were lost when the Carpy home in St. Helena was destroyed by fire.[16]

Bourn's loss on this transaction had to be considerable. Estimates range from a low of some three hundred thousand dollars to a high of two million. This loss meant that all the expenses that Will had incurred during the construction of the Greystone Cellar would never be recovered.

At this time, Will decided to look upon the Napa Valley as no more than a summer retreat. He had Willis Polk draw a plan for his own home, but nothing got beyond this stage. Instead, Will and Agnes and their daughter, Maud, who was to celebrate her twelfth birthday in November, confined their visits to the Napa Valley to summer trips to Madroño. In such visits there would always be a hospitable time of great dinners, family talk, and the easy joys of country living. The new house at Madroño continued to assume shape, and as work progressed, the ultimate task of completing the house was turned over to the Napa architect W. H. Corlett, who was to redraw some of the plans and keep the local builders headed in the right direction.[17] In a very real sense, Madroño became a special place to Will and Agnes, where their visits brought them away from the social whirl of San Francisco and where Will did not have to make daily decisions regarding business.

Sometime in late October or early November, Will received a letter from Horace Moody, Zaidee's husband since 1890, in which Moody indicated that he thought he knew of an English syndicate that might be willing to buy the Greystone Cellar. Will was insulted by the general inference in Moody's letter that Will was bored with the day-to-day business of running a wine cellar, but he never let his sister know this. However, Zaidee knew about her husband's letter, for on November 8, 1894, she wrote to her mother that Horace had written to Will about helping to sell the winery. She indicated that Horace thought "Will commenced it as a whim, got into it, and did not like the confinement to business it necessitated."[18]

This letter from Horace Moody was almost the final straw in Will's relationship with his brother-in-law. He had been doubtful about Moody ever since he courted and married Zaidee, for he considered him as something of a fortune hunter and not the best choice of husband that Zaidee could have made. Fortunately, Will did not have to see Moody on a regular basis, because he and Zaidee lived on the East Coast, but he did hear from his mother and from his sister Maud that Moody was trying, with minimal success, to build his own fortune in the railroad business by investing with an English firm in a short-line railroad in the South.

As 1894 neared its end, William Bourn allowed his name to be placed on the ballot as a candidate for a Board of Freeholders to consist of fifteen elected officials who were to put together a charter for the City and County of San Francisco. As a man who believed in the future of San Francisco, Will—who hated public exposure—was elected to the Board of Freeholders on November 6, 1894.[19]

On December 26, 1894, one day after Sutro's second Cliff House went up in flames, William Bourn was sworn into office by Alfred J. Evans, Registrar of Voters for the City and County of San Francisco. However, even before Will began to serve his term under Mayor Levi Richard Ellert, he found himself subjected to harsh criticism for having a conflict of interest, in that he was an important figure in the San Francisco Gas Light Company and also was owner of considerable stock in the Spring Valley Water Company. Not wishing to endure this kind of negative publicity, Will withdrew from the Board of Freeholders, as did one other man. This left thirteen men, who worked hard to put together a new charter only to have it rejected by voters in the 1895 election.[20]

Despite this discouraging foray into San Francisco politics, Will remained a true believer in the future of the city by the Golden Gate. To him, San Francisco was indeed a city of promise, and while political squabbles would be a part of San Francisco's growth and the constantly changing nature of its population, there was no reason to be doubtful about its future. The very location of San Francisco on the rim of the Pacific, its great harbor, its Mediterranean climate, and its close proximity to the riches of the gold mines of the foothills of the Sierra Nevada and the fertile agricultural lands of the coastal valleys and the great valleys of the Sacramento and San Joaquin rivers assured its future—a future that William Bourn believed would fulfill every promise.

13

Expanding Horizons

In the beginning of 1895, William Bourn learned that conditions at the Empire Mine continued to deteriorate. Ever since George Starr's departure for South Africa, his replacement, Robert Walker, had gone through one barren zone after another. The owner, James D. Hague, received no profit from the mine, but he had a daily payroll to meet and all the expenses associated with searching for gold. In addition, there were complaints from investors who were not realizing any return from their stock. Rumors reached Bourn that the mine might soon be for sale. Will also kept in touch with Hague, who was becoming very discouraged.

Bourn did not offer to purchase the mine, because he thought that would seem wrong in that he had sold the Empire to Hague. Still, he made up his mind that if Hague wished to rid himself of the mine, he would buy it back and put all his efforts into working through the barren zones. He still had faith in the Empire, and he believed the mine had many rich years ahead. Will decided to wait until Hague was ready to call it quits, then he would step forth and try the "Bourn Luck" once again.

Meanwhile, Will continued to work to bring about a merger of the San Francisco Gas Light Company with George H. Roe's Edison Light Power Company. As Bourn saw it, the City and County of San Francisco had to combine all gas and electric companies supplying the city; this was the only solution to the chaotic competition that did not serve either customers or producers with a fair and reliable system. But even as Will talked to other owners, they listened but did not act. Bourn was convinced that the time for action lay not far in the future, so he kept in touch with the owners of the various utility companies and waited for the right time to act.

All in all, in the beginning of 1895 it seemed to Bourn that he was playing a waiting game. As a firm believer in change for the future of San Francisco as well as for California and the United States, Will was not content to see the city, state, or nation rest upon past laurels. As a child born of parents who had seen the rowdy times of the Gold Rush years in San Francisco and who had himself seen the impact of the Comstock Lode upon the fortunes of San Francisco, Will did not want the city to become mired in legends of its frontier past while the challenges of the future bypassed it.

The past and the future combined in the February 26th wedding of forty-year-old Maye Champney Bourn to fifty-one-year-old James Ellis Tucker of Winchester, Virginia. Tucker, a widower, was a Civil War veteran whose service for the South began when, as a sixteen-year-old schoolboy at Vevey, Switzerland, he made his way to Paris. There, he was "commissioned by Mason and Slidell . . . to bear dispatches to the Confederacy." His ship was wrecked when it reached the blockaded harbor at Charleston, but young Tucker managed to dive overboard and swim to shore with his messages, which he then delivered to President Jefferson Davis. Following this, Tucker joined the Second Virginia Cavalry under General Jeb Stuart, saw action in many of the major battles of the Civil War, was wounded more than once, and "witnessed the surrender at Appomattox."[1]

Although Maye Bourn had had other opportunities to marry, no man had previously caught her fancy, and many other suitors gave up during their flings at courtship. But the tall, good-looking, likable Tucker captured Maye's heart. Maye's choice for a husband suited Will all the way. He liked Tucker, who was employed by the customs office in San Francisco, and he enjoyed his ability to tell stories and make his adventures in the Civil War and later in Mexico as a mounted soldier of the Empress Guard right up to the execution of Emperor Maximilian come alive.[2]

In many ways, the marriage of the diminutive Maye, who was just one inch over five feet, to the jovial Tucker seemed a perfect match. Tucker also liked to socialize, and like Maye, he enjoyed belonging to clubs and lodges. He had no objections to the fact that Maye was a Catholic and a Democrat in a family of Episcopalians and Republicans, nor did it bother him that Maye was an ardent supporter of the national rights for women movement.

The marriage ceremony was conducted by Dr. Lathrop at the Church of the Advent, and the day of the wedding was a show of elegance by the

Bourn women. All wore beautiful gowns designed and made for them by the dressmakers of the White House, a firm founded by Raphael Weill in 1884 at the corner of Post and Kearny.[3] For this very special occasion, Weill—a genial, short, plump, dignified man who was well known for his superb taste in the finer things of life—had seen to it that his dressmakers used all their talents as they took the finest materials to create beautiful gowns for Maye's wedding.

After this family event, Will and Agnes agreed that the time had come to build a new San Francisco home on a small lot that Will had acquired at 2550 Webster Street in the Pacific Heights area. Both agreed that Willis Polk might be just the architect to design their home and oversee its construction.

Bourn and Polk met and talked at great length about the type of house that would be a place for family life as well as lend itself to entertaining friends and business acquaintances. Polk saw that the small lot would require the use of almost the entire property for the house, and he suggested a variation of an English townhouse. The building would not have a basement in the normal sense. Instead, he would use the ground level as a basement, and above it, he proposed to build three more floors. He suggested the installation of an elevator to run from the ground floor to the third floor, with a stairway to the fourth floor. The principal rooms were to be situated on the second floor, where they would be well above the street to allow them to receive more light and have better views. Altogether, the house was to have twenty-eight rooms. The second, or main floor, was designed to be quite open, with a central hall to connect and unify all the rooms. Everything on the main floor could be seen at once upon entering the deeply recessed front door, which opened into a vestibule. From that point forward, a wide corridor extended to the rear hall and a free-hanging staircase with a newel post to be carved out of a tree trunk.[4]

Throughout the house, as Polk designed it, there were to be fourteen fireplaces, so that all rooms except the servants' quarters on the top floor had fireplaces. Next to the entry, Polk's design called for two reception rooms, one with a vaguely Georgian design, the other rustic. Polk suggested to Bourn that Bruce Porter be commissioned to paint a landscape mural on the wall surfaces of the central hallway. In addition, he proposed that Porter's talents in stained glass be put to use to create windows to filter additional light to the staircase landings. In the dining room, Polk proposed bringing in natural light by having a wall of glass surrounding a great free-standing fireplace.[5]

The outer surface of the house was to be made of rough clinker bricks with a glassy surface that gave the exterior a shingle-like quality and provided a rich-looking but durable veneer. They were also inexpensive, because such bricks were usually discarded after firing. For the roof, Polk proposed slate both for its durability and for the contrast it would make with the clinker bricks. Altogether, Polk's estimated cost for designing and building this elegant townhouse came to $50,000.[6] After reviewing and refining the initial plans, the Bourns gave Polk the go-ahead to build their new home, though they knew they would not be able to move into it and leave Taylor Street until sometime in 1896.

This same spring, Will met with Bruce Porter and talked to him about the wall mural and the stained-glass windows. Porter was delighted with this commission and agreed to take on the job. As the two men talked, Porter told Bourn about the publication of the first issue of *The Lark,* a sixteen-page magazine "printed on yellowish, bamboo-fiber paper." He explained that he and Gelett Burgess, a former topographical drawing instructor at the University of California, had received praise in the *New York Times* two weeks after the first issue of the magazine, which included Burgess's poem "Purple Cow." In the review, the critic referred to the young publishers as "'*les jeunes,*' those of California, forsooth, and delightfully young they are."[7]

Although he was older than the young writers, editors, and artists of San Francisco's new literary frontier, Will felt at home with such creative people. Quite possibly, *The Lark* brought back memories of his own early entrance into the world of little magazines. In March 1872, when he was only seventeen, he had joined Harold Wheeler in taking over the publication of *The Cub,* which had been started the year before by Alfred A. Wheeler, who remained on as the editor. Selling for five cents per copy or twenty-five cents for six months, *The Cub* was devoted to the "Amusement and Improvement of Boys and Girls." A ten-page magazine printed on rather cheap paper, its cover sported a bear cub sitting with front paws extended in the fashion of a Yosemite National Park bear begging for a handout. The usual contents of the magazine consisted of a poem or two, a couple of ongoing serials, notes and queries, editorials, holiday tramps, puzzles, book reviews, a column "Concerning Dress," and advertisements at the front and back of the magazine from such firms as the White House, I. W. Taber's Art and Photographic Gallery, assorted booksellers, real estate brokers, liquor and wine dealers, Fireman's Fund and other insurance firms, grocers, druggists,

George C. Shreve & Company for jewelry and silverware, and even an ad for St. Mary's Boarding School for Young Ladies at Benicia.

This early experience with magazine publishing was a fond memory for Will, and no doubt he wished he had time to join his young friends in such a joyful publishing venture as *The Lark.* Even if he did not contribute to this venture, in later years he was associated with such publications as *Western Field,* a Pacific Coast magazine devoted to hunting, fishing, and other outdoor sports, and with the publications of the Academy of Pacific Coast History issued by the University of California. Like many individuals who have been involved with publishing in one way or another, Will's love of the written word drew him to ventures that promoted the expression of creative thinking.

2 By the beginning of 1896, work was moving along briskly on the Bourns' new home at 2550 Webster Street. The outer walls and roof were completed, and Willis Polk was beginning work on the interior. This proceeded more slowly because the quality of lumber and other materials had to be first rate, and Polk wanted to be certain that his carpenters, cabinet-makers, plumbers, and electricians made no mistakes. He also wanted to be certain that his artistic intentions were carried forth from his plans to the final touches.

During this time Bourn received word from Hague at Grass Valley that he was ready to give up the Empire Mine. As Hague explained, the mine had become a great hole in the earth consuming money at a much greater rate than even his worst nightmares might have indicated. Caught in a situation that appeared hopeless, Hague offered to sell the Empire back to Bourn.

Upon reassuming control of the Empire Mine, Will saw that the grounds, mill, and other buildings had not been kept up. However, this was something he could remedy once he settled in to the hard work of bringing the mine back from failure to success. He was convinced that the mine was not played out, but he realized he would need to explore the depths for new gold-bearing ore, and he knew that sinking the main shaft to deeper levels and cutting drift tunnels to follow potential leads was going to require significant expenditures. To get ready for this, he formed the Empire Mines and Investment Company to take over all assets and issue stock to raise funds for new development.

It had been eighteen years since Will had first assumed control of the

Empire. At that time, he had encountered a situation much like the one he now faced. Without hesitation, he accepted the new challenge and resumed shaft sinking. The miners worked in the cool darkness where the only lights were the electric bulbs at the station levels and the carbide lamps they wore on their hats. They moved downward into new depths while Bourn paid their wages and all the expenses of mining. He insisted that sooner or later his Cornish miners would cut through the barren zones and strike another rich deposit of gold-bearing ore.

The months of 1896 rushed by, and Will returned to San Francisco to assist Agnes in supervising the move into their new Pacific Heights home. As Will and Agnes entered the home through the deeply recessed carved front door, Polk pointed out the 1896 completion date on the massive door. Then they passed through the vestibule into a richly decorated corridor that extended to the rear hall. By the entry, they saw the finished work on the two reception rooms, one decorated in a pseudo-Georgian style and the other in a rustic fashion. They followed Polk from room to room as he explained the varieties of woods he had used and what his intentions had been as he planned each room. They stopped to admire Bruce Porter's dreamlike landscape mural, and they looked upward from the unique newel post carved from a solid tree trunk and saw the sunlight suffused through Porter's luminous stained-glass windows above the two staircase landings. Room after room caught their attention as they moved through their new home. The room that fascinated them most was the dining room, where natural light beamed through a wall of glass to focus on the massive free-standing fireplace.[8]

In many respects, the home seemed forbidding on first glance, and to some individuals the darkness of its exterior carried over into the interior and became almost a barrier. To Will and Agnes, the home offered many light and airy touches, but its very size presented a challenge. Now they had to furnish their mansion and make it a livable home.

Even as Will and Agnes talked over the furnishing of their new home and consulted with young Bruce Porter, whose taste in interior decorating was highly valued, Will became caught up in crucial changes in the San Francisco Gas Light Company. In conversations with President Joseph B. Crockett, who had headed the firm since 1885, Bourn agreed that the struggle between rival electric and gas firms had to be solved before their competing interests caused the financial downfall of all of them. Consequently, by December 11, 1896, the San Francisco Gas Light Company merged with George H. Roe's

Edison Light and Power Company to form the San Francisco Gas and Electric Company with capital stock holdings of $20,000,000.[9]

Joseph B. Crockett was named president of the new San Francisco Gas and Electric Company. The choice of Crockett was a wise move, because he had experience that included service as an engineer for the City Gas Company and with the San Francisco Gas Company, where he had worked and studied under such veterans in the business as William and James Beggs, who had learned the business under the late Peter Donahue. Furthermore, young Crockett had been a driving force in the 1891 construction of the "North Beach gas plant on a site on Bay Street between Laguna and Webster." At the time of this plant's construction, it was considered one of the best plants in the United States, and it had the largest storage capacity of any plant west of Chicago.[10]

Bourn knew that the consolidation of these two companies into the San Francisco Gas and Electric Company was but an initial step. Ultimately, it would be necessary to bring about the merger of as many firms as possible, perhaps all firms, into a single source for gas and electricity. The time was at hand for many new developments in supplying light, heat, and power for the city. In this very year of 1896, newspapers such as the *San Francisco Call* were asking for the replacement of gas street lamps with electric street lights. Once the constant competition of various companies supplying gas and electricity became a thing of the past, the future would mean the establishment of fair and equitable rates, and the installation of standardized electric lines and gas pipes that would be more reliable than the mixture of competing supply lines of various companies.

3 During 1897, Will returned to working almost full time at the Empire Mine. He decided to begin sprucing up the grounds, and he called upon his good friend Willis Polk to design a cottage for his family to brighten the landscape of the mining property.[11]

After considering what might fit into the landscape of the Sierra Nevada foothills and the working environment of the gold mine, Polk decided that the proper material for the outer walls of the house was the same quartz rock that was pulled from the depths of the Empire. The doorways and windows would be framed on the outside by brick. In many respects, this design was similar to many of the structures found in Grass Valley and Nevada City as well as other foothill mining towns.

Polk's design for the interior of the Bourn cottage called for untreated redwood boards to serve as panelling and exposed redwood beams to form a flat overhead ceiling with the beams running above and across the open room. All trim for the doors and windows was to be of plain wood, and the fireplace at one end of the living room was to sit on a raised brick hearth. Above the opening of the fireplace Polk designed a plain wood mantel to rest on four supports. In addition to the living room, the interior of the cottage was to contain a dining room, kitchen, pantry, four bedrooms for the family, and quarters for the maids.

Twelve acres of grounds were laid out so that a curving drive ascended toward the house from either side. Extending downward from the front of the cottage there was to be a lawn, a terraced garden, two low fountains, and an area for a cascade of water to empty into a long rectangular pool. Ultimately, this garden area would include vines to crawl up the quartz walls of the house, yew hedges, and a lotus pond.

In back of the stone cottage there was room for a garden to grow cut flowers for the house. Polk's design for the Bourn cottage was a tranquil garden setting to stand in contrast to the surrounding forest of pines and the tall headframe above the Empire's main shaft as well as the stamp mill, the blacksmith shop, the mine office, and the other buildings associated with the gold-mining process.

Polk had suggestions for other buildings to accompany the stone cottage. His scheme, as he outlined it, called for new company buildings with a less sparse utilitarian appearance, and he even proposed the construction of homes for the principal employees in charge of the daily operations of the mine.

Will liked Polk's ideas, but in his usual manner, he insisted that things be done in order. This was a trait that he appears to have developed in his youth, for his was never a scatter-gun approach to any problem. Everything required a specific plan, and nothing was ever left to chance. To Will, chance was reserved for gambling, and even then, the idea was to reduce the influence of chance as much as possible. Consequently, even though he liked Polk's ideas for the other buildings around the Empire, he insisted that first of all the cottage be finished. Once that was done to his satisfaction, he would consider Polk's plans for other buildings on the grounds.

As Polk put his crew to work building the Bourn cottage, Will focused his attention on the mine. Although he had not yet found a paying lead of gold ore, he continued to forge ahead. Day after day, his miners drilled, placed charges of dynamite, blasted into the quartz walls, and continued downward into the earth following the direction of the main incline shaft past the 1,800-foot level, which showed no promise of paying ore. As the weeks and months passed, the incline shaft reached the 1,900-foot level, then the 2,000-foot level, and as the year 1897 drew to a close, the depth of the mine reached 2,100 feet. Even at this depth there was no sign of the lost Ophir lead or any other gold-bearing lead. All that Bourn and his crew had to show for months of hard work and a steady outlay of cash was a deeper hole in the ground. To the Cornish miners, it must have seemed as if their jabberwocks, or gremlins, saw to it that the hardrock miners were not going to strike anything but one barren zone after another. This was not a happy end to 1897, and both the miners and Will Bourn wondered at the beginning of 1898 whether it would be worth the expense and work to continue this underground search for the elusive lead of gold-bearing ore.

4 The year 1898 began with the excitement of men rushing for gold in Alaska. West Coast ports such as Seattle and San Francisco were jumping-off places for those who dreamed of striking it rich in the Yukon. Passenger fares on Alaska-bound ships soared during the peak of the rush, at times going as high as $1,000 for a miserable little bunk. Even then, the fare was just the beginning of the cost, for the real stake amounted to at least several thousand dollars if a miner hoped to make a go of it once he reached Skagway, the major gateway to Alaska's interior. This town of twelve thousand tents and a hundred wooden business establishments was where the gold-hungry miners and the saloonkeepers, gamblers, pimps, whores, hardware dealers, real estate speculators, newspaper reporters, photographers, sign painters, confidence men, barrelmakers, carpenters, bankers, and merchants stepped ashore to set up business or to make the 550-mile journey over the mountains to Dawson.[12]

Among the many bound for Alaska during this mad pursuit of gold in 1898 was William Alston Hayne, a suitor of Maud Bourn. Hayne hoped to strike it rich in the Yukon, because he believed that in order to ask for Maud's hand in marriage, he needed a fortune of his own to prove his worth to the Bourn family. But whether he was rich or not, Maud was in love with Hayne and eagerly awaited his letters from Alaska and the Yukon Territory.

The other major event at the beginning of 1898 was the explosion aboard the battleship *Maine* in Havana harbor on February 15, 1898. Immediately, the Hearst newspapers picked up the rallying cry "Remember the Maine," and William Randolph Hearst called for a declaration of war against Spain. He already had correspondents awaiting such a war and even had Frederick Remington in Cuba waiting to illustrate the battles that Hearst anticipated.

On April 24, 1898, Spain declared war on the United States, just four days after President William McKinley ordered a blockade of Cuba. During the campaigns of this war, San Francisco became a jumping-off port for the naval and army forces that sailed across the Pacific to invade and conquer the Philippines. In San Francisco, soldiers camped on the hillside of the Presidio as they awaited the call to board ship and sail off to war. Parties and fiestas were held to entertain the troops, and band music played as they marched aboard ships and sailed out the Golden Gate to fight the forces of Spain.

Other celebrations during 1898 were of a more private nature, but they were equally boisterous as friends and relatives said farewell and then welcomed home loved ones who sailed north to Alaska or who returned from the Yukon either rich or broke. More often, these men returned with empty pockets, dashed hopes, and stories of the great hardships they had to endure in the terrible cold of winter in the Yukon Territory.

To Will Bourn, however, the great event of 1898 was the return of a bronzed and healthy cousin George Starr and his family from South Africa. In their first conversations, Starr was excited about the gold rush in Alaska. He talked of getting his family settled and then heading north to see this new gold strike of the American West. Then he talked to Will about the gold mines of South Africa and told him how much he had learned and how he had been paid a great sum of money for his work as a mining engineer.

At first, Will wondered if his cousin would even be interested in going back to the Empire Mine to assume control once again, but when he brought it up, Starr told Will that he was not sure what his answer would be until he had explored the depths and examined the future possibility of the mine. If things looked promising, he would accept the position as manager; otherwise, he would turn it down.

Starr found upon exploring the mine that his "theory of the split in the Ophir vein had been proved true, and that as soon as the large 'horse' [the mass of rock between the enclosing wall of a vein] had been driven through, the vein was as strong and true as ever." At the 2,100-foot north drive, Starr found a rich ore body. "Very large areas of north and south ground were unexplored. A probably valuable reserve was in a parallel vein known as the Rich Hill [which had not been worked since 1880], in other parallel veins, and in extra-lateral rights. Lack of sufficient development was the chief cause of underground troubles." In addition, Starr thought that the condition of the surface equipment was deplorable. Things were run-down, but worse yet, the mine had outgrown the company's plant.[13]

After his examination of conditions, Starr sent Cousin Will his assessment. He also wrote that he would accept the position as manager, provided that a fund of $200,000 be established to reequip and open the property.[14]

Bourn submitted Starr's proposal to the executive committee of the Empire Mines and Investment Company, but they did not believe that the ore Starr reported was sufficient to justify such an expenditure. Upon receiving this answer, Starr called their attention to the mine's history of forty-seven years of production "of more than $7,000,000, with but a small percentage of profit, the chief cause being lack of development and a plant not suited for economical or expeditious working under existing or future conditions."[15]

It took very little time for Bourn and the executive committee to send an answer that had Will standing solidly behind Starr. The letter was dated May 9, 1898, and it read as follows:

> Dear Sir:—I have the pleasure to inform you that the executive committee have accepted your ideas and that you were this day appointed Managing Director by the Board of Directors. You will be given a free hand in the equipment and development of our property with the understanding that if necessary to carry out your plans the sum of $200,000 will be furnished you, and that on the completion of the plant the necessary expenditure for 600 feet per month of development, consisting of shaft sinking and drives will be allowed. We sincerely trust that including the cost of the above development you will succeed in bringing all costs down to $7 per ton.
>
> Yours very truly,
> W. B. Bourn
> President[16]

As work progressed underground, Starr took on another task at the Empire Mine. This was the rebuilding of the stamp mill, which he considered inefficient for the amount of ore that needed to be crushed around the clock. In July 1898, Starr had the old stamp mill pulled down as he began construction of a new mill. He handled the whole job so efficiently that not more than ten stamps at a time were idled. While this was taking place,

Starr also changed the track rails on the incline hoist, replacing the old rails with new thirty-pound rails in the shaft and on the headgear within forty-two hours. Meanwhile, as work went ahead on the stamp mill, underground development continued with results that exceeded even Starr's hopes.

At the 2,100-foot level, the miners struck a rich ore body that extended some 1,740 feet. This meant that as the work went ahead underground and above ground, Starr was able to hold the cost of development to about seven dollars per foot. By the end of the year, he knew he would not use any of the $200,000 allotted to him and that he would be able to return a profit and a dividend to the stockholders of the Empire Mines and Investment Company.[17]

As George Starr worked at a feverish pace in developing the new strike at the Empire Mine, work on the cottage moved along. As this project neared completion, Will and young Polk talked again about the other needs for the grounds of the Empire Mine. They agreed upon a new mine office building that would also make use of quartz rock from the mine and upon a cottage for George Starr. In addition, they talked about possibly adding another cottage and building a clubhouse with a bowling alley, billiard tables, a kitchen capable of serving a crowd, a dance floor, and plenty of room for gatherings of mine officials and their families as well as a proper place to entertain visitors. Also, outside the wide front veranda of the clubhouse, Bourn wanted a tennis court, because he enjoyed playing tennis.

While work at the Empire mine progressed smoothly and efficiently, the same could not be said about the gas and electric business in San Francisco. During 1898, competition among companies supplying utilities became fierce, even though the firms had arrived at "a pseudo truce by tacitly respecting each other's service zones,"[18] a truce that was never respected. During this period, the San Francisco Gas and Electric Company found itself involved in a gas war with the Spreckels gas corporation, the Pacific Gas and Improvement Company, and the Equitable Gas Light Company. The latter was a newcomer, and it had started a gas war in February 1898. Before the year came to a close, Bourn found that his San Francisco Gas and Electric Company had to lower its price of gas to $1.25 per thousand feet in order to compete, and even that losing price appeared to be headed lower. All this worried Bourn, for he realized that not only would profits cease, but more and more gas would be used as prices fell. There was only one way out of this wasteful gas war—merger. If there could be a reduction in companies, there would be an opportunity to establish a gas and electric system that would use consistent rates and established lines to keep the utility business functioning in a reliable manner for customers and suppliers. If not, the new charter for the City and County of San Francisco, passed on May 26, 1898, promised the authorization of municipal acquisition and ownership of public utilities as of January 1, 1900. The only way for utility companies to avoid that was to act with greater responsibility.

As the pivotal year 1898 headed into the foggy days of summer for the San Francisco Bay region, the new Ferry Building designed and almost finished by the late Arthur Page Brown was completed by Willis Polk. It opened for business on July 13, 1898, with a 235-foot tower modeled after the Giralda tower in Seville. While San Franciscans looked upward to the great clock face and marveled at their new Ferry Building, the fog of summer often covered the clock and the top of the tower. Inland, the Central Valley and the foothill communities of the Sierra Nevada baked in the summer heat.

During these months, Will looked forward to the coming of fall and then the holidays. However, he was worried about his sister Zaidee, who had returned home to visit but was not in good health. As October began, Zaidee entered a San Francisco hospital, where she died on October 15, 1898, with a suddenness that came as a shock to Will and his mother and sisters and other members of the family. Her funeral was held in St. Helena, and she was buried in the Bourn family plot close to Madroño. Will was devastated by her death. He stared with a numbness in his mind as he read the tombstone bearing the final facts: "Zaidee Frances Bourn Moody; Daughter of William B. Bourn I and Sarah Chase; Born San Francisco June 5, 1859; Died San Francisco October 15, 1898." Zaidee was only thirty-nine, just two years younger than he, and Will found it difficult to accept her death. She had been deprived of life before she had a chance to see her dreams come true.

To Will, Zaidee's death was a terrible marker for the end of 1898. It was as though a punishment of final loss had to go along with all the gain and joy the other events of the year had brought.

14

The New Century

Will Bourn saw the beginning of 1899 as the end of one century and the beginning of a new era, but there was still business left over from the past. He faced the second phase of a lawsuit brought against him in 1890, which challenged his handling of his father's estate. The dispute had its origin in 1884, when he was asked by his mother and sisters to assume control of the family's affairs.

Will believed that this whole matter should not have been put into the hands of lawyers, because he saw no reason to have a private problem escape the confines of the family and face settlement by litigation. His sister Zaidee had been a key figure in the first lawsuit, but Will believed that she had been talked into the lawsuit by her husband, Horace Moody. This nasty business had to be blamed on somebody other than a blood relative, and Horace Moody was a prime candidate. Will had never liked the man and firmly believed that Moody had put the whole scheme together for his personal gain.

Moody's role in this was bad enough, but Will was hurt by the willingness of his mother and sisters to go along with these lawsuits. After all, he had not asked to handle his father's estate. If the women of the Bourn family had not prevailed upon him, he would have turned everything over to an attorney whose objectivity would not have been questioned. Instead, his mother and sisters had insisted that he assume full responsibility for the investments, mining interests, real estate, ranches, and timberland that made up his father's business portfolio. Like such men as Crocker, Stanford, Hopkins, Ralston, Huntington, Sutro, and other California dreamers and schemers, Will's father had made wise investments in the American West and had accumulated a fortune to pass on to his heirs.

Now, in the early part of February 1899, Will read the latest document from E. J. McCutchen, one of the attorneys representing his mother and sisters, and he was saddened by what he believed was their mistrust. The cold, impersonal words of the lawsuit made it clear that if he could not afford to do as his family requested, he was expected to borrow whatever funds he needed to fulfill their demands.

He was allowed to deduct from his settlement $12,000 he had paid for a cemetery lot and vault at San Francisco's Laurel Hill Cemetery for the use of all the family. However, the attorney's document required that he pay his mother $150,000, or $6,000 per year in monthly installments of $500 for the remaining years of her life, at which time her estate was to be divided equally among her surviving children. Furthermore, this sum was to be "over and above all taxes, trustee's compensation and expenses connected with said trust or trust fund." [1]

The settlement for his sisters Ida and Maud came to $40,000 each at $2,800 per year, or $233.33 per month for the rest of their lives. All this was also to be free of taxes, trustee's compensation, and any other expenses connected with the trust. Again, any funds remaining at the time of the sisters' deaths were to be assigned to their designated heirs.[2]

Maye did not wish to be paid yearly or in monthly installments, because she was not able to save money and was always fending off bill collectors, and she requested that Will pay her $40,000 outright. Zaidee's will left everything to her husband, Horace Moody.[3]

The total amount that Will would have to pay over the years amounted to a minimum of approximately $310,000. There was no certain way of knowing or even estimating the maximum because Will was no longer to be in charge of the trust, and he had no idea who the new executor might be. Furthermore, there was no way of knowing the longevity of his sisters and their potential heirs.

Things were bad enough with the requests issued by E. J. McCutchen, but Will became incensed when on February 20, 1899, he received a letter from J. P. Langhorne, attorney at law at 40 Montgomery Street. In blunt language, Langhorne suggested that Will's accounting of the value of the Bourn estate could not give his mother and sisters any realistic idea of the estate's worth. Langhorne wrote: "it would take an expert accountant to make head or tail of it or determine the value of the estate." Furthermore,

Langhorne indicated that there was no mention of any dividend on Empire stock. Finally, he added a closing insult by telling Will that he was able "to thoroughly dominate the other heirs."[4]

Will agreed to the demands of his mother and sisters. None of this pleased him, but he was determined to put this unpleasantness behind him and to consider his financial losses as one of those things he had not foreseen. He could endure a loss of money more readily than lose the love and affection of his mother and sisters.

2 The good news in the beginning of 1899 was George Starr's success as he continued to go deeper with the main shaft of the Empire Mine. After the completion of the new plant in January 1899, the work underground went ahead at a rapid pace and new, rich ore bodies were uncovered. The miners were now working at the 2,100-foot level and were running drifts off the main shaft that extended 2,500 feet to the north and 1,400 feet to the south of the shaft. In these drifts, the veins ran at a northerly and southerly direction, and the average dip was 30 degrees to the west. These veins varied in depth from a mere seam to one, two, and three feet, and although all the ore in these veins was not of a high quality, there were shoots that were true bonanza in their richness, producing pure specimen gold at their richest. Even the poorest of the sulphurets ran as high as $60 to $200 per ton.[5]

In the remaining months of 1899, the incline shaft neared 3,000 feet, while off the main shaft tunnels or drifts followed rich veins of gold. All this work was done despite the fact that the mine produced a tremendous amount of water that was lifted to the surface first by a Cornish pumping system and then, before the end of 1899, by a hydraulic pump installed at the 1,100-foot station capable of draining the tunnels at the rate of six hundred gallons per minute.[6]

Within the tunnels, a line of bare electric bulbs gave some light, but the miners still wore lamps attached to the front of their caps. Shifts worked around the clock, and the six ore cars in the working tunnel were loaded with ore brought down by hydraulic drills, dynamite, and picks and shovels. The ore was then loaded into the so-called Rand "U" type cars, which could be tipped from the side and held 1,200 pounds each. When the cars were filled, they were drawn by mules kept underground for the duration of their working lives. There they lived in stalls and were provided hay and water, and some became personal favorites of the miners.

As the ore cars reached the shaft level, each car was tipped from the side, and its load was dumped into bins at the shaft. Within these bins, the skip cars were filled with 3,500 pounds of ore. Altogether, there were three compartments within the incline shaft. Two were for haulways to carry ore to the surface, and the third contained a pumpway to hold water headed for the surface and the track bed for the thirty-pound steel rails that guided the man-cars up and down the shaft. The cars were attached to a cable controlled from the ninety-four-foot headframe by an operator in the hoist house who monitored the speed and the stops and starts of man-cars going down or up the main shaft. Power was generated by a Pelton wheel—an iron waterwheel with rows of double cup-shaped buckets around its rim that were moved by jets of water flowing into these metal cups at a high velocity.[7]

Within the shaft, lighting was provided by electric light bulbs placed fifty feet apart. At the principal underground stations at various levels, there were electric return signal bells as well as a telephone communication system from these stations to the hoist and machine shops.

The loaded skips were pulled to the surface at a speed of a thousand feet per minute. At the top of the headgear, the loads from the skips were dumped on the grizzlies (an iron grating that caught the heavier stones), and the finer particles of ore fell into the lower ore bins. During this process, the coarse pieces of ore fell into another bin that held 150 tons. Just below this latter bin was a No. 5 Gates crusher, which received a steady stream of quartz when it was in operation. From here, the waste rock—which had no value at this period of the mine's operation—was dumped into another bin, and from here it was carried by iron cars to a waste dump.[8]

The hoisting works of the mine were easy to see because the wooden framework of the headgear was ninety-four feet high, anchored to its foundation by six cement piers. Each of these piers was eleven feet deep with a 4½-foot base that narrowed to 2½ feet at the top. The main support timbers were Oregon pine, as was the main framework of the headgear. Within the hoist house were two six-foot cable reels with eight-foot friction bands "driven by paper frictions 24 inches in diameter, 13-inch face, operated by two 10-foot Pelton wheels, each with three nozzles controlled by hydraulic gates."[9] At this time, the capacity of the hoist to pull from a three-thousand-foot depth was 750 tons during a twenty-four-hour period. Although the Pelton wheels supplied water pressure of 420 feet for the operation of the hoist, pumps, and compressor, there were back-up engines to supply power in case of a failure in the primary system.

The pump, compressor, and boiler house were located in back of the collar of the shaft and extended under the incline framework of the headgear. About thirty feet behind all this was a large building that housed the blacksmith, machine, and carpenter shops. Above the shops were changing rooms for the men who worked underground. Here the men were required to strip off their work clothes and undergo a search before they changed into the clothing they would wear home. Their lunch pails were also searched to make sure that no "high-grading" (stealing) of gold was taking place. The changing rooms were heated by hot water that passed through interior pipes, and the miners often hung wet clothing on these pipes to dry.

After the ore was crushed, it was passed into lower ore bins, each of which had a discharge door on the bottom. From these bins the ore—which still needed a complete crushing—was sent by iron cars to the ore bins in the stamp mill. Each bin held six hundred tons, and the ore passed from these bins through the forty-stamp mill, where it was finely crushed over vanners (separating tables of metal) and then washed into a slime plant. By this time, the ore was the consistency of liquid mud. Next, the pulp was assayed to determine its richness. After enduring a thundering pounding by the 850-pound stamps, which dropped only seven inches at a rapid rate, the resulting slime was run into an iron clean-up bowl placed at a forty-five degree angle. Mercury was mixed with the ore slime, and cannon balls were placed in the bowl to revolve in an opposite direction to the turning pan. Thus the ore slime was finely ground, and a continuous flow of water flushed out the waste materials, leaving only a high-grade gold-mercury amalgam in the Berdan pan.[10]

In the latter months of 1899, Bourn traveled to Grass Valley to spend some time at the Empire Mine. During this visit, he inspected the new construction above ground and was greatly pleased by what he saw. The collar of the mine shaft was arched with granite. All the buildings of the mining plant were covered with galvanized iron and built on rock foundations without any timber resting lower than four feet from the ground. To further protect the buildings against decay and fire, the floors of the mill and other buildings associated with the surface work of the mine consisted of asphalt laid on concrete foundations.

Even more fire protection came from Monitors (high-pressure nozzles mounted in a swivel frame) spaced around the plant and from an artificial lake that provided both beauty and an emergency supply of water. This reservoir received its water from the supply used for power at the Empire.[11]

The office for the Empire Mine was built of stone taken from the depths of the mine. Within this building were both general and private offices, as well as rooms for maps and drafting and for assaying the gold content of ore. Finally, there were the retort room and the storeroom for mining supplies.

All the working components of the mine were striking examples of what a deep hard-rock gold mine should look like. In fact, both Bourn and Starr saw the Empire Mine as something that would appeal to mining engineers and stockholders. However, the real showplace was the natural park and beautiful lawns, shrubbery, and flowers around the Empire Cottage—as the new Bourn residence was known—as well as the cottages built for George Starr and other officials of the company. The whole expanse of the Empire Mine, including the buildings and grounds, was surrounded by a high stone wall like one would expect to see surrounding the grounds of an estate of the landed gentry.

Another building still on the planning board was a clubhouse for the use of officials and their families. It also was to serve as a place to entertain guests and hold meetings. The clubhouse was to include room for a dance floor, a bowling alley, and an area for billiard tables. A large kitchen was included in the design so that meals for large and small groups could be prepared on the premises. Outside the entrance was a wide porch or veranda, and beyond this Bourn had included a plan for a tennis court.

Will hoped to complete the clubhouse within a few years, but the construction took longer than expected. As the building projects were either completed or nearing completion, Will began to run short of money. Even though the mine was working a rich load, it took time and money to mine the ore, bring it to the surface, mill it, and treat it with quicksilver amalgam to extract the gold. To help pay off his mounting expenses, Will borrowed $100,000 from his mother on September 12, 1899, with a promissory note to pay it back within sixty days after demand.[12] No doubt Will must have felt that the money the lawsuit had forced him to pay his mother and sisters in the early part of the year would not prevent work at the mine from continuing without his having to go into debt. But this was not the case, although he never complained to the family about it.

As 1899 drew to a close, family events assumed the center stage. In November, Will and Agnes held a party for their daughter, Maud, to celebrate her sixteenth birthday. Then, on December 27, 1899, Will's sister, twenty-eight-year-old Maud, married forty-four-year-old William Alston Hayne II, a native of South Carolina.

Their courtship had gone on for some time, not because either one had any doubt of their love for each other, but because Hayne was troubled that he was not a man of means. Though his family had been well off prior to the Civil War, the war had brought financial ruin. Consequently, when William Hayne learned of the gold strike in Alaska, he had joined the great crowd of men who rushed to the Far North with hopes of striking it rich, because he wanted to become a man of wealth before he took Maud Bourn's hand in marriage. But in the end, William Alston Hayne brought only his great love for Maud to their marriage. He had not struck it rich in the goldfields of Alaska.

The end of 1899 brought Will Bourn good news from George Starr, news that was to start him off with dreams of new riches to come in the new century. Starr reported that the amount of ore mined and milled during 1899 came to over 24,000 tons. While the actual return was kept a closely guarded secret, correspondence between Bourn and Starr and reports for the start of 1900 show that the Empire Mine was beginning to pay handsomely, and Bourn greeted the new century with great expectations.

3 During the first year of the new century, Will began to see a greater return from the Empire Mine, and his other investments were paying a healthy return. His stock in the Spring Valley Water Company was paying a steady 7-percent return, and the only major investment not doing as well as he had hoped was the San Francisco Gas and Electric Company. The failure of this firm to become a paying business was due to the continuing conflict as competing gas and electric companies cut prices and offered other incentives in order to corner the market for gas and electricity. It was an old battle, but as yet no end seemed to be in sight.

Away from business, Will and Agnes became increasingly involved with attempts to create a symphony orchestra for San Francisco, although there was still not enough support behind this effort to bring it to fruition. Still, San Franciscans yearned for the best in music, as was demonstrated by the great crowd that filled "Morosco's Grand Opera House in November 1900, to hear the Metropolitan Opera Company of New York presenting Nellie

Melba in *Romeo et Juliette.*"[13] Most of San Francisco's prominent families were boxholders for this event, Will and Agnes among them.

As 1900 drew to an end, Will received news from George Starr that the incline shaft of the Empire Mine was now over three thousand feet below the surface. In addition, the earnings for the year showed a profit of over $100,000.

As 1901 began, Will's business affairs were moving along well enough to allow him some time off. The Bourns took a train to New York, then boarded a steamship for Egypt. By February 6, 1901, Will wrote to his mother from the Shezireh-Palace Hotel in Cairo, "Today if the fog lifts, I am going to the big pyramid."[14]

After seeing the pyramids, the Bourns sailed to Italy, where they went ashore at Naples. From there, they toured throughout Italy and went on to Paris, where they stayed through May. Then they spent June in England and departed for home.

By late summer the Bourns were back in Grass Valley, where they tried to endure the last weeks of summer in the Empire Cottage. The summer heat was almost intolerable, and it was impossible to sleep inside the stone cottage. During the night the family spread their bedding on the lawn in front of the cottage. Here, they could watch the clear sky above them and finally fall asleep to the steady loud beat of the stamp mill.

During the Bourns' stay at the Empire Cottage, Will and George Starr went into the depths of the mine. They dressed in overalls, rubber boots, and miner's caps, and they carried lamps to provide light. They sat tight in one of the sled-like man-cars and held their heads low as they shot down the incline with the stone roof of the shaft just inches above them. They shot by station after station until they reached the 3,100-foot level. Here, their fast down-shaft ride came to a stop, and they got out of the man-cars and stepped on to the level, wet ground of the station. Then they followed a Cornish foreman into a narrow tunnel about four feet wide and no more than six feet high. They walked between the rails of track used to guide the wheels of the iron ore carts as the mules pulled them to the edge of the shaft where the ore was dumped into a waiting skip. Within the tunnel, Will watched the miners working on the quartz above them as they broke it loose so it could drop into the waiting ore car. Will saw veins so rich that specimen gold in its purest form was present. Some of these had rare beauty, for they bore the imprint of leaves, rock strata, and other natural patterns.

For the Bourn and Starr families, these weeks at the mine allowed the two cousins to discuss the progress of the mine and its possible future. At night they drank pints of beer, ate their fill of Cornish pasties, and talked well into the warm foothill nights about the many aspects of deep underground mining and of their youthful days at the mine when they first saw a steady profit coming from the underground warren of tunnels and drifts that ran in various directions as they followed veins of gold-bearing quartz.

The two cousins also talked about their responsibilities for the lives and welfare of the underground miners who worked deep in the earth for $3.00 per day and for the men who worked on the surface for $2.50 per day in the stamp mill, hoist house, and retort room. In addition, Starr impressed upon Bourn the debt the company owed, as a responsible firm, to the welfare of the people of Grass Valley. To Starr, the mine and the community were interdependent. As the cousins talked about this relationship during the warm summer nights of 1901, Will formed a deeper appreciation for the community of Grass Valley and its vital contribution to the success of the mine.

At the end of August, the Bourns were driven through the red clay foothills upward through thick groves of second-growth pines and firs to the railroad station at Colfax, where they caught the passenger train bound for the San Francisco Bay Terminal in Oakland. From the windows of the train they saw the country change from the Sierra Nevada foothills to the beginning of the upper Sacramento Valley with its rich, dark soil and many groves of tall valley oaks. Beyond the growing community of Sacramento, the Southern Pacific headed southwest to the San Francisco Bay Area. At Oakland, the train came to a halt at its East Bay depot. From this point, the Bourns boarded the ferryboat and crossed the bay to San Francisco's Ferry Building, where a driver and carriage awaited their arrival. After he loaded their luggage, he drove them to their imposing home at 2550 Webster Street, where a cold wind swirled the first wisps of fog along Pacific Heights. They heard the distant sound of foghorns, which must have been like music after the heat of Grass Valley.

For forty-three-year-old William Bourn, the immediate business at hand in San Francisco was the problem of the ongoing war between the San Francisco Gas and Electric Company and its major competitors, the Independent Gas and Power Company founded in 1901 by Claus Spreckels and his sons A. B. and John D. Spreckels; the Pacific Gas Improvement Company controlled by C. O. G. Miller; and the Equitable Gas Light Company, which was founded by A. J. Chisholm in February 1898.[15]

At the same time, another son of Claus Spreckels, Rudolph Spreckels, a director of the San Francisco Gas and Electric Company, launched an investigation into the affairs of the firm because he believed that President Joseph B. Crockett was mismanaging it. As chairman of a committee of five directors, Spreckels hired engineers and accountants to make a thorough examination of the company's operations. Their report showed that things were in bad shape: "Methods of management were antiquated. Plants and equipment needed overhauling."[16] Faced with such a damning report, Crockett submitted his resignation effective January 15, 1902.

As 1901 drew to a close, Rudolph Spreckels nominated William Bourn as the new president of the San Francisco Gas and Electric Company, with his tenure of office to begin on January 16, 1902. The old directors, who were to remain on the board, were Rudolph Spreckels, Captain A. H. Payson, Daniel T. Murphy, and C. Osgood Hooker, who like Payson was a personal friend of Will's. The new directors, all from the San Francisco financial community, were Frank B. King, William J. Dutton, George H. Collins, E. J. McCutcheon, and Louis F. Monteagle.[17] Will knew all these men and respected their individual talents.

4 During the first three months of 1903, thirteen new banks were incorporated in San Francisco. To Bourn, this marked either the beginning of good times or a signal of distress. Knowing something about the banking business, Will tended to be on the conservative side, and he hoped that this sudden boom in banking was an indication of a stable economy.

As the fog and rain of winter gave way to the sunny days of March and April, Will looked forward to visiting Madroño while the grass was green and the wild flowers in bloom. He was, he realized, developing a case of spring fever. He decided he needed a right-hand man, but this would have to be someone he trusted fully and someone capable of dealing with the problems of the gas and electric business as well as reports from the Empire Mine and developments at the Spring Valley Water Company (Will was beginning to think he should enlarge his portfolio of water company stock and give some thought to future involvement with that utility). For all these affairs, and for personal reasons of friendship and trust, he wrote to his cousin, William Ingalls, in Brooklyn and offered him an administrative position if he would move to San Francisco.

Ingalls's reply was positive. He wrote to Bourn that he would settle his affairs in the East and come to San Francisco in late May or the beginning of summer. Will looked forward to renewing his friendship with Willie.

The beginning weeks of May 1903 brought excitement to people who loved Yosemite Valley. On May 15, President Theodore Roosevelt joined California's Governor George Pardee and John Muir for an evening trip across the San Joaquin Valley to the Southern Pacific terminal at the town of Raymond in Madera County. The next day, the party went by stage to the Mariposa Grove of Big Trees. What was not known by the public until a few days later was that Muir and Roosevelt, accompanied by two rangers, camped away from the crowd and the guards in a lesser-traveled area of Yosemite National Park. Here, President Roosevelt, a great outdoorsman, slept on the ground, and during the second night four to five inches of snow fell upon the blankets of the campers. Roosevelt's talks with Muir convinced him that Yosemite Valley should not remain a California state park but should be included as part of Yosemite National Park. This did not happen until 1906, but Roosevelt's trip in 1903 struck the telling blow to private interests and the winning move for all nature lovers—including William Bourn, who considered Yosemite Valley a beautiful national treasure.

In July Will was happy to greet Will Ingalls. Both men hit it off as though they had skipped but a day since they had stayed together in 1874 when Bourn's father died. Best of all, Ingalls was quickly able to pick up the many aspects of Bourn's business affairs, which took a tremendous load off Will's shoulders. Now, he not only had cousin George Starr heading all operations at the Empire Mine but also cousin William Ingalls acting as his secretary and administrative assistant with regard to the complicated affairs of the San Francisco Gas and Electric Company, as well as being his close confidant regarding the rest of his business activities.

In the second week of August, Will told Ingalls they were going to make a trip to the Empire and from there travel into the Sierra Nevada. As he explained, he and William H. Crocker and Joseph Grant wished to look into possible sources of water for both domestic use and for the development of electricity. The future of San Francisco as well as the future of California, Will told his cousin, would be dependent upon their ability to provide water for drinking, domestic and agricultural use, and the production of cheap electric power. To Bourn, the old methods were becoming obsolete. Population growth in San Francisco and other cities, as well as the overall increasing population of California, required a change in thinking about the role of utilities in the lives of Californians.

As they rode the train through the Sacramento Valley, Ingalls found the valley amazingly fertile and beautiful. He was astounded by the acres of wheat that grew for miles on both sides of the railroad tracks, and as they moved into the upper Sacramento Valley and slowly headed upgrade into the foothills toward Colfax, he observed great orchards of fruit trees and vineyards for both table and wine grapes. Everything impressed him so much that he later wrote to his brother, "I do not wonder that Californians have large ideas." [18]

As Ingalls admired the agricultural beauty along their route, Will talked to him about Grass Valley. With a completely straight face, he told his cousin that he should not expect much in the way of accommodations, for it was only a mining town. Then he stretched his tale even more as he said "that the Empire buildings were broken down and in bad condition as it did not or would not pay to rebuild them." [19]

After they got off the train at Colfax, George Starr was waiting to drive the party downgrade to Grass Valley and up to the Empire Mine. Ingalls was amazed by what he saw, and he realized that his cousin had pulled his leg. As Ingalls wrote to his brother, "you can imagine my surprise when I reached this cottage to find a beautiful modern building with all the conveniences and lovely grounds about the house all beautifully kept with the loveliest roses and plants comparing favorably with some of the places in Tuxedo." [20]

It had been twenty-nine years since William Ingalls had been pulled up short by Bourn's sharp sense of humor, and he smiled as he looked about the grounds and buildings of the Empire Mine, for what he saw was a model plant for an underground mining operation, one that mining engineers came out of their way to visit. After an evening of good food prepared by Katie Moriarty, the Irish cook, and conversations where he heard Will and George Starr explain the operation of the mine to Crocker, Grant, and himself, he looked forward to the next day when all of them would be taken into the depths of the mine.

On Sunday morning, after the men had enjoyed a large breakfast, they walked over to the mine. In the changing room they put on miners' clothing and walked to the shaft. Here they boarded the man-cars, which Ingalls described as looking like long sleds or toboggans. "Our first stop," Ingalls wrote to his brother, "was at the 1,100 foot level, here we went through one of the tunnels to where we saw some miners working. While on this level we saw a mule used for hauling the ore, that had not seen daylight for four years."[21] They stayed a short time at this level, then returned to the shaft and boarded the man-cars for a swift ride to the 2,700-foot level. Here, in another tunnel, Bourn pointed out good and bad quartz so they could see the difference. After this, they returned to the surface, having been underground for about an hour.

In the late afternoon, Bourn, Starr, Ingalls, Crocker, and Grant traveled the short distance to neighboring Nevada City by a trolley line that ran between this mining town and Grass Valley. Here, George Starr had hired two teams and two carriages and had them loaded with the men's personal gear for their trip into the Sierra Nevada.

On the first night, the men stopped at Washington City, a mining town located on the South Fork of the Yuba River, where they had their dinner. After this, they traveled upward and northeast for six miles to Gaston Ridge, another mining community. It was ten o'clock at night when they arrived in the town of Gaston, where they got rooms for the night. They were dusty and tired, but they all took time to have baths before they turned in.

On Monday morning the party made an early start and traveled to Bowman's Dam, where they got rooms and had lunch in a boardinghouse. From here, they could see the water behind the dam and the high granite country in the mountains nearby. The country reminded Ingalls of Switzerland. In the afternoon, they drove to two more lakes higher in the granite area. Here they could see lingering snow patches that had not melted during the summer, and they decided to hike to another lake beyond these two. The hike proved to be too much for Will Ingalls as they moved above 6,200 feet, and he had to return and wait for the other men. That night, they stayed at the boardinghouse at Bowman's Dam, and Bourn remarked that "in some respects he considered the country we were in more interesting than the Yosemite."[22]

On Tuesday, August 18, 1903, the men headed for Emigrant Gap, where they planned to board the Southern Pacific and travel to Reno, Nevada. A local train took them as far as Truckee, where, in what Ingalls called the toughest and wickedest town in the country, the men waited for the overland mail train to Reno.

After spending the night in Reno, Bourn and his party took the Virginia and Truckee Railroad to Carson City, where they had lunch in the city's best hotel. After this, they loaded their gear into a canvas-covered, three-seated mountain wagon drawn by four horses. They traveled the length of the Carson Valley, which Ingalls described as charming and fertile, then at the extreme end of the Carson Valley, they came to Woodfords after passing many ranches with good grazing land and large herds of cattle. They stopped for the night at Daniel Woodford's, where the owner was expecting them and had prepared a big dinner. They were, as Ingalls wrote, "living like lords."[23]

The next day they moved upward following the rough road that ran beside the West Fork of the Carson River. They leveled off as they arrived at the lower end of Hope Valley and a fork in the road. From here, the road to the right crossed Luther Pass and dropped downward to the Upper Truckee River and the beginning of Echo Pass just beyond Meyers, the former Yank's Station. But because they planned to inspect the high-country watersheds of this part of the Sierra Nevada, they took the left fork, which headed up Hope Valley toward the Carson Pass. Beyond here, they reached the turn-off to Blue Lakes.

After a hard climb for the team, the party reached Upper Blue Lake just in time for lunch. Then, after crossing a divide that was 8,700 feet in elevation, they dropped down to Blue Lake, where they were to spend the next two nights in a log cabin built in 1878. This was the headquarters of the Standard Electric Company of California, founded in 1899 by Prince André Poniatowski[24] and his brother-in-law, William H. Crocker. By this summer of 1903, Crocker wanted to see how work was progressing on two new dams in the Blue Lakes area, and he invited Bourn and his cousins, as well as Joseph Grant, to visit the construction site. Crocker also wanted to show Bourn the water and electric system that his company was developing.

At this high elevation, work had to be done during the short summer season after the winter snow melted and before the first storms of fall. Crocker had a large crew of many nationalities as well as some Washo Indians working on this job. The overall construction was in charge of W. Frank Pierce and his assistant, Randall Ellis.

Of all the men on this construction job, it was Chief Mayo who fascinated Ingalls, who had never met an Indian. Not only was he surprised that Mayo could speak English, but he was captivated by the chief's intimate knowledge of the flora and fauna of this high granite country.

In the afternoon, Crocker took his guests down to Deer Valley, where the crew was hard at work on the Little Blue Lake Dam, which was to supplement the storage capacity of the upper dam on Blue Lake. After visiting this site, the men walked upward to Meadow Lake, where Crocker told them another dam was to be built. Meadow Lake was a magnificent sight, set in a basin with white-gray granite forming its sides, while the nearby boulders gave the appearance of having been polished by ancient glacial activity.

After one full day and two nights at Blue Lake, the Bourn party loaded its gear into the wagon and headed downgrade to the valley. From here, they followed the pioneer wagon road west and upward past Red Lake, then switchbacked through the granite until they reached the summit of Carson Pass. Here, they left the wagon and walked back to a point where they "saw the marks of the ropes on the trees where a block and tackle had been fastened to pull up the emigrant wagons."[25]

As they continued downward on the wagon road, they stopped to eat their lunch at Tragedy Springs. Here, they saw three graves and carved on a nearby tree the names of three men who had been killed at this place in 1848. Joseph Grant was touched by what they saw, and he took up a collection from the others to have a brass plate made to contain the names of the dead and be firmly attached to one of the nearby boulders so there would be something lasting to indicate who was buried in this lonely spot.[26]

That night, the men stayed in one of the electric company's older cabins at Bear River. The next morning, they headed toward Electra, where the company had a powerhouse on the Mokelumne River. They stopped to eat their lunch at Mill Creek, where the power company had another small station some twenty miles from Electra. After lunch, the men left the wagon and switched to saddle horses for the remainder of the trip over a mountain trail and down into the canyon where the waters of the Mokelumne River turned the generators of the Electra powerhouse. On their way into the canyon, they put their luggage on their horses and walked down the steep switchback trail.

"The plant," Ingalls wrote, "is extensive and shows an investment of an immense amount of capital. The house where we stayed is a very fine building like a country club, with all the conveniences."[27] After they ate dinner, they were given a tour of the powerhouse. It was very clean and had large wheels run by water power. At this time, the plant could produce 10,000 kilowatts, but the ultimate goal of the designers was to produce as much as 60,000 kilowatts of electricity. Although the design of the powerhouse had been conceived by Dr. Frederick A. C. Perrine[28] of the electrical engineering department of Stanford University, the man in charge of the mechanical and hydraulic equipment at the Electra plant was W. R. Eckart, who had been an engineering officer of the navy during the Civil War, had designed the first locomotive built in California by the Donahue Iron Works, and had designed and built the Lake Tahoe steamer *Meteor* for the Bliss family of Glenbrook, Nevada.

What Bourn and his friends saw during this high mountain trip was the possibility of developing a great water and electric system using the water in the lakes and rivers of the Sierra Nevada. Here, in many respects, was the future of California, and it was a future that captured Will Bourn's imagination. As he saw it, he was involved in the gas and electric business at a key moment in history. Furthermore, he now understood more completely the role that the Spring Valley Water Company could play in supplying water to San Francisco and possibly other communities.

As the summer of 1903 ended, Bourn finished months of discussion and offers and counter-offers with the Equitable Gas Light Company, the Pacific Gas Improvement Company, and the two utility companies owned by Claus Spreckels and two of his sons. In buying these firms, Will hoped to halt the rate war started by Claus Spreckels.[29]

Although Will had to pay a considerable amount, he had no trouble buying the Equitable Gas Light Company and the Pacific Gas Improvement Company. It was a costly buy-out. Will's company paid Spreckels $5,000,000 in San Francisco Gas and Electric Company bonds, giving Spreckels a profit of $1,214,000.[30]

But the victory was Will's as he moved to consolidate as much of San Francisco's utility business as he could. Upon closing his deals with these companies on September 1, 1903, he was much closer to gaining full control of a chaotic system that he planned to remake into one that functioned without price wars and duplicate lines and pipes for the same service. Although Bourn saw his plans as acting for public good, it troubled him that he was often the target of newspaper cartoons and editorials picturing him as a greedy capitalist. As he looked forward to future changes in the utility business, he hoped he might rid himself of his terrible public image.

15

Growing Fortunes

Five years into the new century, Will Bourn could look at his business empire as though he were a successful cash-crop farmer. Instead of producing grain, fruit, or produce to take to market, his specialty lay in growing fortunes. As 1905 moved into the fall season, the Empire Mines and Investment Company showed net profits of well over two million dollars from the last six months of 1900 through most of 1905.[1] Although this was a major source of Will's income, it did not include returns from his holdings in Spring Valley Water Company stock or his large portfolio of investments in bonds, stocks, and real estate.

As 1905 neared its end, Will Bourn as president of the San Francisco Gas and Electric Company was about to close a deal to sell this utility company to the California Gas and Electric Corporation, which was planning to merge the two companies to form the Pacific Gas and Electric Company.[2] Although Bourn might have considered holding on to his firm or even offering to buy out the California Gas and Electric Corporation, he had become weary of constant attacks by the local newspapers in cartoons and editorials. Not only did such scurrilous attacks offend him, but as a man who never wished to see his name in the newspapers, Will found these ruthless portrayals more than he wished to endure. He dearly loved San Francisco and contributed money and time to its cultural and economic needs, and he was hurt by this constant personal vilification. Consequently, he was receptive to an offer to buy the San Francisco Gas and Electric Company.

Bourn had been approached by Eugene de Sabla and Frank G. Drum of the California Electric Corporation in February 1905 about the possibility of buying his company, but the actual buy-out was delayed until the purchasers could secure enough capital for the transaction. With the incorporation of the Pacific Gas and Electric Company on October 10, 1905, this new firm had a "capital of $20,000,000 in common stock and $10,000,000 in 6 per cent cumulative preferred. Issues of $10,000,000 in 5 per cent collateral trust bonds and $4,500,000 in 6 per cent debentures." This capital allowed them to buy the California Electric Corporation, but the transaction did not take place until the first week of 1906. Money was available to purchase all the outstanding stock of the San Francisco Gas and Electric Company for $15,848,433.33. In addition to this money, Bourn and the other major stockholders of the San Francisco Gas and Electric Company were to retain the corporation's identity for an unspecified time. Meanwhile, the shares of stock in the San Francisco Gas and Electric Company were deposited with the Union Trust Company to serve as security for PG&E's new bond issue. Bourn and the other officers of the San Francisco Gas and Electric Company agreed to this arrangement on the condition that all their stockholders were to receive "$65 per share in PG&E bonds and $25 per share in cash."[3]

By January 2, 1906, PG&E was able to assume control of the California Gas and Electric Corporation and San Francisco Gas and Electric Company, but the new company still had to pay off the San Francisco Gas and Electric Company, which was backing its bonds. When they did this at the beginning of the new year, they had to pay holders of San Francisco Gas and Electric Company stock $90 per share, or an increase of $25 per share since October 1905.[4]

Two months before the actual sale, Will wrote to his mother at Madroño and indicated his feelings about the business. "I will be glad," he wrote, "to get the responsibility of this public concern off my shoulders. It has brought me a notoriety that had not been at all pleasant, but I think the result of the administration should be satisfactory to all shareholders."[5]

Within this same letter, Will discussed the burden of the ranches that he and his mother had owned for many years. Principally, he was concerned about the upper and lower ranches in the Napa Valley, which were not associated with Madroño, and he indicated in his letter that there was an offer from a potential buyer named Jimmie Howland. Will then stated: "What an elephant all these ranches have been. They are expensive luxuries excepting for those who farm for a living."[6] Both ranches had considerable acreage, but neither offered anything more than a minimal return in rental income from ranchers who leased the land for grazing livestock. The total income barely paid the yearly taxes, and it did not meet the expense of maintaining fences, keeping accounts up to date, and worrying about potential wildfires starting on this uncultivated land during the long, dry months of summer.

Will did not suggest that the disposal of these ranches had to be settled at once. Still, with the gas and electric business almost out of his hands, he was more than willing to question the luxury of clinging to unprofitable property. It was as though he wished to begin 1906 with all business problems resolved, so he could focus his attention on ventures that offered a steady, yearly return with prospects of substantial growth.

2 As the year drew to a close, Will saw his wife and daughter off as they took the Southern Pacific ferry to Oakland to board the cross-country train to New York, where he had made reservations for the family at the St. Regis Hotel. As soon as he had completed the last details of the transfer of ownership of the San Francisco Gas and Electric Company to the PG&E, he planned to join them in New York, for they were bound for Egypt, Italy, Monaco, and then on to Paris and perhaps England.

In no more than five or six days, Will completed all the business that required his personal attention and turned over any immediate or future problems to cousin Will Ingalls in the San Francisco office. Then he traveled to Oakland and caught the Overland Limited for New York. On January 1, 1906, he sent a telegram from Ogden, Utah, to his wife to let her know he was on his way to join them for their long-awaited holiday. Three days later, Will arrived in New York where Agnes and Maud met him at the station. When Agnes saw him, she was distressed at how he looked. He was suffering from a bad cold, and he was exhausted and "very unlike himself." After a good night's rest, Will felt better, and while Agnes visited family members, Will and Maud went to see the play *Alice-Sit-By-The-Fire.*[7]

After completing all the last-minute arrangements for their cruise, Will wrote to his mother from the St. Regis Hotel and told her that they were sailing for Italy on January 9. He indicated his trip to Egypt was much on his mind as he longed for the rest that sailing up the Nile should bring.[8]

The day they boarded the steamship, Agnes wrote in her diary that "We sit at the Capt.'s table."[9] She was enchanted by the smooth sailing down the bay, for they were able to walk on the deck and watch the distant city on the fading shoreline as the light of the moon outlined it.

The next morning, as they moved out to sea, the ship encountered deeper swells. This was too much for Agnes, who had to spend their first day at sea in the cabin, too seasick to stroll on the deck. The very thought of food kept her confined to bed. Her bout with seasickness was over in one day, and by the second day she was able to join Will and Maud for meals and meet fellow passengers and talk to them about their vacation plans. The company of fellow travelers on the Atlantic cruise brought about a kind of civilized congeniality that made it easy for people who did not know each other to meet and talk as though they had been friends for years.

Sometime during the first few days at sea, the Bourns were introduced to Arthur Rose Vincent. He had an easy and pleasant manner, and he told the Bourns that he was returning to Ireland from a short time in Siam but that he was to go back there again as an assistant judge of His Britannic Majesty's Court. He went on to say that Mrs. Tobin Clark, a social leader of San Francisco's Irish community and a friend of the Bourns, had suggested that he introduce himself so he would know somebody during his Atlantic crossing.

Thirty-year-old Vincent was a good-looking man from Summerhill, Cloonlara, County Clare, Ireland. He had a certain flair and a background that fascinated twenty-two-year-old Maud. Born in Mhow, India, where his father, Colonel Arthur Hare Vincent, was stationed with the 3rd Hussars, Arthur was educated at Wellington College and Trinity College, Dublin. He had been a member of the Irish Bar since 1900 and had served in the Judicial Service of the British Foreign Office since 1903. In 1903, he had been stationed in Kisumu, East Africa, as a magistrate; in 1904, he had served as town magistrate of Mombasa; and in 1905, he had been a second assistant judge in Zanzibar until he had received his appointment to Siam.[10]

To Maud, Arthur Vincent possessed all the qualities of a hero from a romantic adventure novel. He had the grace and wit of an educated man of the world, and he spoke of travels and appointments of importance in lands that bore names with a ring of romance about them. Though one leg was slightly shorter than the other because of a hip injury he had suffered as a boy, this seemed to add another aspect to his character. In Maud's eyes, he was a Byronic hero who bore a slight flaw that enhanced his stature.

During the rest of the Atlantic crossing, Maud became better acquainted with Arthur Vincent, and when the ship made its first European stop at Gibraltar on January 17, Maud bid farewell to Arthur but promised to answer his letters. To Will and Agnes, who had enjoyed Vincent's company, the friendship between Maud and Arthur had merely been a shipboard flirtation, and they believed they would not see Vincent again unless by chance their paths were to cross in a similar manner in the future. But to Maud, it had been much more than a passing romance, and she promised herself that if the opportunity presented itself for them to see each other again, she was more than willing to carry on from where they had left off.

Three days after the ship's stop at Gibraltar, it sailed into the bay at Genoa, Italy. After the ship had docked, the Bourns and other passengers of this Cook's tour were lodged in various hotels. As Agnes wrote in her diary on January 20, 1906, "We arrive ashore about eleven and walk to Cook's—then to Eden's Palace—a delightful hotel—in a garden full of lovely and interesting trees and plants."[11]

During their five and a half days at Genoa, the Bourns visited many of the sights of the city. Using their Baedeker, they tried to see as much of Genoa's historic past as they could. They rented an automobile and hired a driver, and in this manner they saw the terraced gardens of the Villa Pizzario and the views of the bay from the hills above the city.

On Friday, January 26, they were back aboard ship and bound for Cairo. A cold wind blew off the water, and the sky was a brilliant blue as their ship sailed away from Genoa. The Bourns were excited as the ship cut through the Mediterranean on its voyage to the north coast of Africa and the mouth of the Nile River. They sailed along the coast of Italy and passed the islands of Corsica, Capri, Sardinia, Sicily, and Malta.

Three days after leaving Genoa, they sighted the fabled Alexandria on the horizon. As their ship drew closer, they could make out "a few straggling palaces and a minaret here and there, and the masts of ships."[12] They had an excellent lunch in a hotel, and afterward they viewed parts of the city and then were driven to Pompey's Pillar and on to the catacombs.

In the late afternoon the Bourns left for Cairo. On their journey they passed through the fertile Nile Delta country, where they saw palm trees, camels, donkeys, Arab villages, and boats with triangular lateen sails. A little after seven o'clock in the evening of January 29, they arrived in Cairo and were taken to the Savoy Hotel. Here, they had a fine view of the Nile and the sprawling city.

After breakfast the next morning, Will and Agnes went to look at a *dahabeah,* because Will wanted to cruise up the Nile on one of these large passenger boats that had once sailed the river by using their lateen sails to catch the wind. By 1906, these vessels were equipped with steam engines. From what the Bourns saw of such vessels that belonged to Cook's, they appeared quite comfortable. Before they made arrangements for their cruise, they agreed to stay in Cairo for a while so they would have time to see the city and visit the Pyramids.

Their tours around Cairo gave them a good view of the city and its historic sites. They were intrigued by the mosques and made a point of spending time in the important museums. Then on February 2, they moved to another hotel, which was better than the Savoy.

Up to this time, they had only a distant view of the Pyramids. Then the desert winds began to blow so hard that they waited from day to day for them to ease up so they could travel overland to the Pyramids. On Sunday, February 4, the day was clear and the wind had died down. They drove out to the Pyramids, and Agnes thought that the afternoon was "a dream of loveliness—the verdant and fertile valley of the Nile . . . the majesty of the Pyramids. They are marvelous and the Sphinx—something to study for days, months."[13] Everything the Bourns saw fascinated them, and they took time to ask questions of their guide. Will and Agnes wanted to come away from their experience with as much historical information as possible. More than that, they knew that one day at the Pyramids would not satisfy them, and they looked forward to all the other visits they planned to make during their stay in Egypt.

On the evening of February 11, the Bourns entertained guests aboard the *dahabeah Nitocris.* In the morning they would begin their cruise up the Nile, but that Sunday evening they celebrated their Egyptian tour with a sixteen-course dinner. Agnes described this as an Arabian dinner, but she claimed it was not her idea of a good meal. Still, she kept two copies of the menu, which she treasured enough to insert between the pages of her diary.

On Monday morning, the *Nitocris* cast away its mooring lines and began the trip up the Nile. During this voyage, the vessel made frequent stops so the passengers were able to travel by donkey to visit the Pyramids. The Bourns were fascinated by the statue of Rameses II (1292–1225 B.C.), which had once stood fifty-six feet tall but now lay tumbled on the ground. They also saw the tomb of Pharaoh Merenptah, who Agnes Bourn noted was the "Pharaoh of the Red Sea." Then they saw the tombs of Amenhotep II (1447–1420 B.C.), Rameses III (1204–1172 B.C.), Rameses IV (1172–1166 B.C.), and Seti I (1321–1300 B.C.), which had beautiful reliefs carved in the stone. This phase of their twenty-eight-day Nile River trip was something the Bourns would never forget. They savored every moment, even on those days when the wind blew such great clouds of sand that the vessel had to put ashore and everybody had to remain off the decks until the hot winds of the desert ceased to blow. But even this discomfort added to their feeling for the Land of the Pharaohs.

The Bourns returned to Cairo on Monday, March 12, 1906, and took rooms at the Shyrizah Palace. While Agnes rested on this first day back from their Nile adventure, Will and Maud went shopping. In the next two days, the Bourns did their share of buying gifts and souvenirs. Time passed quickly, and on Thursday, March 15, they boarded a steamship and sailed away from Cairo to the mouth of the Nile and into the Mediterranean.

Six days later, their ship docked in the Bay of Naples. Their long tour of Egypt was fresh in their memories, but they quickly shifted their attention to the cultural heritage of Italy. Within the next seven days, they saw a bit of Naples and Sorrento, but most of their time was spent in Rome, where they visited the Coliseum, marveled at the art in St. Paul's and St. Peter's, and walked through the gardens of the Vatican. Then they stopped to see the Sistine Chapel and the work of Michelangelo.

The Bourns traveled quickly at this point of their journey. Unlike their time in Egypt, they moved through Italy as though they were on a tight schedule. By April 7, after having spent two very cold days and nights in Genoa, they arrived by automobile in Monte Carlo.

Here, all their traveling caught up to them. Agnes suffered from a cold, and Maud had an upset stomach. Will was weary, but he looked forward to visiting the casino to try his luck. To him, putting down his bet on the turn of a card at Monte Carlo was a gambler's dream. Poker games at the Palace Hotel in San Francisco were one thing, but Monte Carlo offered something he had looked forward to ever since they left Italy and crossed into the French Riviera. For the moment, however, he saw to the care and comfort of Agnes and Maud. The time for the casino would come, and he awaited the challenge.

3 April 18, 1906, 5 A.M. in San Francisco, California; April 18, 1906, 2 P.M. in Monte Carlo, and it was a rainy day. The previous evening, Will went to the casino to try his luck. In her diary Agnes simply indicated: "Will remains until the closing. He returns from Monte Carlo ahead." [14]

In San Francisco April 17 had been a festive evening for many friends of the Bourns. They had attended the second night of the visiting Metropolitan Opera Company's offering at the Grand Opera House on Mission Street between Third and Fourth Streets. The house had been packed with music lovers eager to hear the great Enrico Caruso perform the role of Don José in Bizet's *Carmen.* The women in the boxes and the diamond circle wore their finest gowns. "Metallic brocades, rich velvets, sequined materials predominated." [15]

The opera was not the only attraction in San Francisco that evening. The Columbia Theater on Powell Street was featuring Victor Herbert's *Babes in Toyland,* and the dashing John Barrymore was appearing at another theater in Richard Harding Davis's *The Dictator.*

The political news that people were talking about was yet another scandal involving Mayor Eugene Schmitz and Abraham Reuf, better known as Boss Reuf, for there were rumors that both men were accepting bribes. There was also talk of natural disaster on that fine evening, for Italy's Mount Vesuvius continued to take its deadly toll upon the Neapolitan countryside as its lava flows destroyed towns and villages.

After this magnificent evening in San Francisco's Opera House and in its theaters, people flocked to North Beach to enjoy a good meal in such popular restaurants as Luna's and Coppa's. Even members of the opera's cast entered these restaurants to the applause of the diners.

April 17 passed into April 18. Party-going San Franciscans returned to their homes, and visitors found their way to their hotel rooms.

At 5:12 A.M., April 18, 1906, "Police Sergeant Jesse Cook stopped to chat with Al Levy, a young produceman at the corner of Washington and Davis." Suddenly, Officer Cook noticed that nearby horses had become terrified of something. Then he heard a distant, deep rumbling sound. Had he been a trainman, he might have thought that somehow a freight train had found its way onto Washington Street. He did not look at his watch, but no more than six seconds had passed since 5:12. He turned and stared up Washington Street. It was impossible! As he said later: "The whole street was undulating. It was as if the waves of the ocean were coming toward me, and billowing as they came." [16]

The initial shock lasted for forty seconds of incredible intensity. "With a terrifying, wrenching shudder the earth began a crazy dance that toppled towers and chimneys, crumbled rows of simple frame houses to splintered kindling, threw cornices and whole walls into the streets, and twisted steel rails and bridges and pipelines like wet clay." [17]

Church bells clanged with senseless fury, and hundreds of thousands of people thought it was Judgment Day. Inside buildings, dishes, glasses, and framed photographs flew off shelves and walls to smash into pieces; bookcases fell, and books flew against walls and floors; furniture shot across rooms or tipped and slammed to the floor; waterpipes burst and sent geysers into the air; toilet tanks overflowed and water ran across bathroom floors, flowed beneath doors and flooded one room to another. Gas lines broke and filled nearby rooms with dangerous fumes; and electric power poles snapped or fell and took the hot lines in a sparking jumble onto the ground and pavement. Then the movement of the earth stopped as suddenly as it had begun. But only ten seconds later a jarring second punch hit with a terrible power that lasted another twenty-five seconds. When this ended, smaller tremors continued as though directed to take care of anything not already destroyed.

Even after the devastation of an earthquake that would have measured somewhere about 8.25 on the Richter Scale—to be developed in later years by Charles F. Richter of the California Institute of Technology—the next great worry for survivors of the earthquake was fire. Fire Chief Dennis Sullivan was mortally injured when the smokestacks of the California Hotel crashed down on the roof of the third story of the new fire station on Bush Street between Grant and Kearny. Sullivan's wife was only slightly injured, but Chief Sullivan suffered serious chest and head injuries, and he died three days later in the hospital at the Presidio. Sullivan had developed plans for using water from San Francisco Bay in the event of a disaster, but his plan had not been passed on to his men.

Still, the firemen of San Francisco proved to be more than resourceful as they raced their horses and pulled fire wagons to the scenes of the first fires, only to discover that the water mains were broken. They did the best they could by using water from cisterns that had survived, from sewer storage tanks that had not ruptured, and water from San Francisco Bay. Still, even in the first hours of the fire, the firemen knew they could save only a part of San Francisco. The fire was to last from Wednesday, April 18th, to Saturday, April 23rd. During that time "585 firemen with few more than fifty pieces of equipment—steam engines, hooks and ladders, and chemical units—faced the mile-wide fire front without water, without the leadership of their chief, and without adequate communications."[18] Yet they managed to bring the blaze to an end.

San Francisco had been saved, but much of the city was destroyed by the earthquake and fire. Four hundred and ninety blocks were gone. The flames had destroyed twenty-eight thousand buildings. "The City Hall and its records, the libraries, the courts and jails, the theaters and restaurants had vanished. The heart and guts of one of the world's best loved cities were gone."[19] And as the Bourns were to learn upon their return to San Francisco, the City by the Golden Gate now could lay claim to "The Damndest Finest Ruins."

4 On Thursday, April 19, 1906, Will, Agnes, and Maud heard about the great disaster, and Agnes wrote in her diary, "We learn the news of the earthquake and fire at home."[20] She stated it as a matter to be put down as part of the record, but she had no knowledge at this point of the terrible disaster that had wiped out 4.11 square miles of San Francisco and resulted in 315 people killed outright, 6 shot for looting, 1 shot by mistake, and 352 people missing for a terrible total of 674 lives lost.[21]

What the Bourns did not learn until they arrived in California was that their home on Webster Street had survived, as had the home on Broadway owned by Sarah and Ida. As Will was to learn when all accounts had been settled, the Fireman's Fund Insurance Company, which found itself with $11.5 million in claims and only $7 million in total assets, managed to pay off its policy holders. This was accomplished by forming a new company that was free of debt and offering policyholders a settlement of 56½ percent cash and 50 percent stock in the new corporation to pay off their claims. Six other American companies paid their policyholders in full, but six German insurance companies and one Austrian company refused to pay any claims. Added to this, twelve other American companies either failed to pay or paid as much as they could and then went out of business.[22] All things considered, Will was proud of the company that his father had once headed and in which he held many shares of stock.

This same morning of April 19, Will sent home cables and money that he had won at the casino to help both friends and family in this time of great need. The newspaper headlines and stories about the earthquake presented a grim account. From what the Bourns could tell, the earthquake had spread south and north and to the east of San Francisco.

Still, the extent of damage was not to become clear to them until they reached home. Then they would learn that the terrible power of the earthquake along the San Andreas Fault had toppled the top of the tower of Mission San Juan Bautista, caused the collapse of many buildings at Stanford University, and caused the death of more than one hundred inmates and staff members at the Agnew State Insane Asylum near San Jose.[23] From the Santa Cruz Mountains in the south to Fort Bragg in the north, the path of destruction was twenty to forty miles wide. Along this trail of terror, the earth shook with fury in Oakland, Berkeley, and other East Bay communities; to the south it rattled Gilroy, San Juan Bautista, San Jose, Palo Alto, Redwood City, and Burlingame; and to the north it startled and panicked the people of San Rafael, Sebastopol, St. Helena, Sonoma, and Santa Rosa, where every brick building in town was leveled.

In the Santa Cruz Mountains south of San Francisco, "acres of splendid two-hundred and three-hundred year old redwoods were whipped into splinters as whole mountainsides slid into sharp valleys below."[24] Train tracks slid into the Pacific Ocean. Just south of San Francisco, a commuter train of four cars fell onto its side, but by sheer luck not one passenger was injured. Within less than two minutes after the devastating earthquake, San Franciscans had fled into the streets wearing their nightshirts and whatever else they had grabbed in the way of clothing. Once outside, they saw a scene of chaos where buildings had collapsed, streets had buckled, tall electric poles had snapped or fallen to carry sparking lines with them, sirens wailed, and terrified animals ran or stood and shook. To all who had survived, it was clear at once that San Francisco had changed forever.

On that morning of April 19, Will Bourn purchased tickets for the next train to Paris, but they were not able to leave until the morning of April 20. The next day, they were in Paris. Here they remained until April 27, when they traveled to the seaport of Cherbourg and boarded the SS *Amerika* and sailed for the United States.

Sunday, May 6, 1906, the *Amerika* dropped anchor in New York. The Bourns stayed overnight at the Manhattan Hotel, which they did not like, but during the day they found time to visit relatives in Brooklyn, including the Ingalls family. At 4:30 P.M. on Monday, May 7, they boarded the overland train and headed for California.

Four days later on the western slope of the Sierra Nevada, the Bourns got off the train at ten minutes after noon at the Colfax station. The George Starr family was waiting at the depot for them, and they had "a special train to take us to Grass Valley." This was the Nevada County Narrow Gauge Railroad, which ran between Nevada City and the Southern Pacific depot at Colfax.[25]

The trip from Colfax to Grass Valley only covered twenty-two miles, then the Bourns and the Starrs had a short drive to the Empire Mine. Here at the beautiful stone cottage they were greeted by Katie Moriarty, the large Irish cook and keeper of the Bourns' Grass Valley home. Agnes was very happy to see the reliable, motherly Katie. After all the terrible news of the great earthquake and fire in San Francisco, Katie was a staunch symbol of all that home stood for to the Bourns.

After three days of rest at the Empire Cottage, days and nights when most of the conversation centered around the great disaster in San Francisco, Will was ready to travel out of the foothill country to see the extent of the damage and visit his mother, sisters, cousin Willie Ingalls, and all his San Francisco friends. This was a time to come to the aid and comfort of people who had been through a terrible disaster.

On Tuesday, May 15, Will and Agnes caught the Southern Pacific train at Colfax and traveled to the San Francisco Bay Area. Their first view of the city was from the bay, and although they could see the terrible scar where once the heart of the city had been, Agnes wrote, "One does not realize the awful calamity from the Bay."[26]

Once they landed at the Ferry Building and walked into the open to look up Market Street, the impact of disaster became clear with a terrible shock of recognizing the loss of landmarks and the total devastation. But restoration was already under way. The Ferry Building had not fallen, nor had it been torn down as some engineers wanted. Instead, a scaffolding was built around the lower part of it, and the building that was San Francisco's grand entrance was being repaired.

Up Market Street and then on to the other streets that fanned off Market, debris was being cleared away by wagons and hauled to waiting Southern Pacific gondola cars on special tracks that had been laid to help in the clean-up. Much of this rubble was then dumped in Mission Bay, but when that became too full, the rest of the debris was loaded onto large barges and towed out to the vicinity of Mile Rock, where it was dumped.

The Bourns were relieved when they reached their home on Pacific Heights and saw that it remained standing. Inside the house, servants had picked up fallen objects and put them back, or if they were broken, thrown them away. The relief at seeing their home much as they had left it was more than the Bourns had expected. Still, San Francisco was not where they wished to stay for the next few months. As they left the city and headed up the bay toward Napa County and St. Helena, they knew that they would return to help in the rebuilding of San Francisco.

It was good to see all the family gathered at Sarah Bourn's home at

Madroño. Will's sisters and the two brothers-in-law were staying there until San Francisco was ready for daily living. Will and Agnes were pleased to learn that the city home of his mother and Ida on Broadway Street had survived with no damage. It, too, was anchored in rock and also was west of Nob Hill and the fire line.

Agnes noted in her diary entry for Thursday, May 17, that Will's "mother has a terrible cold, and seems very feeble. The others remarkably well after their anxiety and hardships."[27] For seven days and nights, Will and Agnes enjoyed the company of family at Madroño, then on May 24, they traveled to Burlingame to visit friends who had not been as fortunate during the earthquake.

After one day down the Peninsula, Will and Agnes returned to San Francisco. As they traveled along Mission Street, they were appalled by the terrible devastation. Although the clean-up continued at a rapid pace throughout San Francisco, it was not pleasant to live there. Will decided that it would be better if the family made its headquarters at the Empire Cottage. For the next few months he was to make trips from Grass Valley to the city to take care of business affairs and lend his financial backing where it was needed in the recovery and rebuilding of San Francisco.

5 That summer of 1906 at the Empire Cottage was a wonderful interlude in the lives of the Bourns. During the latter part of May and nearly all of June there were more thunderstorms and showers than usual. This cooled the air, and the heat of the Sierra Nevada foothills did not arrive until July. Everybody enjoyed the use of the Clubhouse, which Willis Polk had finished building in 1905. The tennis court was also completed, and Will enjoyed a daily game of tennis against anybody who would give him a good game.

During this idyllic summer at the Empire Cottage, Will had time to indulge in many activities for pleasure only. George Starr taught him to play billiards on the tables in the Clubhouse. Here, Will played with his usual competitiveness, playing with determination to become as good if not better than his cousin or any other player.

At other times, Will and Agnes enjoyed the company of Arthur and Mary Hallock Foote, who lived in the beautiful North Star Mine home designed by Julia Morgan. Agnes and Mary became especially close, and they thoroughly enjoyed each other's company during the summer of 1906.

In June, Willis Polk paid a short visit at the Empire Cottage. Polk was on his way back to San Francisco after a visit with the architect Daniel Hudson Burnham in Chicago. After dinner on the first evening, Will and his friend Polk talked at great length about the rebuilding of San Francisco. Both men feared that city leaders would not follow through on the plan that former mayor James Duval Phelan and the Association for the Improvement and Adornment of San Francisco had commissioned Burnham to draw for them in 1904. Ironically, the major objection to such a grand scale of city planning had been the need to remove blocks of business buildings as well as homes in order to follow the design of Burnham's plan. But now the earthquake and fire had taken care of that aspect of rebuilding the city, so Bourn and Polk saw no reason that this plan should not go ahead.

To Bourn and Polk, as well as to such men as James D. Phelan, John Galen Howard—the Massachusetts-born architect hired in 1901 to take charge of the campus plan for the University of California—and the University of California's President Benjamin Ide Wheeler, the Burnham master plan for the City of San Francisco was the ideal that should be followed in rebuilding. Ordinary streets were to be replaced by magnificent boulevards. There was to be a new civic center where fountains splashed. Reservoirs were to be built at high points in the city to provide water that would cascade through open aqueducts and flow in and out of a system of manmade lakes. The old idea of geometric platting was to give way to open community gardens that would replace the checkerboard aspect of almost useless small backyards.[28] Finally, the high point of the Burnham Plan called for a great amphitheater on the sides of Twin Peak that would overlook downtown San Francisco.

Yet even as Bourn and Polk talked about a new San Francisco, the forces against such a grand design were forming. The Downtown Business Men's Association withdrew its support for this bold move, then M. H. de Young, owner and publisher of the *Chronicle,* used his newspaper to lead the fight against the Burnham Plan. As de Young put it: "The crying need of San Francisco today is not more parks and boulevards; it is business."

By the Fourth of July, the true summer of the foothills had arrived and Will began to suffer from the heat. Early in the morning the temperature would be seventy degrees, but by early afternoon it climbed to one hundred degrees. Within the Cottage, the heat was unbearable, and the family slept outside on the lawn at night. Here, a light breeze gave some relief from the heat. On July 4, there were fireworks for all to watch, and Agnes commented in her diary that "The fireworks are very pretty in the evening—especially the green lights among the pines."[29]

In the latter part of July, the William H. Crockers visited the Bourns at the Empire Cottage. By this time, the weather had become very warm. Agnes wrote that July 24 was the hottest day of summer, and both Will and the Crockers felt the heat very much.

Five days later, Will, Agnes, and Maud traveled to San Francisco. After the summer heat of Grass Valley, they found foggy San Francisco a cold, windy city of ruins. Agnes was depressed by the sight of workmen continuing the clean-up and carpenters and craftsmen hard at work rebuilding the city. On Van Ness Avenue, though, there was a steady stream of lumber wagons and a new version of the Emporium open in a white frame building, flying the American flag as though it had become a symbol of recovery. "The City is a sad sight," Agnes wrote, "and Van Ness Avenue gay like a country fair."[30] Here she saw a bustling retail area come to life like a western boomtown. There were stores that looked as though they had grown out of the ground overnight, colorful flags above buildings, hastily opened restaurants that belonged on some carnival midway, and throngs of people who crowded the street as though they were boomers for a new land rush.

By August 9 the Bourns were back in Grass Valley, for they had mixed feelings about their stay in their Webster Street home. While they had been happy to see old friends, the Bourns were like survivors of a terrible disaster. They knew they had been very lucky, yet they had a feeling of guilt. Although they were largely unscathed, many of their friends had lost their homes and personal belongings.

In a very real sense, the Bourns now felt more at home in the Empire Cottage, for here there were no signs of destruction. They enjoyed the company of the Footes, the Starrs, and many other friends in Grass Valley and Colfax. It was an easy-going life and always offered the enjoyment of the out-of-doors and the closeness of the magnificent Sierra Nevada.

However, the time at Grass Valley in the months between May and October 1906 was not limited to a long vacation for Will Bourn. On June 23, 1906, he purchased the River Mines Company in Nevada County. The transfer of syndicate took place in Carson City, Nevada, but the company office was listed as 2550 Webster Street in the City and County of San Francisco.[31] This, of course, was the Bourn family home, but since the loss of the company's downtown office during the earthquake, all Bourn's business activities had to take place in either his San Francisco residence or the office of the Empire Mine.

On October 1, 1906, the Bourns were back in their San Francisco home. This time, they returned to stay. Even so, it was clear that they had some misgivings about leaving Grass Valley, for Agnes wrote: "We all return from the Cottage, am sorry to leave it."[32]

At this time, Will's interest in the Spring Valley Water Company became more than that of a casual buyer of stock in the company. On October 6, he traveled with his friend Captain Albert H. Payson to San Mateo to look over conditions at the Spring Valley Water Company's three dams in San Mateo County: Pilarcitos Dam, hidden in the hills; San Andreas Dam; and the Crystal Springs Dam. Payson, who had been a director of the San Francisco Gas and Electric Company in 1901, was now associated with the Spring Valley Water Company. On this trip to the company's dams, Payson gave Bourn a tour of the damage caused by the earthquake. To Bourn's amazement, almost the only damage was to pipes a few hundred feet distant from the Crystal Springs Dam. These were broken in two or thrown completely out of the ground by the force of the earthquake. Other damage showed that the road and fence crossing the causeway "were parted and left with an eight-or-nine-foot offset. Yet the strength and flexibility of this large dam brought it through all the shaking without any damage."[33]

As the two friends talked about the overall damage caused by the earthquake, it became clear to Will that the company's city water mains as well as pipelines off the mains to buildings would have to be replaced. Also, a complete examination of the major dams and pumps and all the pipelines would be necessary.

Will talked at great length with Payson about what would have to be repaired as a result of earthquake damage. Will trusted Alberto—as he called him—and knew that Payson's assessment of expenses involved in putting the water company back into operation on a full-time basis would be as accurate as he could expect without fully examining everything owned by the company. That, he knew, would not be possible until he had accumulated enough stock to be able to take over the company. All this, of course, remained a confidential matter between the two friends, but Bourn made it clear to Payson that he intended to take over the Spring Valley Water Company within the next two or three years.

After Will's return from his field trip, he had to consider all the aspects of such a business move. No doubt there would be many expenses involved in repairing the earthquake damage—and there was still the possibility that the pipeline that ran beneath San Francisco Bay from San Mateo County to Dumbarton Point might have to be replaced either in part or in full. Then there was the need to check the aqueduct that ran all the way to Suñol in Alameda County to be sure that everything was all right up to the entrance of the current water supply from that area into the water filtering and pumping station. Finally, Will realized that there would be a need to control as many sources of water in Alameda, Santa Clara, and San Mateo counties as he could. He knew that San Francisco's need for water would continue to grow.

However, there was one aspect about the possibility of owning the Spring Valley Water Company that did not excite Will. That was the fact that once again he would be in charge of a public utility. With this responsibility would come the continual grief of having to plead his case in order to get rate increases, and as in the gas and electric business, Will was not eager to face the kind of press that would come with his ownership of the water company. All these factors had to be taken into consideration as he faced an opportunity that truly excited him.

As the last months of 1906 drew to a close and San Francisco was well on its way in the long process of rebuilding, Will received good news from the Empire Mine. The net profit for 1906 came to $210,466.52.[34] Once again the true foundation of Bourn's wealth was the family's private reserve deep within the earth below Ophir Hill. Despite the great tragedy of the earthquake and fire, the Bourn Luck held true even in this time of disaster.

16

Water, Land, and Politics

California's need for water was something that William Bourn understood very well. Most of the state was semi-arid, and until a major water system was developed, there was the constant threat of drought when local reservoirs would run low. Even in normal fall and winter seasons, the San Francisco Bay Region had a rainfall history that showed twenty-five inches of rain as an expected annual amount. Anything more was considered a bonus. Anything less became a problem.

In the foothill country of Grass Valley, water power was vital to the operation of the Pelton waterwheels that provided power for machinery at the Empire Mine. In the Napa Valley, water was vital to Sarah Bourn's vineyards at Madroño as well as to the other vintners. In San Francisco, the need for fresh water had always been a concern for a city on a peninsula bounded by salt water. All these factors added to Will's decision to acquire the controlling stock in the Spring Valley Water Company, even though he did not like the political aspects of running such a company. As long as the City of San Francisco controlled the price of the water it bought from the Spring Valley Water Company, Will knew that if he took on the ownership of this firm, he would also face a constant battle with the city.

Will had taken an active interest in the Spring Valley Water Company as early as 1904. At that time, he became a regular investor in its securities, and he encouraged others—including his mother—to invest. He considered ownership of securities issued by the company to be both wise and prudent. During 1904 and 1905, Will talked to Captain Albert H. Payson, an officer of the company, about the firm's status and learned that the Spring Valley Water Company was in a position that made it financially and physically vulnerable. At this time, Will formed a syndicate to protect the company.[1]

After the Earthquake of 1906, the company faced tremendous expenses to repair damage and replace miles of broken pipelines and water mains. All this cost the company well over $600,000. During this trying period, Captain Payson became the company's president. Through his close friendship with Payson, Bourn became privy to the financial, physical, and political problems that faced the company. He learned from Payson, as well as from public hearings, that the City and County of San Francisco was setting water rates for the company so that it could earn only a 4 percent profit, which hardly covered operational expenses and the need for future improvements. Payson became so discouraged about future prospects for the company that he tried to persuade the Board of Supervisors of the City of San Francisco to offer $32,000,000 for the company. This was a very low price, and Bourn talked Payson out of this as he believed that such a price was "practically placing the property on the bargain counter."[2]

Realizing the need to prevent such a giveaway, Will made up his mind to move quickly. He had no faith in the overall attitude expressed by the company's board members, and he did not trust the political motives of San Francisco's Board of Supervisors. All these factors convinced Bourn that he had to use his money and business sense to save the Spring Valley Water Company, because he considered the water company indispensable to San Francisco.

By the summer of 1908, Will had acquired a controlling interest in the company. On August 21, 1908, he wrote to his New York broker, James Laidlaw of Laidlaw and Laidlaw: "Conditions have made it necessary for me to take over the management of the Spring Valley Water Company, and for the last two weeks, I have been up to my neck in water, in fact, I am now suffering from water on the brain."[3]

As he assumed management of the company, Will began to hire his own men. He retained his friend Captain Payson and appointed him vice president and acting executive chairman of the firm. Then he brought cousin Will Ingalls into the firm to serve as his secretary. Next, he hired young Samuel P. Eastman, who had attended the University of California as a mechanics student but had left in 1905 before obtaining his degree.[4] In adding young Eastman to the list of the firm's officials, Bourn made a wise choice, because Eastman was bright, a quick learner, reliable, and trustworthy. He was a young man who was willing to work long hours and was quickly able to grasp the many aspects of the water business.

With his complement of company officers hired and in place, Will had time to devote to other matters. He and Agnes leased Sky Farm in San Mateo County from the Crocker Estate and began using this as their country home.[5] Here, Will was close to the heart of the water company's holdings. Not far from Sky Farm were its major reservoirs: Pilarcitos Dam in the Coast Range, which captured the water of Pilarcitos Creek as well as run-off from the watershed, which had a yearly rainfall that ran between twenty and thirty inches; San Andreas Dam; the Old Crystal Springs Dam, which had impounded water from Laguna Creek but became a causeway between two lakes when Herman Schussler's engineering triumph resulted in the concrete Crystal Springs Dam, which backed up the water of San Mateo Creek.

In addition to these dams in San Mateo County, Bourn was interested in the development of the Alameda County water system. Here, the water company controlled most of the water rights for the Pleasanton area. Underground gravel beds provided a water source that added to the company's supply. A rough shack covered the filtering and pumping station at Suñol—a shack that Bourn hoped to replace. From this station at Suñol, water flowed through an aqueduct to Dumbarton Point. From there, it was pumped through a pipeline beneath San Francisco Bay to another pumping station near Belmont in San Mateo County. From here, the water was pumped up the mountainside and allowed to flow through a pipeline that carried it downward to Crystal Springs Reservoir.

While Will and Agnes enjoyed their stay at Sky Farm, the home's location on the border of the water company property in the Township of Hillsborough made it easy for Will to become thoroughly acquainted with every aspect of the Spring Valley Water Company.

2 William Bourn assumed the office of president of the Spring Valley Water Company on July 31, 1908. One of his first projects was to seek out the history of the water company, because he believed that in order to plan for the future, he had to know the firm's past. He wanted to have a grasp of the year-by-year advancements that went into its formation. In this undertaking, he would learn of the water company's acquisition of property and water rights, and its construction of dams, aqueducts, pipelines, pumping stations, and storage facilities within the City of San Francisco.

In the early years of San Francisco—long before it began its population growth during the Gold Rush—the basic water supply for the city came from Mountain Lake and Lobos Creek, which flows out of the lake within the borders of the Presidio. In addition, there were some wells, and for the future there was the water of Lake Merced.

By mid-1858, the Spring Valley Water Company was incorporated by George H. Ensign. The new firm was authorized "to lay down pipes, in the public streets of the City and County of San Francisco." Within this agreement there were two provisions that were to be a headache for the water company for many years: it agreed that water rates would be set by five commissioners, who were to be appointed by San Francisco's Board of Supervisors, and that for twenty years San Francisco had the right to purchase the company at a price to be determined by a Board of Commissioners.[6]

Six years after its beginning, the Spring Valley Water Company increased its capital stock to $6,000,000, divided into sixty thousand shares priced at $100 per share. During this time, William F. Babcock became chairman of the firm. In that same February 1865, the water company absorbed the San Francisco Water Works, which dated back to 1857. This move gave the Spring Valley Water Company a monopoly of the water system for the City and County of San Francisco. William Babcock had the backing of the banking firm of Pioche, Boyerque and Parsons, a firm which—under Pioche's specialty of buying Spanish and Mexican land grants—was able to add thousands of acres of watershed land to the holdings of the Spring Valley Water Company.[7]

Within ten years of its beginning, the Spring Valley Water Company had purchased large tracts of land in San Mateo County. Here it controlled the watershed from the coastal mountains and was able to capture the rainfall in catchment basins and storage reservoirs. At this time, in 1868, the firm purchased the water rights to Lake Merced at a cost of $150,000 and sought out such investors as Darius Ogden Mills and William Ralston of the Bank of California; James Ben Ali Haggin and Lloyd Tevis, who were partners in banking, land, mining, utilities, and railroads; and John Parrott, a financier and shipping magnate. The addition of these capitalists to the firm opened the doors for more money, more acquisition of land and watersheds, and more expansion. Tevis and Parrott became trustees and acted as key decision-makers of Spring Valley; Mills, Tevis, Ralston, and William Babcock were stock and bondholders and key financiers.[8]

In 1874, William Ralston—Comstock Boomer, flamboyant builder of the Palace Hotel, owner of the Bank of California—saw his overextended financial empire begin to fall apart as the United States endured another year of recession. However, Ralston came up with an idea to save his investments. He began buying stocks and bonds in the Spring Valley Water Company with the idea of gaining control of the firm. When he had accomplished this, he planned to sell the firm to San Francisco once the coming September election of supervisors put a majority of men into office who would back the idea of buying the water company from him. He borrowed wildly to gain control of the firm and managed to raise $6 million to acquire almost fifty thousand shares of Spring Valley Water Company stock. Now, all he had to do was wait until after the election, when he would sell the water company to San Francisco for $15,500,000. All he needed was a popular vote to swing things his way.[9]

But San Francisco's newspapers began a full attack on Ralston, referring to him as a masked highwayman, a seasoned holdup man, and a swindler who would pick the pockets of San Francisco's taxpayers. Even Mayor James Otis, who would die of diphtheria a year later, threatened to veto any measure to purchase the water company. The result was that Ralston's plan failed, and San Francisco made a decision to buy its own watershed lands and develop its own water system.

As for William Ralston, all his luck failed him, and by August of 1875 he had to resign as president of the Bank of California and give up his ownership of the Palace Hotel and practically everything else that he had built up as his personal fortune. Then in the late afternoon of August 27, 1875, after signing over the Bank of California to the Board of Trustees, the flamboyant Ralston walked to present-day Neptune Beach to take his usual swim in San Francisco Bay. A boy swam with him for a while and then gave up because of the tide, but Ralston continued onward. This was his last swim and his last day of life. His body was later washed ashore, as though even the depths had rejected him.[10]

After William Ralston, control of the Spring Valley Water Company was assumed by men from the highest socioeconomic circles of San Francisco's society, men like Charles W. Howard, Antoine Borel, S. C. Bigelow, Charles Mayne, Albert H. Payson, and others. All were listed in the *San Francisco Blue Book,* belonged to either Pacific or Union clubs, as well as the Bohemian Club, and were included in the *Social Register.*[11] In short, they were men of position, power, and influence. From them and their predecessors, William Bourn learned the history of the acquisition of land, watershed rights, and storage areas during the growth and development of the Spring Valley Water Company.

Grant, remise, release, convey and quitclaim.
Grant, bargain, and sell and convey.
Remise, release, and quitclaim.
Grant, bargain, sell, convey and confirm.

These were the opening lines for a series of land transactions that constituted the ballad of buying land, watersheds, creeks, lakes, catchment basins, and holding tanks for the water company. The measurement of acquired land went by acres, *varas,* miles, surveyors' markings and maps, crudely drawn sketch maps, and the beautiful *diseños* of Spanish land grants. But no matter how the refrain was marked, the final ballad was about the buying of land and watershed rights by the Spring Valley Water Company. From its early beginnings, the company's acquisitions included San Francisco County: Francisco Street Reservoir, Lombard Street Reservoir, Clay Street Reservoir, College Hill Reservoir, Laguna Honda, Lake Merced, Mountain Lake and Lobos Creek within the Presidio, as well as the Point Lobos Pumping Works.[12]

San Mateo County contained the following water company properties: Crystal Springs, Pilarcitos, and Lock Creek lands for a total of 15,404.06 acres. Added to this were the San Andreas lands consisting of 2,198.50 acres. Also, the San Mateo County land included the Searsville Reservoir and the acres surrounding it. There was more, much more. There were the Buri Buri Ranch, San Mateo Creek, Rancho Cañada de Ramundo, the Quinn Tract, and Rancho de las Pulgas. Added to these tracts of land and water rights were Rancho Corral de Tierra, Bear Gulch Creek, Rancho El Corte de Madera, Dennis Martin Creek, Alembique Creek, Hallett Rancho, Mountain Home Ranch, San Francisquito Creek, San Gregorio, Tunitas, Purisima, and Pescadero Creeks—thousands of acres of watershed, freshwater creeks, reservoirs, and sites for other reservoirs—all in San Mateo County.[13]

It was a small kingdom, but this was not all of it. Across San Francisco Bay, maps of the Spring Valley Water Company holdings showed the following in Alameda County: Alameda Creek, Calaveras Creek, Laguna Creek; lands along a country road from Suñol to Alameda Canyon to Niles; Rancho Arroyo de la Alameda with control of the water for Alameda Creek, a site for the Niles Dam, plus reservoirs, pipes, flumes, aqueducts, and mains.

Added to this were many holdings in Santa Clara County that ran from the Bernal Rancho to land near Mission San Jose. In 1908, 2,300 acres of farmland in Alameda County near Pleasanton had been added to the water company holdings.[14]

This amazing collection of ranchos, city lots, water rights to creeks, springs, and lakes, holding reservoirs in San Mateo County, and the plans for new reservoirs in both Alameda and Santa Clara Counties constituted the empire of water that Will Bourn had acquired. But with such vast holdings came tremendous responsibilities. Former landowners who had sold out to the water company might become bitter and even hostile as the value of land they once owned increased in value. Then there was the responsibility to the City and County of San Francisco to deliver on a promise to supply it with all the water needed for all purposes. There was also the responsibility to neighboring farmers, ranchers, and townsfolk to assure them that their own water supplies would not be depleted by the great thirst of the Spring Valley Water Company.

Ultimately, all this fell upon Will's shoulders, and he did not take such responsibilities lightly. His duty, he believed, was to all citizens in this vast area affected by the activities of the Spring Valley Water Company.

3 Even as the Spring Valley Water Company called for Bourn's close attention in 1908, he managed to find time to accept the position of president of the Pacific Union Club on April 22, 1908. One of the first things that Will wished to consider was a new home for this prestigious organization. During their long history, the two clubs that made up the Pacific Union Club had never had a decent home. Founded in 1852, the Pacific Club's first quarters had been the southeast corner of Kearny and Commercial Streets in the former Diana Saloon, Steve Whipple's gambling hall. The Union Club, organized in 1854, had its first location in the Parrott Block. In 1889 the two clubs had joined together to form the Pacific Union Club, but when Will took over the office of president the organization still did not have a permanent or suitable location. Since the 1906 earthquake and fire, everything had been put on hold. Bourn "suggested that he be given authority to appoint from the body of the Club such special committees as he deemed necessary to carry forward any special needs of the Club, and this was promptly granted."[15]

Among the first things Will suggested was that the club should proceed, through a Board of Directors, to plan for a new clubhouse. With this in mind, he asked Willis Polk, who was now associated with D. H. Burnham and Company, to attend a meeting on December 4, 1908, to add his suggestions for such a building. During his talk with the Board of Directors, Polk advanced the idea of buying the burned-out shell of the Flood Mansion on Nob Hill and using it as a framework for a new building.[16]

Polk's architectural vision for the new clubhouse included the addition of east and west wings to the building. From the main entrance, there was to be a wide hall that would extend 150 feet to the rear, where it was to terminate at a large window. Within the plan, Polk added two cross halls to intersect the central hall and extend for the full width of the building. The entrance corridor was designed to lead directly into a central court, which was to be forty-four feet square and thirty feet in height. Here, Polk called for a ceiling made of stained glass and sculptured relief. These last two touches, as well as others, called for offering contracts to two of Polk's and Bourn's friends—the stained-glass artist Bruce Porter and the sculptor Arthur Putnam. The decorative material to be employed in this area was gray marble, except for eight detached Ionic columns, which were to stand on either side of the entrances to the halls and were to be made of white Italian marble.

On the east side of the structure, Polk's design called for a large lounging room, and on the west side there was to be a spacious dining room. Both rooms were to be forty feet by seventy feet, with ceilings twenty-two feet high. The lounging room was to have an elaborate ceiling and was to be finished in oak, while the main dining room was to be finished in oak in an Elizabethan style.

The club's library was to be on the second floor, its motif based on an apartment in the Chateau de Chantilly near Paris. The library shelves were to have capacity for ten thousand volumes. Finally, the room was to be paneled in heart redwood to give it a western flavor. Redwood and other local materials were also to be used in the card room, the billiard room, and the French room. The second floor was also to include rooms for club members who needed accommodations.

Polk added another spectacular feature in his architectural plan. In the basement, he called for the construction of a Pompeiian swimming pool with Doric columns of marble and a predominate use of red, blue, and gold colors.

The swimming pool was the only break from a quiet and subdued atmosphere in Polk's design.[17] In general, the building was to be a reflection of its membership. Within these walls, many of San Francisco's most important men would meet to dine, drink the best wines, and discuss business, politics, civic affairs, cultural activities, and scandals within the ruling class of prominent San Franciscans. Here, in this remodeled home that had once belonged to a saloonkeeper who got rich on Nevada's Comstock Lode, the movers and shakers of San Francisco's business, political and cultural worlds would have their Nob Hill bastion. Here, the policies that would shape San Francisco's future would be expressed even before they became policies.

Will Bourn provided much of the financing and carried the major note for construction costs of the new home of the Pacific Union Club, as well as the purchase of the Flood Mansion. On December 1, 1908, Bourn also agreed to take over the Bohemian Club's $60,000 loan from the First National Bank, and a day after that, he persuaded William Crocker to subscribe to $10,000 of Pacific Union Club bonds.[18]

Work proceeded at a rapid pace. In less than a year, Polk's construction crew completed the building. The total cost amounted to $399,820.45, which included Polk's fee of $27,894.45.[19] The cost of providing a grand new home for the club was quite reasonable, for Polk's vision of a proper meeting place for San Francisco's business elite was one that was to be a monument to capitalism.

4

Even though Will Bourn delegated considerable authority to Captain Payson, cousin Willie Ingalls, and young Sam Eastman of the Spring Valley Water Company, he was a hands-on owner who insisted on knowing every aspect of the company's business. If his employees noticed something that should be called to his attention, he did not require that suggestions or information pass through a chain of command before reaching him. A good example of this close attention to detail was his reaction to a March 23, 1909, letter from Superintendent W. B. Lawrence, who notified Bourn that since "the earthquake of 1906, the bank at the channel at Dumbarton Point has been gradually washing away so that now the mud has been washed from under the two 22″ submarine pipes . . . exposing them to the extent that boats not knowing their location might do considerable damage to them, for which we would have no redress."[20] Lawrence also suggested a way to correct this situation, and Bourn notified him to proceed with the project as he saw fit.

This same year, Will decided to do something about the unsightly shack that covered the water filtering beds at Suñol in Alameda County. It was hardly dignified to have such an ugly building covering the spot where the gathering of water from Alameda County entered the pipelines that ran to Dumbarton Point. Here, it joined the pipelines beneath San Francisco Bay to the pumping station in San Mateo County and then to Crystal Springs Reservoir. Such an important aspect of San Francisco's water supply should be more imposing.

To change all this, Will contacted his good friend Willis Polk and asked him to design a proper building. Will suggested a dignified treatment and mentioned that a water temple would be fitting for this site. All this began in 1909, but it was a year before the project was completed, as Polk drew one design after another until he produced a beautiful water temple that was "inspired by the Temple of Vesta at Tivoli."[21]

Within this same period of 1909–1910, Bourn instituted a fence design for the Spring Valley Water Company. This called for the use of "6 inch × 6 inch × 8 feet redwood posts with a pyramid top set 2 feet deep in the ground 16 feet apart on straight runs. On curves and corners this distance is shortened up considerably, depending on conditions. These posts are painted green, with the exception of the pyramid top which is painted white. Elwood lawn fence 58 inches wide with a 4 inch mesh dipped in green paint . . . is stretched between the posts. One strand of barbed wire, also dipped in green paint . . . is stretched from 6 to 8 inches above the top of the Elwood Mesh."[22]

Item after item, detail after detail, nothing seemed too small or too great to escape Will's attention. He was in every way a man whose mind cataloged, classified, and clarified all information regarding the Spring Valley Water Company, the Empire Mine, real-estate holdings, farming lands that were part of the water company holdings, and all the other business and social activities that were part of his daily, weekly, monthly, and yearly schedule. He was a man with a passion for information, a man who wanted to know all that was possible to learn about any activity in which he became involved. He dreamed only grand dreams, for to him small dreams were the nightmares of small minds and the currency of corruption.

Most of all, Will detested corruption and vile behavior. To him, attempts to skirt the normal rules of civilized behavior were the hallmark of men who failed to follow the patterns of cultural decency. Consequently, when he was told that the owner of the *San Francisco Chronicle* refused to pay his water bill because he did not believe he should pay the same rate as other customers, Will was certain that M. H. de Young had simply misunderstood. To show him every courtesy possible, Will sent A. S. Crawford, who had worked for the *Chronicle* for seventeen years, to have another talk with de Young. For the second time, de Young refused to pay for his water at the same rate as other customers. He told Crawford that he considered the water rates "nothing short of robbery, and he would have the Company and its methods of robbing the people written up in the *Chronicle*."[23]

Startled by such behavior, Will believed that de Young had either misunderstood Crawford or that something else was troubling him, because this did not reflect the kind of manner that Will expected from a man in his position. Consequently, on the morning of October 8, 1909, Crawford was sent to the Chronicle Building for a third and final discussion with de Young.

During this talk, Crawford told him: "You are the only consumer who is not paying according to the ordinance." De Young replied: "Your company is robbing the public of San Francisco, but I will not stand for it. I have a verbal agreement to pay $1,000 a year for water and that agreement cannot be taken from me until the end of the year. If this rate is taken from me I will publish every complaint against the water company that I can get hold of."[24]

Having no alternative, Crawford informed de Young that if he did not pay his bill his water would be cut off. Upon hearing this, de Young said: "If you cut the water off I will detail a man to look up every complaint against the Spring Valley Water Company, and I will publish them and rip your company up the back and wide open. Your company is made up of a lot of crooks, and I will show them up."[25]

Crawford replied: "Mr. de Young I am surprised that you should make such a brazen threat. If it gives you more comfort and satisfaction to persecute the Company through your paper rather than compensate it for water supplied your building, then go ahead and enjoy yourself."[26]

Having said this, Crawford left de Young's office and returned to the Spring Valley Water Company offices, where he dictated everything that had occurred during his conversation with the owner of the *San Francisco Chronicle.*

When the fixed time for the payment of the *Chronicle*'s water bill had passed, Crawford tried phoning de Young but had no luck. He tried to see him for another conversation, but when he was unable to arrange a meeting, Crawford ordered water service to the Chronicle Building halted.

A few hours without water were all it took. The *San Francisco Chronicle* paid its water bill. But true to his word, M. H. de Young became a lasting enemy of the Spring Valley Water Company and of William Bowers Bourn.

Such action baffled Will, and he was puzzled that a man like de Young would behave so badly. Still, Bourn realized that as head of the water company he had become a fair target for various vested interests. This was a fact that he did not like to recognize, but he realized that this unpleasant aspect of his business was something he would have to endure.

But Will was not prepared for the trouble he was to have with the newspaper. From 1909 to 1920, he was forced to bring lawsuit after lawsuit against the Chronicle Publishing Company. Some lawsuits were to get the newspaper to pay the proper amount for its water, but other lawsuits were brought against the *Chronicle* for its use of libelous language about the Spring Valley Water Company. The newspaper called the company a fake and imputed it with the "sin of being a cheat, a fraud, a thief, a pilferer."[27]

5 By December 1, 1909, there were properties of the Spring Valley Water Company located in the City and County of San Francisco, San Mateo County, Santa Clara County, San Benito County, and Alameda County, and the total company land within these five counties amounted to 81,676 acres, or 128 square miles of land representing a total area three times that of the City and County of San Francisco.[28]

With the maps for this area spread out before him, Will looked with both astonishment and concern at the holdings that represented the water company. Much remained to be done to keep the water company functioning and growing to its full potential. A new dam in Alameda County was needed. For this project, he was already in touch with William Mulholland, who was in charge of building the 250-mile aqueduct that was to tap the Owens River in the Eastern Sierra Nevada for water for thirsty Los Angeles.[29] Once work was finished on the water temple at Suñol, a new aqueduct to the pipes going underneath San Francisco Bay at Dumbarton Point would have to be built. The biggest expense for the water coming from Alameda County—at this stage—would be laying new pipes underneath the bay. Bourn knew that the Pulgas Tunnel from Dumbarton Point would be costly, but he was to be stunned at the final cost of replacing these pipes—the interior cement and the laying of pipelines for the Pulgas Tunnel was to come to $4,300,000.[30]

It seemed that nothing came easy or cheap for any of the projects associated with the Spring Valley Water Company. But even as this costly operation continued and grew, it gave San Francisco better service. However, it became clear to Will that the City of San Francisco gave its cooperation only when absolutely necessary and that the city's ultimate goal was to buy the company for as little money as possible. Failing to achieve that goal, it was altogether feasible that the city's politicians might attempt to seize the Spring Valley Water Company through a suit of condemnation.

Even as Will worried about the problems associated with the water company, other business matters had to be considered. The acquisition of such great acreage for water rights also offered an opportunity to use the surface for agriculture. To facilitate this, Will had Sam Eastman contact potential sharecroppers who would farm water company land and in return pay the company a percentage of their crop sale for the right to use the land. In this way, Bourn began to see reports of sugar beets from the Pleasanton area that were sold to the Spreckels Sugar Company. On other water company land, crops varied from alfalfa to cabbage, from vegetables such as corn, cucumbers, string beans, potatoes, pumpkins, and tomatoes, to various fruit crops such as grapes and pears. In addition, the company also owned its own herds of sheep, cattle, and dairy cows. The Spring Valley Water Company received from the growers a share of the profits that ranged from one-fourth to as much as one-half.[31] These revenues plus earnings from the sale of livestock resulted in a large bonus and a welcome addition to the yearly profits of the water company.

There were other problems to be faced as a result of the vast stretches of land owned by the company. Even before Will had become involved in the water business, the company had accumulated problems that had not been solved, and in these cases, Will was now to be the final arbiter.

One concern left over from the previous administration was the water company's dealings with the Ocean Shore Railroad. This short line had been incorporated in 1905, and its owners hoped to complete a little over eighty miles of track between San Francisco and Santa Cruz to fulfill its slogan "Reaches the Beaches." The objective was to provide easy transportation to Santa Cruz's famous Boardwalk and its great, sandy beach, but during its fifteen years of existence, the Ocean Shore Railroad never fully realized its goal of a direct route to Santa Cruz.[32]

This railroad caused many headaches for the Spring Valley Water Company. As early as 1905, the company won a lawsuit against the Ocean Shore Railroad for $35,000 after the railroad laid tracks across part of Rancho Laguna de la Merced without obtaining permission from the water company. Later, Spring Valley had other difficulties with the railroad when it used the name Spring Valley to replace Daly City on the railroad's map. The water company also had to threaten to sue the railroad in order to force it to pick up scattered timbers it had dropped on cropland that the water company had leased to a truck farmer.[33]

Other problems Bourn faced included making water agreements with the East Bay communities of Pleasanton, Livermore, Dublin, Niles, Irvington, Decoto, Centerville, and Newark. All these communities were dependent upon the creeks, streams, and underground water supplies of southern and eastern Alameda County. The other East Bay communities of Alameda, Oakland, Piedmont, Fruitvale, San Leandro, Emeryville, Berkeley, and Richmond received their water service through the Peoples Water Company and the Richmond Water Company.[34]

However, the biggest problem for the Spring Valley Water Company was the City and County of San Francisco. Its failure to be reasonable about allowing an increase in water rates made things so difficult for the company that on November 29, 1909, William Bourn wrote to Mayor Edward Robeson Taylor and the Board of Supervisors of the City and County of San Francisco and offered "to sell the Entire Physical Property of The Company (Free of Debt) for the Sum of Thirty-five Million Dollars." Then in a letter to the stockholders of the Spring Valley Water Company, on December 24, 1909, Bourn admitted that the offered price of sale was too low but that he believed that civic duty would have to override a higher price. Despite this offer, San Francisco turned down a chance to buy the Spring Valley Water Company for a bargain price.[35]

6

In all lives, there are certain years that stand out, years when events mark turning points or dramatic changes. For the Bourns of San Francisco, 1910 was such a year.

During the second week of January 1910, William Bourn expressed his continuing concern about San Francisco's future water supply. "If the City," he wrote, "purchases the Spring Valley Water Company that supply, if properly developed, will last for at least forty years. It is a fair presumption that the intelligence of the community will grow in the next forty years, and the logical addition to the water supply will be waters from the Sierras carried down in the San Joaquin River and filtered through the Spring Valley Water system."[36]

Will's disgust with the politicians of San Francisco had reached the point where he did not care if it was known that he had little faith in the city's officials. From his point of view, the logical move was for the city to buy him out and then proceed with its own plan for the future water supply of San Francisco.

The city planned to build a dam and back up the waters of the Tuolumne River to flood the Hetch Hetchy Valley in Yosemite National Park. The plan had its beginning under Mayor James Duval Phelan in 1901, and by 1910 it had developed sufficiently to warrant consideration by the secretary of the interior. Bourn eagerly enlisted in the fight against this project. He did not believe it necessary to dam the Tuolumne River, because he knew there were other areas in the Sierra Nevada that promised a greater water supply without destroying part of his beloved Yosemite. He tried to make it clear to the politicians of San Francisco that if they purchased the Spring Valley Water Company it would not be necessary for them to seek water in the Sierra Nevada for some time to come. But the city was hell-bent on following Phelan's plan.

Will began contacting members of the water commission of the U.S. Army Corps of Engineers, government officials of the East Bay cities, and Sierra Club officers. He wanted to find as many people of persuasion as possible to join in the fight against San Francisco's water plan, because he intended to battle in every way possible to halt this desecration of Yosemite National Park.

Before the battle ended, conservationists from many walks of life joined behind the Old Testament figure of John Muir in what was to be a losing war to protect the broad public interest against narrower municipal ambitions. On January 4, 1910, the citizens of San Francisco passed a proposition to incur a debt of $45 million to acquire, construct, and complete a public water utility to draw water from Lake Eleanor and the Tuolumne River and its tributaries.

Ironically, even as Will Bourn fought San Francisco's Hetch Hetchy project, he became involved in the construction of a cyanide plant at the Empire Mine. Here was a potential polluter of nearby Wolf Creek as well as underground water tables, but Bourn and George Starr agreed that a better method than mercury amalgamation was needed to free gold from impure sulfides, and the use of potassium cyanide appeared to be a more practical method.

The design of the plant included equipment to take crushed ore from the stamp mill and pass it through a washing process in a solution of potassium cyanide. After sixty to ninety-six hours in the cyanide, the solution was percolated through sand into a vat with a sloping bottom to facilitate the sluicing out of the tailings. After the gold-rich solution passed through this vat, it passed through the Merrill-Crowe zinc-dusted method, in which the zinc-gold precipitate was collected in two filter presses with two thirty-six-inch frames. The final process involved fluxing the mixture with borax, soda, and silica, then moving this melted mixture from presses in the tilting furnaces and casting it into gold bars for shipment to the United States Mint in San Francisco.[37]

The cyanide plant at the Empire was not the first one put into use in a California gold mining operation, but it was another aspect of the Empire operation that would stand as an example of how to run a gold mine. As in all his business ventures, Bourn wanted the very best technology available.

Even as Will took time to go over the details of the cyanide plant with cousin George Starr, he also had pressing family affairs on his mind. Twenty-six-year-old Maud was engaged to marry thirty-four-year-old Arthur Vincent, whom she had met during the family's Atlantic voyage in 1906. Will and Agnes were happy for Maud, but they were not pleased with the fact that Arthur Vincent had been a judge for His Majesty's Court for Zanzibar since 1909. Neither of the Bourns wanted to see their daughter become a resident of Zanzibar. It was bad enough to see their only child leave the United States, much less have her take up residence on a thousand-square-mile island off the east coast of Tanganyika—an island protectorate of Great Britain noted for its production of cloves.

The wedding of Maud Bourn and Arthur Rose Vincent took place on Wednesday, March 30, 1910, at Saint Matthew's Episcopal Church in San Mateo, California. It was one of the highlights of San Francisco's spring social season. The wedding invitation indicated that the ceremony was to take place at high noon. Enclosed with this invitation were two cards. One card noted that a special train would leave the San Francisco depot at 11:15 A.M., and that there would be conveyances in attendance at San Mateo to take guests to Burlingame. After the ceremony, all guests were invited to a wedding breakfast at Sky Farm in Burlingame.

The church was filled with guests. The bridesmaids were Marjorie Josselyn and Clare Vincent, the sister of the groom, and the flower girl was little Helen Crocker, who carried a large basket of spring flowers. According to the story in the *San Francisco Call,* the bride's gown was made of "imported white satin, trimmed with masses of rare, old lace . . . elaborately embroidered with seed pearls. In her tulle veil was caught a spray of orange blossoms, and she carried a magnificent shower bouquet of white orchids."[38] Tall, handsome George Starr stood in as the groom's best man. All the women wore their most beautiful gowns, most of which had been designed especially for Maud's wedding.

After the ceremony, the guests traveled by cars that Bourn had in waiting to Sky Farm. Here, almost in a toast to the Empire Mine—where all the workers had been given the day off on this special occasion—"gold cloth stretched over poles . . . from the carriage drive to the doorway, and the whole front of the spacious mansion was hung with velvet banners in honor of the day."[39]

The bride and groom received guests in the living room, which was filled with American Beauty roses, white lily of the valley, pale pink blossoms, and asparagus fern. Gifts of initialed diamond brooches set in platinum were given to the bridesmaids and the flower bearer, and the best man was given a stickpin of diamonds and sapphires. When the bride tossed her bouquet to the waiting crowd, it was caught by a surprised little Charles Crocker.

After the wedding day, Maud and Arthur took one of the Spring Valley automobiles and drove to Grass Valley. Here, they honeymooned in the Empire Cottage for two weeks, using the company car to make day trips into the Sierra Nevada and travel around the Gold Country as the grass of the foothills was beginning to turn green.

Upon their return from Grass Valley, the young couple visited with the Bourns for a few days, then took the train to New York, where they boarded a ship and began the next phase of their honeymoon, which included a European tour, a trip to Egypt, and a three-month period while they visited friends and relatives of Vincent's in Ireland and England. During their stay in London, Arthur looked for another position because he had given up his judgeship in order to marry Maud. But nothing turned up, and he must have wondered what he would do after the last part of their honeymoon, which was to take them on a tour of Asia before they returned to settle down in Ireland.

When the honeymoon ended, the Vincents found Will and Agnes Bourn waiting for them in Ireland. Will had already started to make plans for their future. He had begun negotiations with Lord Ardilaun of the Guinness family to purchase Muckross and the eleven thousand acres surrounding Muckross House, an Elizabethan-style mansion in County Kerry, built in the 1840s for Henry Arthur Herbert. Located below Torc Mountain, the house commanded a grand view of the Lower and Middle Killarney Lakes. Will loved the site of this great home, and he was not daunted by its enormous size. The house contained one hundred rooms and sixty-two chimneys for the fireplaces that were the mansion's only source of heat.

The Herbert family had gone into debt just prior to 1861, when they had the honor of hosting Queen Victoria and Prince Albert as they visited Ireland. Not only did the Herberts have the queen and her husband stay at their home; they also had to provide lodging for Edward, the Prince of Wales; Prince Alfred; and the Princesses Alice and Helen. For the queen's visit, the Herberts purchased new dining room furniture, new tapestries, and a Persian carpet. Their greatest expense was incurred as a result of the queen's fear of fire. To ease her worries, the Herberts prepared a ground-floor bedroom and went to the added expense of installing a steel fire escape.[40] After the visit of Queen Victoria and her retinue, the Herbert family faced a debt that even their progressive farming and copper mining operation could not manage to pay off. By 1889, they sold Muckross to the Standard Life Assurance Company. This firm kept the house and farm until 1899, when the company sold it to Lord Ardilaun, whose wife was a Herbert. Still, as much as Lady Ardilaun loved the home, by the time William Bourn began talking to them during that summer of 1910, the Ardilauns were quite ready to part with Muckross.

In addition to Muckross House and the vast acres around it, the sale offer included Muckross Abbey. This Gothic edifice and its connecting buildings dated back to A.D. 1330 when M'Carthy More, Prince of Desmond, began construction of the abbey for Franciscan monks. The abbey had a long history of suppression. Soldiers under the orders of Henry VIII drove the monks—even killing some—from Muckross Abbey in 1542. The Franciscans returned to the Abbey in 1600, under the reign of Queen Elizabeth I. This stay was interrupted in 1629 as a result of the penal edicts of Charles I, then the final suppression of Muckross Abbey took place in 1652, when Cromwell forced the monks out for good.

All this was fascinating to Will, who loved English history and yearned to see the day when he might be appointed ambassador to England. If that never came to pass, he was more than willing to settle for being a landholder in Ireland. Although he was about to buy Muckross House and all its land for Maud and Arthur, it was as much for the fulfillment of his own dreams as it was for finding a home and a way of life for the newly married Vincents.

Sometime during August 1910, Will completed all the necessary documents for the purchase of Muckross. The final price was approximately $200,000, and by September Will wrote to his mother about the purchase. It was as though he might have thought that his mother would understand why he had bought farming land for Maud and Arthur, even if the young couple had doubts about becoming Irish landholders.

Before leaving Ireland to return to California, Will made it clear to his daughter and son-in-law that he would see to it that they received a combined yearly income of $25,000. In addition, he let them know that he would pay the operational costs of Muckross, which were to run as high as $65,000 per year. Still, Bourn believed that his son-in-law would be able to help defray some of these expenses by running a good farming operation and even adding to this income by promoting tourism.

What Will failed to recognize in his dealing for a way of life for Maud and Arthur was that he was buying his own dream and asking them to live it out. At no time during this whirlwind of using his drive and his money to achieve a beginning for the Vincents did he stop to ask them what they wanted to do with their lives. His drive to forge ahead, to carve a destiny as he had been doing all his life, seemed to be all that mattered. In a very real sense, it was as though he believed that if he saw a future in Muckross, then there had to be a future. All it would take was some backing from him until things were started. Then once Maud and Arthur got the hang of things, once they learned how to operate a farm, they would become successful. Having set the wheels into motion, having turned the future prosperity of Muckross over to them, Bourn bid the young couple farewell as he and Agnes left for London to catch a steamship to New York.

7 With family affairs settled to his satisfaction, Will returned to the water wars. By the beginning of 1911, he was fighting the City of San

Francisco on two fronts. One battle was against the city over its decision to dam Hetch Hetchy. The other battle was over the city's refusal to buy the Spring Valley Water Company at what Bourn considered an extremely fair price.

Upset by what appeared to be a movement in the United States Department of Agriculture to give San Francisco the right to dam Hetch Hetchy, Will wrote to Gifford Pinchot, Chief Forester, to express his outrage. He wrote: "Do you think the Yosemite National Park should be dismembered unless absolute necessity so required? Should aid have been given by the National Government to the 'people' of San Francisco in their method of obtaining the Spring Valley Water Company? Better far to have protected San Francisco against itself."[41]

During this same year, Will continued his discussions with officials from the city. He made it clear to Sam Eastman and other officers of the water company that he wanted all records to be complete and up-to-date at all times. As he explained to them, he expected a long battle with San Francisco, and he had every reason to believe that city officials would try to secure the water company's assets through condemnation if they could not get the company to sell to them for whatever price they decided to pay.

To back up his historical materials regarding the Spring Valley Water Company, Will hired the eminent historian Hiram Martin Chittenden to compile a complete study of the company's water supply system. At this time, Brigadier General Chittenden was fifty-three years old. He had retired from the U.S. Army after spending many years as the chief engineer and builder of highways for Yellowstone National Park. He was highly respected for his knowledge of the American West and was the noted author of *The Yellowstone National Park* and *The American Fur Trade of the Far West.*

To assist General Chittenden in the preparation of this *Report on the Water Supply System of the Spring Valley Water Company,* Bourn hired A. O. Williams, a first-rate civil engineer who possessed a good knowledge of rivers and streams and run-off systems in general. However, the bulk of the report was in Chittenden's capable hands.

By the time Chittenden completed this report, he had examined the following systems that constituted the resources of the company: the Peninsular System, the Alameda System, the Coast Streams, Artesian Supplies, the Coyote System, and the San Joaquin River. At no point did he consider the use of a dam in the High Sierra. Even without such a source, he believed that the supply system of the company was more than adequate for San Francisco up to 1950 and perhaps even beyond that date. "So far as *quantity* is concerned," he wrote, "there is no present *necessity* for a resort to the Sierra, and will not be for an indefinite period of time." The key statement of this report was the following: "If there were no Sierra, San Francisco could still face the problem of a future water supply with perfect equanimity."[42]

Even as Chittenden worked on his report, John R. Freeman was putting together a report for the City and County of San Francisco, which was to come out in 1912. This document stressed the absolute need for building a dam that would flood Hetch Hetchy Valley. Freeman went so far as to claim that the lake behind such a dam would make the cliffs of the valley appear taller, and that such a lake would be a tourist attraction.[43]

Though water was Bourn's main concern during 1911, it was not the only thing on his mind. He also was involved in early planning for the proposed Panama-Pacific International Exposition, which was to celebrate the completion of the Panama Canal. Will served on the original board of directors of this committee beginning on April 14, 1911. Along with his friend, William H. Crocker, Bourn was on the Foundation Committee.[44]

Thanks to the efforts of Bourn and Crocker and the others of the original forty-two subscribers for the planned exposition, a financial foundation was established and a high level of subscriptions enabled the raising of the balance of money. As chairman of the finance committee for the exposition, Will called upon the wealthiest San Franciscans to contribute to the project. The concept that was the focus of this exposition's plan was to produce "a microcosm so nearly complete that if all the world was destroyed except the 635 acres of land within the Exposition gates, the material basis of the life of today could have been reproduced from the exemplifications of the arts, inventions and industries there exhibited."[45]

In the early stages of planning for the exposition, Will had enough influence to see that his friend Willis Polk was appointed to head the architectural commission. However, Will's ongoing fight with San Francisco over its designs on the Spring Valley Water Company forced him not only to resign from the board of directors on July 13, 1911, but also to refrain from extending his water system to the exposition because of pending litigation between the company and the City of San Francisco. As a result of not being able to get water from Spring Valley, the officials of the exposition had to locate another source. This was discovered at the west end of Golden Gate Park, where they found an underground flow near Captain Amundsen's sloop *Gjoa*.

Even as Will's resignation reached the Board of Directors from Ireland, where the Bourns had gone to visit, he retained his interest in the exposition. Knowing that Will wished to be kept up to date on the exposition's progress, Sam Eastman wrote to him at Muckross on July 27, 1911, to let him know about the final selection of the site for the exposition. It was to "comprise lands between Fort Mason and the Presidio, thence Ocean Boulevard around the Presidio including Lincoln Park adjoining Fort Miley, thence to Golden Gate Park, thus assuring ample space for all exposition purposes. Proposed Ocean Boulevard will be world famous for beauty, besides being a permanent military highway from Fort Miley to Fort Mason. This plan including parks and running from bay to ocean, giving four miles of frontage on Golden Gate, offering unlimited scenic beauties and architectural possibilities, and particularly appropriate to the celebration of the greatest maritime event of the age and of the great seaport."[46]

During this period of the Bourns' visit to Muckross, Will and Agnes were caught up in the excitement of associating with royalty when Agnes was presented at the Court of St. James. During this early part of the twentieth century, the Bourns—like most wealthy American families—were enchanted with the trappings of royalty. It was as though they had gone as far as they could within the structure of the society of the very rich in America, and they yearned for something beyond the society they knew in San Francisco, New York, and the popular resorts frequented by their friends. Travel had become tiresome, because they had been to the capital cities of Europe time after time, and even such exotic destinations as Egypt and Alexandria were only worth so many visits. What the Bourns and others of their class wanted was not obtainable in the United States, but there was the chance to be on the fringes of royalty in England. To Agnes and her daughter Maud, this was as close as they could be to the fortunate few who were born into an exalted position in life, and the Bourns enjoyed every moment of this taste of royalty.

By the fall of 1911, Will and Agnes were back in the Bay Area and were dividing their time between Sky Farm on the Peninsula and their mansion on Pacific Heights in San Francisco—a home that seemed dark and confining after living at Sky Farm, where the house and the outdoor world complemented each other. On October 13, 1911, Will was one of the featured speakers who followed President Taft during the exposition's groundbreaking in Golden Gate Park. Bourn spoke about the spirit of San Francisco. As a son of a Gold Rush pioneer, Will had heard and read about the rough-and-tumble days in the boom years of San Francisco, and now, as one of the city's prominent citizens, he spoke with intimate knowledge of the growth of this modern metropolis located on the shores of the Pacific and the gateway to Asia. Throughout his speech, he put his emphasis on San Francisco's never-say-die spirit, for he had seen the city grow out of its ashes and ruins to begin again with optimism and a renewed sense of purpose. Now, with completion of the Panama Canal less than four years away, he stressed the importance of San Francisco as one of the great maritime cities of the world. To Will, San Francisco remained the City of Promise.

Even as he looked forward to this international celebration to which San Francisco would play host, he continued to indulge his great love of music. Since the founding of the Music Association of San Francisco, Will had devoted both time and money to push for the formation of a San Francisco Symphony Orchestra. As the second president of the Music Association, he looked with pride at the opening night of December 29, 1911, as the orchestra played under the direction of Henry Hadley and Mme. Martha Richardson, prima donna soprano of the Paris Opera Company, appeared as a guest soloist.

8 The beginning of 1913 saw the shaping up of a major battle between the Spring Valley Water Company and the City and County of San Francisco. On January 23, 1913, Bourn wrote to Sam Eastman with instructions about his future relationship with the city. "From this day," Bourn wrote, "you will please consider that our relationship with those connected with the Administration of the City is one that will not permit the exchange of further information or reports by this company to the City, other than pertains to the accounts of the company, and matters of daily routine in reference to water supply."[47]

At this time, San Francisco was convinced that it would receive permission from the Department of the Interior to proceed with the Hetch Hetchy project. However, one last piece was missing from the city's grand plan to form its own water supply system, which was the need of the very system owned by the Spring Valley Water Company. Even though the supervisors hated the thought of having to deal with W. B. Bourn, they were caught in a trap of their own making. Without the complicated water system of the Spring Valley Water Company, the city was faced with the coming of a future water supply from the Sierra Nevada that would require having its own local reservoirs, pipelines, pumps, storage tanks, and all the other aspects of a water system.

Beginning in May 1913 and continuing through June, the Spring Valley Water Company filed a complaint against the City and County of San Francisco and the Board of Supervisors for an increase in water rates beyond the usual small increases the rate board usually granted. Appearing before the Board of Supervisors for these meetings were William B. Bourn, Samuel P. Eastman, and E. J. McCutchen, attorney for the water company.

The transcript of these meetings filled over sixty legal pages. At the beginning, Eastman read a long history of the water company. Within this history, he included the growth in San Francisco's population from 34,000 persons in 1850 to 416,912 persons in 1910. He then pointed out that in 1850 San Francisco was able to get along with 2,500,000 gallons of water per day supplied to it by a company called the San Francisco Water Works, sometimes referred to as the Bensley Company.[48] By 1910, the amount of water needed per day for San Francisco had increased to 12,995 million gallons.

To ensure a steady supply of water, the storage policy of the Spring Valley Water Company was to have enough water in its reservoirs to equal at least a three year's supply. As Eastman pointed out, it was necessary to have this much water stored because of the varying annual quantity of rainfall. Here, Bourn's people had gathered rainfall records for the past fifty-one years that showed an average rainfall per year of 25 inches. However, this figure was somewhat misleading, because they pointed out that the amount of yearly rainfall could vary from a low 7.40 inches per year to a high of 50 inches per year.

Within this report to the supervisors, Eastman gave a history of the acquisition of watershed lands in San Mateo, Alameda, Santa Clara, and San Francisco Counties. In addition, the company's report listed its major reservoirs and their water-holding capacity. San Mateo County reservoirs included Pilarcitos with a capacity of 1,000 million gallons; San Andreas with a capacity of 6,000 million gallons; Crystal Springs with a capacity of 22,500 million gallons; and Portola with a future capacity of 3,000 million gallons of water.[49]

In addition to these reservoirs, the water company possessed valuable water resources in the East Bay, where it owned watershed land on Alameda Creek and its tributaries, as well as water rights in the Livermore Valley near Pleasanton and in Suñol Valley and the Calaveras and San Antonio Valleys, which included land in both Alameda County and Santa Clara County. These holdings consisted "of many thousands of acres of land, water rights, reservoirs sites, watersheds and rights of way, and a large natural filtering and storage bed of almost unlimited capacity, and a concrete gallery existing under and into the same—all of which give it practically the control of the water output from a watershed of more than 621 square miles." Within these holdings, it was pointed out to the supervisors that the Calaveras Valley was a possible reservoir site that would be able to hold at least 58,000 million gallons of water once a dam was built.[50]

Even as Eastman read from his text, it was hard for the supervisors to grasp what they were hearing. To these men who had no prior knowledge of how the water they used daily came to them, this listing of reservoirs, water rights, and watershed lands was something they could not fully understand. They tended to consider the forests, brush-covered hills, mountains, and the rivers, streams, creeks, and underground sources of water to be part of what they perceived as country land used for cattle and sheep grazing or for general agricultural purposes. Consequently, they put a much lower value upon such holdings than their true value as lands that supplied water. As city men, they thought in terms of city values and found it hard to grasp the value that the water company put upon land they considered wild, open country.

One thing the supervisors appeared to understand was a description of the amount of water that San Francisco received from the Alameda Creek system through a complicated delivery arrangement that was able to supply San Francisco with an average of more than twenty million gallons of water daily. A major reason for their ability to grasp the cost of building and operating this system was the detailed description that Bourn had Eastman read to them. Water from the Alameda Creek system, Eastman read, "flows through a 36-inch pipe, connected with tunnels and flumes and conduits to the westerly shore of the Bay of San Francisco, near Dumbarton Point; from here an intermediate slough and the Bay of San Francisco are crossed by two 16-inch submarine pipes, and two additional submarine pipes 22 inches in diameter, each of the four being about one-quarter miles in length. At the westerly end of the submarine pipes, near Ravenswood, on the west shore of the Bay, the water is pumped through a booster plant under pressure equivalent to a level of 100 feet above tide, and thence flows through a 36-inch iron pipe to the Belmont pumping station, in San Mateo County, where it is lifted to an elevation of over 330 feet above tide, and from there flows in a 36-inch pipe to a place near Burlingame where it connects with the . . . Crystal Springs iron pipe line, 44 inches in diameter."[51] From here, the water flowed into Crystal Springs Reservoir.

This description made it clear to the supervisors that both labor and materials for a water system were expensive and required ingenuity to conceive and build. However, these city men were not fully able to grasp the other costs—such as the need for the land for a watershed—that were both a daily and a long-term expense for the Spring Valley Water Company.

The supervisors also grasped the expense of constructing and maintaining the nine distributing reservoirs within the city and county that held a total of ninety million gallons of water. These reservoirs and the nine pumping stations, as well as the tunnels, flumes, and pipelines that totaled over 545 miles beneath San Francisco's streets, were facts that had obvious costs attached to them. But when the value of the water company was given, the supervisors were startled. What they considered to be wild lands suddenly took on a different description and value as they listened to Eastman read: "The properties now in use for the purpose of supplying the City and County of San Francisco and its inhabitants with water are worth in excess of fifty million dollars, while those which will be so utilized in the immediate future are worth many millions more."[52]

Fifty million dollars! The figure was way beyond the board members. Somewhere they had come up with a value of the Spring Valley Water Company that amounted to thirty-three million, and now they were hearing fifty million. This was not what the City and County of San Francisco wished to pay for the water company. But the figure of fifty million dollars had been spoken. They had heard it right from an official of the Spring Valley Water Company, and they were not pleased with the prospect of trying to convince W. B. Bourn that his company was only worth thirty-three million dollars.

It was bad enough to try to convince Bourn that he should be satisfied on a rate increase that only gave him a 4 percent return for the water company. As he put it, he would not be able to borrow money at that rate for the development of the property to secure a new addition to the present water supply. The last few years had been drought years, and there was no way of knowing whether or not the future would bring wet years or if there would be a longer cycle of dry years.

When asked to clarify his attitude regarding water rates, Bourn replied: "Our attitude is that we wish a rate made that earns the company a reasonable income on the reasonable value of its property. Second, under existing conditions, we wish a protection as to the value of any investment the company has already made to supply the city with water. Third, we wish a protection for any other capital expenditures that we would make."[53]

Unable to face Bourn's request for protection that would include an increase in the water rate to allow his company to proceed with future reservoir development, especially that of building the Calaveras Dam to back up a vast water supply in Alameda and Santa Clara Counties, one of the supervisors switched the conversation to the possibility of a condemnation suit being put forth on the company property by the City and County of San Francisco.

Hearing this suggestion, one he had been expecting, Bourn said: "Supposing the court should find the value of this property is \$45,000,000 or \$50,000,000 or \$40,000,000, or anything like that. Under existing conditions, you will have a very hard time to pass your bond issue. I don't think it will be passed. We are then, or will be then, as we are now. But let me relieve your mind upon one point. It will be the policy of the company to keep up their property, so there will be no deterioration of their property."[54]

However, when asked if there would be any further capital investment, Bourn indicated that there would not be, but that the company would "lean over backwards to maintain the property."[55] This was not completely true, because Will was still considering the possibility of building the Calaveras Dam.

The concept of the Calaveras Dam was brought up by Michael M. O'Shaugnessy,[56] San Francisco's City Engineer, who asked: "Suppose, then, the city will enter into a contract with you to proceed with the construction of the Calaveras Dam, that could, as I say, be made a part of the Hetch Hetchy system, and pay your interest on that. Would you be willing to undertake the construction?"[57]

At this point, Will began to play with O'Shaugnessy and the supervisors, as he replied: "Would you pay us what Oakland will pay us for it?"

Clearly upset by this reply, Supervisor Koshland asked: "What has Oakland offered you?" When Will replied that no such offer had been made, Supervisor Koshland was puzzled. Then Bourn said: "I think the Calaveras Dam, the water from there will be just as valuable any time, or is today, to the Peoples Water Company, or to Oakland, as the Peninsula supply is to San Francisco."[58]

Shifting from one aspect of the water business to another, Bourn clearly caught the Board of Supervisors off guard as he guided it through the many intricate details of past and future moves that the Spring Valley Water Company had to consider as it looked for an ever-greater water supply to maintain the growing City and County of San Francisco. He discussed the possibilities of the Calaveras Dam, of an Arroyo Valle Dam, and of obtaining additional water from the Pleasanton area.

In an attempt to get Bourn to indicate the kind of money that the water company had to spend in order to be assured of a constant growth in its supply of water, his attorney asked him to explain the nature and amount of such expenses.

To give some example of what he meant, Bourn decided to give the supervisors some indication of expenses associated with a new site in Alameda County, namely the proposed location of the Calaveras Dam. Will stated that to purchase lands for this project the company had gone into debt for almost two million dollars.

Even this figure was something the supervisors were not able to grasp within the overall cost of building and operating the water company. Not accustomed to dealing with the many aspects of running a large corporation, the supervisors eventually got around to the one thing that was on their minds: the purchase of the Spring Valley Water Company by San Francisco. Yet even now, they were thinking of offering a mere thirty-six million dollars. When Will heard this, he asked the supervisors to examine the property, to take under consideration the amount of capital that had been spent in order to develop the water company over these many years.

On the third meeting, May 19, 1913, between Bourn and the supervisors, the latter argued over the value of the Lake Merced lands. They kept insisting the value was approximately $2,500 per acre. Will rejected this figure, and said: "You can get values for those lands all the way to $3,000 or $4,000, perhaps $5,000 an acre."[59]

Still, the supervisors would not stay with one subject long enough to understand or follow up on any answer to the questions they were putting to Bourn. As he began to explain the changing value of the Lake Merced lands within growing San Francisco, Supervisor Gallagher switched the topic by asking: "Are you using the Calaveras properties now?" Bourn replied: "Every foot of them. We are using it, not as a reservoir, but we are using all the water that falls in Calaveras—every bit of it is used, all the water that comes to Sunol falls on the Calaveras watershed."[60]

In yet another change in the questioning by the Board, the matter of water rates was referred to once again by Supervisor Koshland. In a long rambling speech, he told Bourn that the supervisors were responsible for water rates and that if Bourn didn't like what was offered, he was quite free to ask the courts for redress. But as far as Koshland was concerned, a 5 percent income on the value of the water company property was absolutely fair.

To this blunt statement, Bourn made it clear that he did not agree, especially when the city had indicated that if it did not get what it wanted, it was prepared to condemn the water company land. And here was something that he could not overlook. As he stated: "the company has no right to go out and ask its shareholders or ask its people, its owners, to go on investing their capital in the company, with a notice, which has since been tremendously magnified by you, that 'you are putting your money in at your peril.'"[61]

The meeting wore on, and Will wondered if anything concrete would ever come after these days of what he called "talk-talk-talky." Then in frustration over the way in which the individual supervisors put value on individual parts or the whole of the water company, he turned to gold mining to illustrate the concept of arriving at value.

"Supposing a ledge," he said, "would go underground, and it would cost you $100,000 to sink a shaft down there. Suppose there is nothing in the mine. If you are a sensible man, your shaft is not worth a hundred thousand dollars, you have an asset that is worth nothing, you have got a hole in the ground, which is profitless, and your mine is worthless. But suppose that you strike rich ore, this shaft is valuable to your mine, it only cost you $100,000, but your mine depends on the value of the ore that you take out of it, and what you can get out of that mine in ore. If you build a dam twenty feet high that impounds so many gallons of water, if, by reason of that dam you can impound three times as much water, your dam site is more valuable—it is a more valuable dam site than a dam site that can impound only 20,000 gallons of water."[62]

Stated in this way, the growing value of the Spring Valley Water Company was a result of purchasing more watershed land, of acquiring more water rights, of building more dams, of laying pipelines, of developing pumping systems, and of designing and building a complex system to deliver fresh, clear water on a steady basis from the company's reservoirs to the buildings, homes, fire hydrants, and faucets of San Francisco. Consequently, any offer for the purchase of the water company at an earlier date had to be re-examined in view of the company's many and continuing improvements.

As the last meeting between Bourn and the Board of Supervisors neared an end, two key questions came up again. One was the matter of a rate increase, and the other was a selling price on the Spring Valley Water Company.

With regard to the 5 percent rate increase that the board offered to the water company, Bourn was specific about what he thought: "I will tell you frankly," he said, "that we could no more go out and get $8,000,000 for 5% than we could fly. We could not do it. I would be considered a crazy man if I should write to anybody in New York and say, 'We want to underwrite a loan of $8,000,000 or $10,000,000 at five percent.' Why, they wouldn't even answer me."[63]

When the supervisors stated that they were willing to offer Bourn $38,500,000 for the company, Bourn was astonished. He referred to an earlier decision by Judge Farrington, who had placed a $50-million value on the company, and said, "you could not, with a fine tooth comb, get the value of this property under $50,000,000 if you tried."[64]

Although there were to be many more attempts by San Francisco to purchase the Spring Valley Water Company for a price that suited city officials, Bourn was to hold fast to his own value of the company. Meanwhile, even as he prepared to travel with his wife to Ireland to visit Maud and Arthur at Muckross, he hired William Mulholland of Los Angeles as chief engineer for the building of the Calaveras Dam in Alameda County. Despite the politicians of San Francisco, Bourn was determined to increase the water-supplying capacity of his company.

Between July 1 and December 31, 1913, Mulholland planned and began the construction of the Calaveras Dam. As he had outlined his plan to Bourn, the dam was to be an hydraulic fill with the following dimensions: "Height at the center from bedrock, 230 feet; thickness at the base, 1,300 feet; width at the crest, 1,300 feet; and a total fill yardage of approximately 3,200,000 cubic yards."[65] There was to be a concrete tunnel, resting on bedrock, built through the dam to care for flood waters during construction, and after completion it was to be used as the rain outlet from the reservoir.

As Mulholland designed it, there was to be a "reinforced concrete gate tower, designed to resist earthquake shock . . . constructed on bedrock." This tower was to be 220 feet tall. When the dam was completed, the reservoir behind it would hold approximately fifty-three million gallons of water, and the upper reaches of Alameda Creek were to be connected to the reservoir by a tunnel that would handle fifty million gallons of water per day.[66]

To build Calaveras Dam and all the other features that were to be part of this mammoth project, a camp was built to house a work force of 650 men; hydraulic pipes were purchased; pump houses were built; and pumping and electrical equipment were installed.[67] Nothing was to be overlooked in a project that Bourn believed would add to the company's water supply. Even though San Francisco was committed to building the Hetch Hetchy Dam, Bourn was certain that even more water would eventually be needed.

Despite all the political difficulties he continued to have with San Francisco's Board of Supervisors, Bourn believed in the future of San Francisco, and he did not wish to stand in the way of his beloved City of Promise. He would continue to look out for the future of San Francisco's water supply even though he was disgusted with the political arena. The failure of the city leaders to realize that the Spring Valley Water Company's system was vital—as the final piece of a puzzle called Hetch Hetchy—was something that Will found beyond belief. Without his system, the Sierra Nevada water would not mean anything to San Francisco. Always an excellent card player, Will knew that he was sitting on a pat hand and that before the game ended, San Francisco's politicians would have to ask for a new deal in order to finish the water game.

17

The Changing Times

By the beginning of 1914, the Bourns were convinced that their years at Sky Farm had been a splendid combination of country living with easy access by train and automobile to the cultural life of San Francisco. During these years, they had seen the building of such Peninsula mansions as William H. Crocker's New Place, Charles T. Crocker's The Uplands, George A. Newhall's La Dolphine, and Harriet Pullman's Carolands. Although the Bourns did not want a home as large as any of these, they realized that their time at Sky Farm had made it impossible to consider living full time in their Webster Street home in San Francisco. They agreed that the combination of country living and the nearness of all the benefits of the city was a desirable way of life.

Agnes and Will considered the pros and cons of building a home in the open country of the Peninsula until they were certain that this was what they desired. Then all that was needed was a proper site on which to build the home of their dreams.

Even as construction of the Calaveras Dam moved ahead and as changes at the Empire Mine were under way, Agnes and Will found just the site for their home by the spring of the year. Will began negotiating for the land, and on April 29, 1914, he wrote to his attorney, E. J. McCutchen, regarding the purchase of the land.

> There is a tract of land of 709 acres belonging to one Husing, situated between Woodside and San Mateo, and right in the heart of

> the Crystal Springs watershed. It is surrounded by land owned by the Spring Valley Water Company.
>
> The public county road, known as Canada Road, runs through the place my wife wants for a suburban home, and our occupation of the place and the creating of a home would, in no way, affect the water supply. A friend of mine has secured an option from Husing, and I propose to have the Empire Mines and Investment Company purchase the property and, like the Empire Cottage, it will be used as the home of the president.[1]

While negotiations with E. A. Husing for the home site went on, Will and Agnes decided that their dream of a country home had to be planned in such a manner so that it would combine all the beauty of country living with a refined architectural style that would blend with the natural setting. There was no doubt on their part that the man to draw the plans for their dream home was their old friend Willis Polk. Though Bourn knew that Polk was busy with other contracts and with his position as chairman of the Architectural Commission for the forthcoming 1915 Panama-Pacific International Exposition, he contacted Willis and received a positive reply.

This country estate was to be the last home that Will wished to build. As things stood, he had the country house at the Empire Mine and the San Francisco house on Webster Street. In addition, he had a great love for Muckross as well as his mother's Madroño in the Napa Valley. But this new home was to combine all the elements that he and Agnes enjoyed. They planned the garden at the same time that they planned the home, for they believed the two should work together to form a perfect blend of the outside world and the man-made interior world of wood and stone.

2 Even as Willis Polk began to make his preliminary sketches to submit to the Bourns, Will found that business affairs were calling for his attention. The news from cousin George Starr at Grass Valley required Will's input. Litigation had been brought against the Empire Mine and Investment Company by the North Star Mining Company. The crux of the suit was that miners for the Empire were working a vein that passed beneath land upon which the North Star held an agricultural title. This accidental

crossing had occurred at the 4,600-foot level, and the miners were unaware of trespass until the North Star filed its lawsuit.

The suit brought a halt to work at that level until the two mining companies decided upon an arbitrary vertical boundary. All this was done without any exchange of money or any measure of bad faith between the owners of the respective companies, but in order for the Empire's miners to continue work at this deep level, they had to dig a winze, or vertical incline opening, that allowed them to go from one level to another without infringing upon the rights of the North Star.

During this time, the management also was involved in a very extensive building program begun in 1913. In order to handle a greater quantity of ore, the stamp mill was being remodeled from a forty-stamp operation to sixty stamps. Each of these new stamps weighed 1,575 pounds and fell at a rate of 102 times per minute to crush the quartz ore. This thundering mill was designed to increase the ore-crushing capacity from 47,000 tons per year in 1912 to 85,000 tons per year in 1915.[2]

To add to the efficiency of the plant, a new hoist was installed to bring heavier loads from the depths of the mine. Power for the new hoist came from a five-hundred-horsepower Westinghouse motor with enough energy to operate at a depth of at least 7,500 feet to bring up skips (ore containers) holding loads of as much as four tons each. But even with this new engine, George Starr kept the old water-driven hoist in place for emergency use.[3]

Meanwhile, the capacity of the cyanide plant was being increased to handle additional tonnage from the new stamp mill. All this called for more machinery to carry on the amalgamation process.

Despite the outlay of money for these improvements, the company continued to show a profit. In 1913, the net profit amounted to $317,823.30, and in 1914, the net profit was $372,647.47.[4]

One other business item of this spring of 1914 was unrelated to the mine or the water company in a normal sense, but water company land was involved. The San Francisco Golf and Country Club asked for and received a lease for 150 acres at the Lake Merced Ranch, where they planned to build a golf course.[5] Bourn thought it a worthwhile activity that would not interfere with the company's business.

Finally, as Will and Agnes got ready for a trip to Europe and then Ireland where they were to visit Maud and Arthur, a preliminary sketch for a country home came from Willis Polk. After Will looked it over, he was appalled at the costs that Willis outlined for what Bourn considered frills. On July 2,

1914, he wrote to Polk regarding the plan and stated: "I suppose, of course, you know why a ship is a female: the rigging costs more than the hull. Does the same pertain to dwellings?"[6]

3 Will and Agnes were visiting Maud and Arthur at Muckross during the beginning of August 1914. Although trouble was brewing in Europe and the possible outbreak of war was a daily topic in the newspapers, it came as a shock when Germany declared war against France on August 3, 1914. On that same date, Sir Edward Grey said: "The lamps are going out all over Europe; we shall not see them lit again in our lifetime."[7]

Although Grey's dramatic statement caught the attention of the English-speaking peoples, it seemed a bit overstated. At least, many people thought the Age of Darkness was not certain to arrive as long as France remained strong and England committed its armed forces to the defense of France and freedom.

To Will, the need to support France in its struggle against the German war machine was obvious. His main concern was that the United States had not delivered an ultimatum to Germany. Instead, news from home indicated that President Woodrow Wilson and the United States Congress appeared to be ignoring this threat to world peace while the United States Army chased Mexico's Pancho Villa in the Sierra Madre Occidental in an attempt to capture and punish this bandit and rebel leader for his raid against Columbus, New Mexico.

Even as the Bourns and Vincents enjoyed their time together at Muckross, daily reports of what was taking place on the Continent put a damper upon what would have been a perfect time. By the end of the first week of August, news of Germany's invasion of Liege on August 4 was reported in Ireland's newspapers, and a shocking story of mass murder during the first day of invasion reported that the Germans were shooting not only civilians but also Belgian priests.[8]

The news from France indicated that its army was prepared to hold out against the invading Germans. Meanwhile, in England, troops were being called into action to form the British Expeditionary Force. It would cross the English Channel to join France in the coming battles that would ultimately form the Western Front, which would run from Switzerland to the Channel. But at this stage of what was to become a four-year World War, nobody envisioned such a long and brutal struggle.

In between talk of war, Will and Arthur discussed the future of Muckross. Bourn had notified his son-in-law in the early part of the year that he would not be able to increase his support of Muckross because he was about to build a country home in San Mateo County and was certain that a good amount of cash would be needed for that purpose. Somehow, Will believed, there had to be a way for Arthur to turn the corner and get Muckross to a point where it would return a decent income. But in asking this, Will was not able to understand that as beautiful as Muckross was to Agnes and him, it simply did not offer a way for Arthur to make a living.

Even though Arthur tried his best to explain this situation, he could not make it clear to Bourn. Time and again, Will made suggestions that were well meaning but did not apply to the situation at Muckross. Here, there was not the kind of soil that Bourn controlled in California and leased out to tenant farmers who returned a sizable yearly profit to the Spring Valley Water Company. In addition to lacking the right type of soil for produce and fruit, the climate of Killarney was too cold and damp to support the kinds of cash crops that Will envisioned. In addition to the profits he realized from various tenant farmers, Will also owned the Solano Irrigated Farms, Incorporated, which consisted of sixty thousand acres of rich farming land in the Sacramento Delta country near such areas as Rio Vista, Cache Slough, Suisun, Montezuma Slough, and Bird's Landing.[9] On this rich land it was possible to grow vegetables, barley, and wheat, while for Bourn's son-in-law, the soil of Muckross offered nothing even close to what Will took for granted.

During their conversations, Arthur, who had been appointed Deputy Lieutenant for County Kerry in 1914, listened to Bourn's concern—a concern that Will had earlier expressed in a letter:

> Now, I want you and Maud to do something for Dad. Just try very hard to get a little nest egg of a few hundred pounds out of your income. When you once can tell me that you have saved a nest egg from your income . . . I shall be very glad . . . and ultimately you will be glad too. Gee! I would like to have a few years of joy, and a few gray hairs less at the same time, but never mind, Mother and Dad will grow younger yet.[10]

What Will failed to take into account in his letters and in his fatherly talks with his son-in-law was that he was responsible—in great measure—for Arthur's being in a position where he had to rely upon him for an income. After all, it had been Will who had asked Vincent to give up his profession as a judge in Great Britain's Foreign Office Judicial Service. Furthermore, the purchase of Muckross in many respects had been Will's romantic idea of having a grand country estate in Ireland, but he had not fully examined the money-making potential of Muckross. So, in this terrible month of August 1914, Bourn and Vincent managed to agree not to disagree as the whole of Europe took an insane move toward destruction.

Even as the men talked about personal finance and the possibility of getting better crop production and more income from tourists who visited Muckross, Agnes and Maud strolled through the garden and spent many hours talking of a forthcoming event. The latter was the coming of a first grandchild for the Bourns. Maud was four months pregnant and due to give birth sometime in January 1915. This joyful news filled Agnes and Will with happiness, and it gave a glow to their final weeks in Ireland before they traveled to England to board their ship for the voyage home.

4 By the beginning of 1915, news from Arthur and Maud filled the Bourn household with a mixture of joy and worry. They were happy to learn of the birth of Elizabeth Rose Vincent on January 13, 1915, but they were worried about Arthur, who had volunteered for the ambulance service as a driver. In this position, he was to serve on France's Western Front as the terrible war settled into trench warfare. Vincent felt that he had to do as much as he could after he was turned down for active service because of a permanent disability.

During this same month, Will and Agnes joined friends in celebrating the forthcoming event of the season. In February the Panama-Pacific International Exposition was to open, and all San Franciscans were caught up in the excitement.

Opening day of the exposition was February 20, 1915, and a large crowd entered the grounds through eight entrances located off the Presidio, Baker Street, Laguna Street, Van Ness Avenue, Scott Street, Fillmore Street, the Yacht Harbor, and the ferry slip. To Bourn, who had been among the early backers of the exposition, the concept of a world celebration had come true throughout the 635 acres—some of it filled parts of the Bay—upon which the dreams of today and tomorrow were expressed in the exhibits.

Many nations were represented, and there were exhibits from most of the states as well as the counties of California. The combination of indoor-outdoor courts, buildings, and towers gave visitors a treat for all their senses. The two buildings that caught the fancy of most visitors were the Tower of Jewels and the Palace of Fine Arts. The Tower of Jewels was 485 feet tall, and it was covered with 102,000 brilliants that shimmered in the breeze off the bay, glittered in the sunlight, and reflected a wide array of colors during the night as colored lights played upon the building. However, it was Bernard Maybeck's Palace of Fine Arts that made a lasting impression and captured the attention of architectural critics, who hailed it as a bold note of individual creativity.

Other exhibits that made a lasting impression were the large-scale models of Yellowstone National Park and the Grand Canyon. The Yellowstone exhibit built by the Union Pacific Railroad showed model geysers erupting and had a replica of Old Faithful Inn that served as a concert hall for the Exposition Orchestra and contained a dining place that quickly became a favorite of those who attended the exposition. Nearby, the Atchison, Topeka and Santa Fe Railway had a large-scale model of the Grand Canyon where spectators were conveyed by eight standard-gauge passenger cars beside a convincing replica of the scenery of the Grand Canyon. In addition, there was a realistic pueblo occupied by Indians, where visitors could stroll trails, climb ladders, and even buy Indian curios and Navajo blankets from the business operated by Fred Harvey.

Another favorite place was the racetrack where both horse races and buggy races were held. Then there was the chance to attend the 101 Ranch Rodeo that took place every day during the first months of the exposition.

As in all fairs, there was an amusement park for carnival rides, exhibits, and games. This area was called the Zone, and within its boundaries there was a working model of the Panama Canal. Visitors to this exhibit were transported on a moving platform in cars like opera boxes. This train took 1,200 people per ride on a twenty-three-minute tour of the Panama Canal. At points of interest, spectators held telephone receivers to their ears and heard lectures from phonograph records designed by Thomas A. Edison. "The model showed boats, trains, 'electric mules,' and light houses in operation, and the ships were timed to pass through the miniature canal and locks at the same pace relatively at which the originals would have passed through the real canal."[11]

Everything about the fair astounded visitors who strolled the grounds and looked at the exhibits. To Will and Agnes, the beauty of the courts and buildings combined with plants and flowers was in the best possible taste.

Added to their enjoyment of the exhibits was the fact that music had not been overlooked or given a minor place during the planning of the fair. Concerts were held, opera singers appeared, and favorite performers of popular music had their days and evenings on stage.

Day after day, night after night, crowds thronged the streets of the exposition. They were rewarded with a sense of something special, something to be remembered and talked about for years to come. It was a world's fair that set a standard of everlasting beauty and excitement as a celebration of human achievement. Most of all, it was a theme park of dreams, and Bourn was proud that he had been among the original contributors to this creative gem that brought great honor to San Francisco.

While the excitement of the opening of the Panama-Pacific International Exposition enthralled Will and Agnes during the first weeks of its operation, it was the exposition's use of indoor-outdoor spaces complementing each other that convinced them that their concept for their country estate matched this idea. Now, with the good months for building not far off, Will wrote to Willis Polk and requested "the approximate cost of building the house, terraces and two pavillions."[12]

As he awaited a reply from Polk, Will began to be concerned, because there were rumors that Willis was drinking too much and that he had become careless with his income to the extent that his wife worried. The more Bourn thought about this, the more he wanted to do something for his old friend. During April, he wrote to Willis and offered to invest $5,000 to $10,000 for him "with more care than I have ever used in my own investments."[13]

Polk rejected Bourn's offer and indicated that he was insulted by the suggestion. The men managed to resume their cordial relationship once Polk had accepted Will's apology for having offered to be of assistance. They resumed their exchange of ideas regarding the country home, and Will wrote to Polk to request that the cost of construction be limited to $204,000. Within this same letter, Will indicated that he wished the exterior of the home to be built of brick and stone and that the roof be tiled. As for the interior, Will requested that for the most part it should be of wood.[14]

The general idea was that the house would have two stories and be of a style that Polk had borrowed from both the Stuart and Georgian periods. Both men agreed that most of the rooms would be large and that they would have seventeen-foot ceilings. There were to be forty-three rooms plus bathrooms and storage rooms. The overall size of the home was to be 36,000 square feet. Polk's plans called for the use of steel I-beams and columns to strengthen the stone and brick walls and the Spanish tile roof.

The U-shape of the house, as Polk saw it, was to contain two wings that stretched out from the entrance and main hall; the major rooms in the base of the U were to be the study, library, drawing room, and dining room. The north wing was to contain the one-and-a-half-story ballroom and the lounge; and the south wing was to contain the kitchen, pantry, and servants' quarters. Between the two wings were to be a courtyard, entrance porch, vestibule, men's and women's reception rooms, other assorted rooms, and a vestibule leading to the main hall.

With work well under way on the new home, Will turned his full attention to business matters. He agreed with cousin George Starr that the Empire Mine should purchase Crocker's Sultana Company as well as a group of other mining claims lying south of the Empire Mine. Another major project that required his attention was the continuing construction of the Calaveras Dam in Alameda County. During this period, William Mulholland consulted with Bourn regarding the progress of the dam. At Bourn's request, Mulholland agreed to remain a consultant on this project until the dam was completed.

The most unpleasant tasks that confronted Bourn were legal battles. First, he had to deal with the condemnation suit against the Spring Valley Water Company by the City of San Francisco in which the city was attempting to secure ownership of the water company for a price well below the firm's true worth. Second, he had his attorneys file a lawsuit against the Chronicle Publishing Company, which had printed a series of libelous articles about the water company during 1914 and 1915, articles that had such headlines as "The Water Hold-Up" and "The Spring Valley Hold-Up," and other defamatory and abusive stories that Bourn found distasteful and disgusting.

In July a problem that had been ongoing for some time was finally solved when the water company settled a dispute with the U.S. government over the ownership of Lobos Creek water rights in the San Francisco Presidio. The government agreed to pay the company $98,937.50 for its titles to the land plus the water rights, dams, and buildings. In turn, Spring Valley agreed to spend $4,000 to build a twenty-five-foot-wide road from 22nd Avenue to 17th Avenue along the southern border of the Presidio.[15]

Though he parted with Lobos Creek water rights as well as the land beside it, Bourn continued to own other expensive land beyond the Presidio in the Sea Cliff area. All this he had purchased from its previous owners—D. Ogden Mills, Lloyd Tevis, and William F. Babcock.[16] With an eye for value, Bourn considered the Sea Cliff region ideal for real estate development.

5 As one of the early contributors to the Panama-Pacific International Exposition, Bourn was pleased to be called upon to speak on November 27, 1915, at ceremonies in honor of France and Belgium. During this day, a crowd of at least five thousand gathered at the French Pavilion. Respects had been made to the statue of Lafayette, which stood in the colonnade of the Palace of Fine Arts, then the throng gathered at the French Pavilion. Here, as the Exposition Band played, the crowd sang "The Star Spangled Banner," "La Marseillaise," "La Brabançonne," and "The Battle Hymn of the Republic."[17]

William Bourn was introduced to the crowd by William H. Crocker. Then Bourn began to speak about the soul of France and the country's love of idealism. As he cited the influence of France's love of honor and country upon the men who fought the American Revolution, he gradually worked his way to the present struggle, in which France stood against the German war machine. He caught the mood of the crowd as he asked: "Is America neutral?"

To this question, the answer from the throng came in loud shouts of "No! No!"

After Bourn's rousing speech, Professor Charles Mills Gayley of the University of California spoke on "France and the World." He was followed by Bruce Porter, who read his long poem, "France in Vision." The final act on this day was reserved for San Francisco's most beloved poet, George Sterling, who read his sonnet, "To France."

It was a stirring day for the huge crowd that had come to the fair to celebrate the heroic deeds of France. In San Francisco, with its large French population, it was a day that would not be forgotten. As a fitting climax, it was announced that once the fair ended, a major portion of the Library of French Thought, Scholarship and Literature that was part of the French Pavilion would be donated to the University of California.[18]

On December 4, 1915, the Panama-Pacific International Exposition closed. The "Exposition Recessional" was played, and taps sounded from the Tower of Jewels as the flag was lowered. At midnight all the lights of the exposition were turned off, and fireworks filled the darkness as the crowd, which refused to go home, sang "Auld Lang Syne." San Franciscans partied through the night as they celebrated the world's fair that had captured all that was good about their time—even as Europe floundered in the darkness of war.

6 As work progressed on the Bourns' country home, Will named it Filoli, a word he had coined by combining the first two letters from the words *Fight, Love,* and *Live.*[19] On December 3, 1915, Will received a memorandum from Willis Polk in which he stated that the cost of Filoli as of that time was $206,225.80. This seemed high, and on December 13, 1915, Will wrote to Polk at his office in the Hobart Building in San Francisco, asking that the following items be excluded from the present allowance for Filoli, to be taken up later: light fixtures, hardware, plumbing fixtures, all mantels, hardwood floors, painting, fire extinguishers, kitchen range and boiler and hood, laundry dryer, and stove. Within the estimate the following were included: inside finish for library and study; terra-cotta trimmings instead of imitation stone; terra-cotta to replace metal cornices; and the roof to be of tile and slate. The allowance for these items was to be $155,000.[20]

Will was clear about what he wanted at Filoli. Concrete floors were not to be considered. The vestibule was to have marble columns, a marble floor, and perhaps marble wainscoting. He wanted the inside stairs to be made of iron with marble treads and marble trimmings. The floors of the pavilions were to be of marble, but all designs were to be simplified. The dining room was to be finished in oak, the library in poplar, and the study in pine or poplar. There were to be no glass doors for the bookcases, and the bookcases were to be five feet tall and ten inches deep, with movable shelves. Over and over, he stressed that simplification was to be the rule at all times. Finally, he made it clear—once again—that he preferred a flat tile on the roof but would settle for a tile with a very slight curve.[21]

After seeing to these details for Filoli, Will shifted his attention to the Friends of France. This same day, a meeting of the organization was held at the Palace Hotel. During this meeting, Will was elected president; Bruce Porter was elected vice president; William H. Crocker became the treasurer, and Porter Garnett became secretary.[22]

As December neared an end, Will arranged for an office for the Friends of France in Room 443, the Montgomery Block, and he saw to it that Porter Garnett was named full-time director. Members did not pay dues, so money was collected through voluntary contribution. For this purpose, coin boxes were distributed throughout San Francisco and the neighboring Bay Area cities. Raphael Weill of the White House had these coin boxes distributed by the department store's delivery system.[23]

In February 1916, Will wrote to Weill and requested some coin boxes so he could distribute them among his friends. As he pointed out, coin boxes might bring in a fair sum of money during any meeting of a board of directors. His assumption proved to be correct, because the first time the coin boxes were returned to the Friends of France, they contained a total of $6,700.[24]

This same month, Will received a progress report on the Calaveras Dam from Sam Eastman. On February 5, 1916, Eastman estimated that the cost of the dam to date was $2,089,535.27, but this did not include the cost of the spillway, tunnel, or conduit. Even with this growing expense for the water company, which San Francisco was threatening to claim through condemnation, Will insisted on completing the project. He estimated the worth of the Spring Valley Water Company to be near $68,000,000, at least two times the value of the company that the City and County of San Francisco cited.[25]

By the spring of 1916, Will was busy planning a trip that would include a visit to Muckross. In addition, he hoped to visit Paris to get some personal feeling of how the war was affecting his French friends and the people of France. Even as he prepared for this trip, he wrote to his sister Ida on May 16 and requested that she telephone him before he and Agnes left so he would know if any members of the family needed money.[26]

This same month, Will decided that Sam Eastman needed a vacation. In his usual manner, Eastman had been working long hours and shouldering an immense responsibility as he carried on his regular water company duties while keeping a close watch over the Calaveras Dam project. Bourn's sense of humor appeared as he wrote:

> At an executive meeting that was held today there were present: W. B. Bourn, President of the Spring Valley Water Company, the President of the French Republic, the King of Great Britain and Emperor of India, the Czar of all the Russias and the Emperor of Germany.
>
> The Kaiser stated that unless the Vice President and Manager of the Spring Valley Water Company took a good and happy vacation

he would send the German Army after him. That seemed to settle it, and the others had nothing to say. Obey, or beware![27]

7 In the summer of 1916, the Bourns traveled abroad again. Although this was not to be a long visit, it allowed time for Will and Agnes to visit Maud and baby Elizabeth at Muckross. But here, as on the Continent, there was turmoil. There was continuing trouble between Ireland and Great Britain ever since Easter Monday, April 24, 1916, when eight hundred men had occupied key points in Dublin in the name of a proclaimed Irish Republic. None of this violence had seemed possible during that Easter Monday, when Dubliners jeered and pelted the arrested men with bits of garbage as they were marched off to jail. But after the British put fourteen men to death before firing squads and then sentenced others by secret court martial to death or prison, Arthur Griffith's Sinn Fein movement had gained popular support.[28]

Added to the Bourns' concern was their worry about Arthur Vincent, who was serving as an ambulance driver on the French front line. Will had been in Paris during August, when he talked with Albert Tierman at the Ministry of Commerce about the progress of the war. At this time, Bourn presented 20,000 francs to Tierman from the Friends of France to be equally divided for aid to blinded soldiers and artists who were in need of support.[29] During Will's visit with Tierman, he heard stories of the terrible trench warfare and learned of the mounting toll of wounded and dead. This was a very high price in human suffering for the cause of freedom, yet Will was convinced that such costs had to be endured.

Upon their return to San Francisco, the Bourns found their lives filled with affairs requiring their attention. Work was progressing at Filoli at a rapid pace, and Will had Agnes take over the task of making sure that the final details were handled according to their wishes. In the meantime, he turned his attention to the Empire Mine. By this time, the cyanide plants at both the Empire and the Pennsylvania mines were in full operation, but at the Empire a Dorr thickener had been installed in the cyanide plant and two Rockwell furnaces added to the refinery to allow for melting more precipitates. With these changes, it was now possible for the Empire to handle a greater tonnage of ore.

By the end of 1916, reports from the Empire Mine for the year were remarkable. The profit was $935,007.41, and for the Pennsylvania the profit was $258,112.59.[30] Yet this was only part of Bourn's yearly income as the majority stockholder. Added to this were profits from the Spring Valley stock, the shared income from leased agricultural lands, and investment income. All this made Will one of the richest men in California and added to his reputation as one of the last Bonanza Kings.

In the last two months of 1916, Bourn backed the Friends of France in the establishment of ambulance units from Stanford University to join the American Ambulance Field Service for duty in France. Among the first volunteers was Joseph H. Eastman, Samuel P. Eastman's brother. In a letter to his brother on November 23, 1916, young Joseph Eastman stated that there were many students ready to volunteer for service in France. To back up his words, he enclosed a select list of twenty names from 125 applications. Then he wrote: "If you feel as we do on this . . . could you put us in touch with someone who is interested and might help."[31]

Within a short time, Sam Eastman let Will Bourn know about this. In turn, Will notified the American Ambulance Field Service that it would be possible to equip four Friends of France units of twenty men each for overseas duty on the battlefields. These field-service units generally consisted of ambulances serving in the field with two back-up ambulances plus the rest of the unit, which contained the following: "a staff car, a Ford repair car (equipped with work bench, forge, vises and other tools), a large ambulance (usually a White two-ton truck) capable of carrying from sixteen to twenty sitting cases, a kitchen trailer with stove and cooking utensils, and three tents capable of furnishing living, dining and sleeping facilities for thirty men."[32]

On February 2, 1917, the Friends of France had a dinner and leave-taking for the twenty-one members of the first unit of volunteers from Stanford University. The young men and their families joined distinguished guests in the ballroom of the Palace Hotel. Among the speakers at this farewell dinner were Dr. Ray Lyman Wilbur, president of Stanford University; M. Julien Neltner, Consul-General of France; Professors George M. Stratton, Gilbert Chinard, and David P. Barrows of the University of California; Joseph Eastman of the Stanford Volunteers; and William B. Bourn.[33]

It was an evening of full-blown patriotism in which the volunteers were presented with brassards bearing the insignia of the Friends of France. Even chivalry and knighthood were mentioned. Bourn's speech stressed that France was fighting for a civilization based on Liberty, Honor, and Justice.

Then in a great show of emotion, he said: "In serving the American Ambulance, in helping France, you will better learn the spiritual and highest meaning of Peace."[34]

As the United States moved closer to entering the war against Germany, a second ambulance unit was sent from Stanford. By March 25, 1917, the University of California's ambulance corps was ready to go, and a second unit was being formed. Then on March 29, 1917, the American League of California was organized at the University of California. The league's purposes were twofold: to offer loyal support to the government to uphold American honor and American rights; and to urge and sustain all citizens in the performance of American duties.[35]

The American League sent a long telegram to President Woodrow Wilson urging him to commit American troops to the war in Europe. Copies of this message were sent to California's senators James D. Phelan and Hiram W. Johnson and to the eleven California congressmen. Even as these messages reached Washington, D.C., the United States was on the verge of entering the conflict. On April 2, 1917, President Wilson appeared before Congress and asked that war be declared between the United States and the Central Powers (Germany and Austria-Hungary).

By the summer of 1917, four California ambulance corps were serving on the front—two from Stanford and two from the University of California. William Bourn received letters from some members of the corps, giving him a vivid picture of this terrible trench warfare. In July he received a letter from Joseph H. Eastman in which he gave a full description of being under a heavy artillery attack. Another letter to Bourn came from A. Piatt Andrew of the University of California Ambulance Corps, in which he informed Bourn that the French needed them to drive five-ton trucks loaded with ammunition as well as other military supplies from the railroads to the artillery batteries and troops at the front.[36]

One of the highlights for the Ambulance Corps volunteers was the arrival of an American flag from California, which was sent from San Francisco after dedication services in the new Civic Auditorium on April 24, 1917. This special flag was intended for the Stanford volunteers who were in the first Friends of France unit. The flag reached the Stanford unit on June 8, 1917, and a ceremony was held at Ligny-en-Barrois during which the "Marseillaise" and "The Star Spangled Banner" were played. A ceremony followed, which Eastman described in full and commented that "You feel full of tingles about this time, and impulse tells you to clap your hands or step into the ranks to then and there shoulder a musket with these fighters."[37]

Throughout the spring and summer of 1917 Bourn received letters from young men serving with the Ambulance Corps of the Friends of France. From such correspondence he learned about the reality of brutal trench warfare: the thundering artillery attacks that sent hot, jagged metal from the sky; the gas attacks that brought a white cloud of acrid, choking, burning chemicals that blistered skin and seared lungs; and the daily slaughter by rifle and machine-gun fire that was known at home as the Western Front.

These letters drove Bourn to spend more time and money backing the Ambulance Corps as well as the men who flew in the Lafayette Escadrille. Will believed that achieving victory was crucial for the way of life that America, France, and England represented.

By 1917, Arthur Vincent was no longer with the ambulance service. After the entry of the United States into the war, he was sent to Chicago by the Foreign Office to head the British Information Service in that city. However, wartime conditions, especially the threat of German submarines to Atlantic shipping, prevented Maud and two-year-old Elizabeth from joining him in Chicago.

Away from his involvement with the war effort, Will gave of his time as a member of the Board of Regents for Stanford University, and he continued to be a key member of the Music Association of San Francisco. New developments in the gold-mining business called for changes at the Empire Mine. In 1917 the California Debris Commission set forth a strict requirement regarding the disposal of mine tailings. Mines would no longer be allowed to dump tailings into nearby streams. For the Empire Mine, this ruling prevented all dumping into nearby Wolf Creek. To obey this new law, the company began to construct an earthen dam that would be 63 feet high and 835 feet long. When this was completed, it would form a milk-colored body of water behind it—water and tailings from the cyanide plant. Another added expense was the plan to enlarge the stamp mill by adding twenty stamps to make a total of eighty. In turn, this called for enlarging the cyanide plant and installing more sand-leaching vats, slime agitators, a new thickener, another filter, and new auxiliary equipment. Finally, Bourn agreed with George Starr that when the new plants were completed, it would pay to build an electric railroad to carry ore from the Pennsylvania Mine to be processed at the Empire.[38]

By September 1917, the initial work on Filoli was completed, and Agnes, with the help of Bruce Porter, had selected and purchased most of the furniture for the house. But when Will and Agnes moved into their new home with its seventeen fireplaces and eleven chimneys, much remained to be done. Although the balustrade of the west wall had been completed in May, only in September were the lawns and shrubs planted. In the fall of 1917, 210 Irish yew trees, grown on the grounds of the Empire Mine from cuttings taken from the yews at Muckross, were dug up, boxed, and brought to Filoli to be planted.

Filoli was the final result of nineteen plans that Willis Polk had drawn for the home. Now, while the ballroom awaited finishing touches and the garage and tea or garden house were yet to be built, Bourn and Polk had a falling out. In great measure, the difficulty between the old friends was the result of Polk's drinking problem, but another part of the quarrel had to do with cost overruns in the building of Filoli. More than once, Will had informed Polk that he wanted to hold the cost of the house close to $200,000, but by the fall of 1917 the estimated cost of building the house, garage, and terrace court was over $300,000.[39]

Ultimately, the cost of building Filoli and the associated buildings and landscaping would run much higher than Bourn had ever dreamed. The water system cost $34,876.18; the gardens and walls $59,486.54; and expenses associated with Filoli's roads and bridges came to $29,199.94.[40] The total for all these costs amounted to just under $425,000. Still to come were the expenses associated with finish work for the ballroom and other costs pertaining to the formal gardens and the farm area west of the house.

The Filoli gardens had their genesis in the minds of three people: William Bourn, who had always loved gardens and who was knowledgeable about plants; his long-time friend Bruce Porter, who in addition to his talents as a painter, stained-glass artist, designer, and poet was noted for his work in landscape gardening, especially for his design of the gardens for William H. Crocker's New Place in Hillsborough; and Isabella Worn—known as Bella—who had worked with Porter at New Place and whose knowledge of plants and ability to create elaborate designs with a unique blend of color combinations made her a highly valued contributor to the ultimate design of Filoli's gardens.

Despite the growing cost of Filoli, William Bourn was well able to afford it. By the end of 1917, his principal investments provided a yearly income of more than a million dollars. Returns from the Empire Mines and Investment Company to its stockholders in 1917 were over a million dollars, while Bourn's other income came from his holdings in the Spring Valley Water Company, agricultural operations of his farms in the Delta, and a very large portfolio of highly diversified stocks and bonds. In short, his growing fortune put him in a position to pay ongoing costs for the building and operation of Filoli as well as yearly expenses associated with Muckross.

In January 1918, Will hired Arthur Brown Jr. of the firm of Bakewell and Brown of San Francisco to design and build the eight-car garage that he referred to as the Carriage House. This represented a definite break with Willis Polk, but at this time Bourn did not believe he could count upon his old friend. He talked over the design of the Carriage House with Brown, and after looking at sketches he agreed that he would like to have a clock cupola with a French cock and weathervane atop it on the roof of the garage. They also talked about the tea house, which was to be built after completion of the Carriage House. Brown was a graduate of the University of California and the École des Beaux Arts. After his studies in Paris, he had remained in Europe for another five years to study, observe, and travel. It was upon his return to San Francisco in that crucial year 1906 that he and John Bakewell Jr. formed the firm of Bakewell and Brown.[41]

On January 25, 1918, William Bourn received honors from Stanford University as his fellow trustees officially thanked him for his gift to Stanford of the flag that he had received from Stanford men serving with the First Ambulance Unit of the Friends of France. This was the flag of the École de Laigne de Ligny-en-Baine, which had been presented to the ambulance unit at the front on a hillside above Ligny-en-Barrois.[42]

A month later Bourn was honored by the Republic of France at a banquet in San Francisco. At this time, he was given the silver medal of "la Reconnaissance Française" for his work in establishing and backing the Ambulance Corps of the Friends of France. Even as he accepted this award, he was involved in sending hospital supplies to Italy, Belgium, Great Britain, and Poland. In the latter nation, his old friend Ignace Paderewski was said to have commented that Poland idolized Woodrow Wilson and William B. Bourn.[43]

With the coming of warmer weather during March and April 1918, the lawns and shrubs around Filoli grew considerably, but by May the weather took a turn for the worse. Will wrote about it in a letter to Arthur: "We had vile weather. I never knew such a May: it was so cold, windy and disagreeable."[44] By the second week of June, summer came, bringing warmth to the newly planted gardens of Filoli just in time for Sarah Chase Bourn's first visit to her son's new home. She came from her Broadway home in San Francisco. Though she was confined to a padded, four-wheeled wicker wheelchair, it did not keep her from looking over Filoli and its gardens. Although there is no record of what she thought of yet another house designed by Willis Polk—not one of her favorite architects—no doubt she had many comments about the garden. Sarah loved gardens, and here was plenty for her to see and compare with her flowers, shrubs, and fruit trees at Madroño.

Even with a busy schedule that took Bourn from business to his continuing work in behalf of the war effort to his ongoing inspections of work at Filoli, he made it his concern to watch out for the health and welfare of his employees. An indication of his "hands-on" style of management comes through in a letter of July 15, 1918, that he wrote to F. W. Nobs, assistant manager of the Empire Mines. Within this letter, he gave the following instructions: "Please tell Mr. Starr I gave my butler, who is taking a rest, a note to him, and in the not far distant future he may turn up in Grass Valley. . . . He has been a good servant, and his wife who will be with him, is a crackerjack. Honeysett is not robust."[45]

With news of victories on the Western Front, Will wrote to Arthur and discussed the possibility of having Maud and Elizabeth come to the United States. German submarines were no longer a threat to ships, and it was simply a matter of getting passports. If that proved to be a stumbling block, Will had another idea: "As far as Maud is concerned she could come out as a representative of the Red Cross—the principal difficulty, as you state, will probably be Elizabeth, but I do hope it can all be arranged."[46]

Between his letters to Arthur at Chicago and Maud at Muckross, Will convinced them that it was safe for Maud to cross the Atlantic. On October 23, 1918—after a visit with Arthur in Chicago—Maud and Elizabeth arrived at Filoli. Mother and daughter were healthy and happy, and joy filled the spacious rooms of Filoli.

Less than two weeks later, it was time to celebrate at Filoli as the Armistice was declared on November 11, 1918, and the years of war came to an end. Now, all that was needed was the appearance of Arthur. On December 20, 1918, he arrived at Filoli just in time for Christmas. Even though the walls of the ballroom were yet to be covered with murals, a great Christmas tree was placed at the east end of the room and a large fire crackled in the fireplace as the Bourns and Vincents enjoyed the holiday season.

During their stay at Filoli, the Vincents and the Bourns traveled to San

Francisco to visit his mother, Sarah Chase Bourn, who now had her daughter Maye and Maye's husband James Tucker living with her. This family gathering included William Bowers Bourn II and Agnes Moody Bourn; the Bourn sisters, Maye Bourn Tucker, Maud Bourn Hayne, and Ida Hoxie Bourn. Tanned, handsome Arthur Rose Vincent, Maud Bourn Vincent, and great-granddaughter Elizabeth Rose Vincent, who became four years old in January, filled out this generational gathering, which sat and stood for a family portrait centered around Sarah Bourn, the pioneer matriarch of the Bourn family.

In late March 1919, the gardens of Filoli were in bloom, the great oaks at the north end of the home were filled with many species of songbirds that had migrated from as far away as Mexico, and the warm sunshine seemed to mirror the sun's rays off the wind-blown fields of green grass. It was a time for picnics, but it also was time for the Vincents to bid farewell and head home to Muckross. They were not in a hurry to leave, but Arthur, though he was a citizen of Ireland, had been born in Mhow, India, where his father, Colonel Arthur Hare Vincent was stationed with the British Army. His place of birth, rather than his actual citizenship, determined the length of stay that he was granted in the United States.[47] So, on March 26, 1919, Maud, who was five months pregnant, and Elizabeth and Arthur said farewell to her mother and father. The visit had been grand, but it ended much too soon.

Thirteen days after the Vincents had left by train, Sarah Chase Bourn died on April 9, 1919. This grand lady was eighty-nine years old and only five months away from her ninetieth birthday. Surviving her were Will, Ida, Maud, Maye, three grandchildren, and one great-grandchild. Her death was reported in the newspapers of San Francisco and the Napa Valley, for with her passing another tie to the California Gold Rush and the boom days of the Comstock Lode was gone. In every sense of the word, Sarah Bourn had been a pioneer. To Will and his sisters, the loss of their mother, who had been the backbone of the family after the tragic death of her husband, left them filled with grief.

Thirteen days after Sarah's death, the California regiments that had fought in the terrible Battle of the Argonne came home to San Francisco. On April 22, 1919, the returning soldiers were greeted by throngs of people. The 363rd and 347th Regiments marched up Market Street, where they saw arches of evergreen and welcome-home banners and heard cheers from the crowds and the wounded soldiers in grandstands built especially for them.

The cheering crowd soon halted the march and turned all of Market Street into a large party.[48]

At Filoli, the Bourns heard about this grand street party. For them, it was a time to rejoice, to be proud of the returning troops, and to remember with pride the early work of the young ambulance drivers from Stanford University and the University of California who had volunteered for duty at the front even before the United States entered the war.

In this same April, the lily-pad pool at Filoli was completed, and the shrubs at the front entrance as well as those that surrounded the house were in full bloom. With the garage completed, Will looked forward to other projects to bring a finishing touch to Filoli and its gardens and grounds. He wrote to a friend about the garage and with pride indicated that "The tower is an imitation of an old Georgian tower. It will contain a clock and bells, and is surmounted by a weather vane. At the top of the weather vane is a magnificent Gallic cock—a real fighting cock—truly an inspiring bird! Whenever I feel blue I look up at this tower and know that Chanticleer is not down-hearted."[49]

In June 1919, Bourn received a letter from the Department of the Interior's U.S. Geological Survey requesting figures on the production of gold and the cost of producing it. To Bourn, this was the same as asking a man to open all his private business affairs so that facts and figures could be used in the future for purposes unknown. His reply to this request on June 11, 1919, was a clear and resounding *no!*[50]

All the Geological Survey could do was give a rough estimate. Even then, it was not close to the actual figures, which by the end of 1919 showed the following profits: $442,879.03 from the Empire Mine and $269,475.29 from the Pennsylvania Mine. As high as these figures were, they were down from 1918, when the profit from the Empire Mine was $682,246.39 and from the Pennsylvania Mine was $336,725.49.[51] Though costs were high in getting gold from a depth that was now over four thousand feet, the quartz in the Grass Valley mining region was extremely rich, and year by year it added to Bourn's fortune.

A month after Bourn turned down the request for information regarding gold production, he received splendid news from London. On July 16, 1919, Maud gave birth to the Bourn's grandson, Arthur William Bourn Vincent. This great news called for celebrating with a fine dinner at Filoli and toasts with champagne and the best wine from Bourn's cellar.

All things were moving favorably for Will and Agnes, and this was a happy time in their life. A month after young Billy Vincent's birth, the Garden House at Filoli was completed and the last bricks were laid in the high garden wall. But their old friend, Willis Polk, was not in good health. For too many years, Willis had acted as though he were immortal, and now high living and the consumption of too much liquor were taking their toll. In an effort to help Willis and to give his wife a vacation away from San Francisco and all the vices her husband easily found, Bourn offered them the Cottage at the Empire Mine for a rest in the warm summer of the foothill country around Grass Valley. When the Polks agreed to Will's offer, he wrote to Katie Moriarty, who not only cooked for the Bourns and other guests but also ran the Cottage. Will let Katie know about Polk's drinking problem and wrote the following: "If there happens to be anything in the cupboard in the dining room, please lock it up in the basement; and if he should want anything to drink, please state that there isn't anything."[52]

Bourn worried about his old friend, and it grieved him that such a talented individual was throwing away his life. To Will, Polk was an old hunting companion, and until their recent quarrel over the last work on Filoli, Willis had been Bourn's master builder. In great measure, Polk's finest work was what he did for Bourn: the water temple at Suñol for the Spring Valley Water Company; the Cottage, Clubhouse, Office, and other buildings at the Empire Mine; Bourn's San Francisco home on Webster Street in Pacific Heights; and most of all, Filoli. In addition, Bourn had also been responsible for getting the Pacific Union Club to hire Polk to take the burned-out Flood Mansion and create a grand headquarters for the members; and it had been Will who had been the driving force to put Polk in charge of all the architectural work of the Panama-Pacific International Exposition. Present difficulties aside, to Bourn, Willis Polk was the great architect of San Francisco.

In September 1919, architect Arthur Brown Jr. and his wife visited the Bourns. By this time, Filoli's gardens were beginning to take the shape that gave a greater sense of completeness. Around the garden house and the nearby wall bedded plants and shrubs were doing well, while flowers and plants were growing around the lily-pad pool. In addition, boxed fruit trees had arrived at Filoli, and the gardening staff was busy with planting. It was a good time to show the Browns the house and the grounds, because the dream called Filoli already gave the feeling of having been there for some years.

As the fall of 1919 passed and the decade came to an end, Will saw the Filoli dream coming true as workmen began the brickwork for the paths, pools, and terraces within the walled garden. More than that, he thought about the years that had passed so quickly since the exposition—years that saw the birth of his grandchildren, years of the Great War when he had been so involved with the struggle to save France from the German war machine, and years in which his business ventures flourished. Now, as he looked back and considered the great sweep of events that had come and gone, he realized that these had been changing times filled with both happiness and despair.

18

The Final Years

The new decade of the Roaring Twenties opened with gala parties at Filoli. Invitations to these parties were prized, for Filoli had become synonymous with elegance. The great home was surrounded by beautiful gardens that formed outdoor rooms with a significant pattern for each room. Designed as an extension of the house, the gardens offered walks of beauty. In addition to the pathways in the garden world of Filoli, strollers had a view of the Coast Range to the west and Crystal Springs Lake to the north. As guests arrived at Filoli, they were greeted at the front door by Sydney Woods, the tall, perfect English butler. If guests were arriving for lunch, Woods served cocktails in the main hall. During these Prohibition years, liquor was brought from the safe for such occasions. After a period of socializing, guests walked through the drawing room to the dining room.[1]

At the elegant Chippendale mahogany dining table, guests were seated in chairs upholstered in tapestry, each chair bearing a symbol for one of the months of the year. Flowers from the gardens filled the room with the colors of the season; or if it happened to be winter, displays of English holly gave a festive holiday atmosphere.

Lunch or dinner with the Bourns was a time for fine food prepared by dark-haired Alma Johnson, their Swedish cook. Along with one excellent course after another, Will had a selection of excellent California and French wines from his extensive cellar. The table was set with beautiful china, and the silver service with a raised initial *B* was made for the Bourns by the silversmith at Tiffany's of New York. Conversation at such dinners covered a wide range of topics from art and music to politics and world travel. These parties sent guests home with memories to cherish and left Will and Agnes happy with the joy of entertaining at Filoli.

Large parties required additional help for the kitchen staff and the full staff of servants on duty. All were easily available, because they lived in the first-floor servants' wing, which had bedrooms and a separate dining room. Often large groups of guests came to enjoy an evening of music or dancing in the elegant ballroom, where a roaring fire in the large fireplace reflected its colors off the ceiling and walls trimmed in gold leaf from the Empire Mine. The room was not yet finished as the Bourns wanted it to be, for the grand chandeliers and Peixotto wall murals were still to come.

At other times, a small group of Will's close friends came to Filoli to play high-stakes poker. Such games were held in the card room, just off the hall and opposite Bourn's study at the north end of the home. Refreshments and food for these games, which often lasted for hours, were brought from the kitchen to the service room east of the card room. These games were not for novice players with a timid streak, because the men who gambled at Filoli were old hands who knew full well that Bourn was a tough competitor in poker or any other game that required skill and daring.

Dinners, parties, musicales, and card games were the indoor events at Filoli. The outdoors provided Will and Agnes with the joy of strolling through the gardens and with nature hikes where they saw coveys of quail that took off with a whirring sound and deer that bounded gracefully for cover or sometimes stopped and stared at the Bourns. At other times, Will and Agnes enjoyed picnics served by the butler and often held on an oak knoll to the right of North Drive. The knoll was called Dundag, after a point of land that goes out into the lake at Muckross.

The beginning of 1920 also saw Bruce Porter and Bella Worn keep a crew of fourteen Italian gardeners busy. During the first months of the year, the paths, pools, and garden terraces were given finishing touches. Then a sundial with a pedestal of carved Vicenza stone was placed in the center of the walled garden. This sundial bore the legend Time Began In A Garden. This reference to the Garden of Eden was a favorite of Agnes's. A stickler for accuracy, she had the sundial adjusted twice a year to capture the sun's shadow with its gnomonic pointer.

2 Even as the Bourns were filled with joy, distressing news came to Will. Once again, the *San Francisco Chronicle* had used what he considered libelous language regarding the Spring Valley Water Company. The newspaper called the firm a fake and imputed it with the "sin of being a cheat, a fraud, a thief, and a pilferer." Attorneys for the water company sued the Chronicle Publishing Company, and the case was brought before the U.S. District Court.[2]

District Judge Bledsoe ruled against the newspaper, and the demurrer was overruled. The second amended complaint called for the Chronicle Publishing Company to pay $50,000 in damages.[3] As far as Bourn and the water company were concerned, that amount of money would not cover their legal expenses; however Bourn was pleased to have won a victory over what he considered irresponsible journalism. Still, he was certain that in future news stories about the company or himself, he could not expect to be treated with either kindness or fairness by the *Chronicle* as theirs was an old quarrel with a rather unpleasant history.

In this same period, the Spring Valley Water Company was noted as the largest privately owned water company in the United States. It seemed to expand without even trying. No doubt, this aspect of the company, more than anything else, brought suspicion about its ethics. In reality, the success of the firm was the result of visionary management. In all his business ventures, Bourn surrounded himself with first-rate employees in key positions. All his people were given the opportunity to proceed with innovative plans to add to the growth and success of the business. This kind of trust from the head of the firm—in both mining ventures and the water business—resulted in the best possible level of worker productivity as well as creative contributions from employees.

Now, in the early months of 1920, Will and Sam Eastman talked about building what would be called the Coyote Reservoir. The purpose of this project was to provide irrigation water for about twelve thousand acres of Coyote River lands that ran from Santa Clara County in the north to San Benito County in the south. This land was acquired in 1917 when the water company acquired parts of Rancho La Polka, Rancho San Francisco de las Llagas, and the San Martín Ranch.[4] From the beginning, it had been Will's idea to sell this land for farms and create the water supply needed to irrigate them. With the completion of the Coyote Reservoir, the water company would be able to sell irrigation water to all these farms in Santa Clara and San Benito Counties.

All was not idyllic in that spring of 1920. The news from Ireland caused the Bourns great concern. On April 4, 1920, war broke out between the Irish Republican Army and the British. On this day, the IRA carried out raids on tax offices throughout Ireland and destroyed tax records.[5] This was only the beginning of the violent and bloody conflicts to come as the British struck back with outright brutality.

As news from Ireland became worse, Will believed that he and Agnes had to get to Muckross to be with Maud, Elizabeth Rose, Billy, and Arthur during this time of great turmoil. Even before the April 4 clash between the Irish Republican Army and the British, Will had written to the secretary of state to apply for passports for Agnes and himself to travel to Ireland and France. He indicated that he wished to visit France to discuss the distribution of funds from the Friends of France for charitable purposes, but it was his request to visit Muckross Estate in Ireland that brought a prompt refusal from the United States Government.[6]

Blocked from traveling to Ireland, the most the Bourns could do was keep in touch with Maud and offer any monetary assistance the Vincents needed during these months of violence. Raids by the Black-and-Tans—a particularly vicious auxiliary force made up of former British soldiers and even former convicts—were reported in the newspapers of San Francisco. These stories were upsetting to Will and Agnes.

By summer's end in 1920, it seemed to the Bourns that the trouble in Ireland had no end in sight. Then on Bloody Sunday, November 21, 1920, the Royal Irish Constabulary and its auxiliaries opened fire on a football match, killing twelve people and wounding sixty. That same night, two IRA men imprisoned in Dublin Castle were killed. As the violence continued, martial law was proclaimed in Cork on December 10, 1920. A day later, the Black-and-Tans invaded, looting and wrecking Cork and destroying the center of the city.[7]

Even as Will and Agnes were caught up in the good life at Filoli, events in Ireland put a damper on everything they did. Reports from Ireland continued to reflect a brutal struggle, and it was hard for the Bourns to have any peace of mind.

On December 21, 1920, William Bourn escaped the worry of the war in Ireland as he attended a banquet at the Fairmont Hotel to honor France's General Robert Nivelle. Other veterans at this banquet were the men who had served as members of the First, Second, Third, and Fourth Friends of France Ambulance Field Service during the Great War. During the banquet, General Nivelle spoke of the common understanding and friendship that joined France and the United States. Then he decorated four members of the leadership of the Friends of France with the Legion of Honor. William B. Bourn and William H. Crocker were made Officers of the Legion, while Bruce Porter and Porter Garnett were made Chevaliers.[8]

It was a grand evening for men who had seen action on the Western Front and also men who had backed the cause of freedom with money, supplies, and a steady belief in the need to be counted in this battle to protect the great democracies of the world. To Will Bourn, it was the end of a heroic time. The close of 1920—even with war in Ireland—offered hope for the future, for if the United States and Great Britain—to name but two nations—could stand and fight a common enemy, the future of freedom seemed to be in good hands.

3 Two weeks into January 1921, Bourn decided to give San Francisco another opportunity to purchase the Spring Valley Water Company. To Will, it was simply a matter of common sense, for once the Hetch Hetchy Project was completed and water began to flow through the 149 miles of pipeline from Tuolumne County, San Francisco would need storage capacity and a system of delivery in order to get its water to the customers. Even though the voters of San Francisco had turned down bond issues to purchase Spring Valley in 1910 and 1915, Bourn convinced the officers and board members of the water company to give the city another chance.

On January 14, 1921, the Spring Valley Water Company made official its offer to sell all its properties, rights, and privileges for "the sum of Thirty-seven million (37,000,000) dollars plus such amounts not exceeding One million (1,000,000) dollars as the Railroad Commission of the State of California shall certify to have been expended by the Spring Valley Water Company since the first day of March 1920 in capital investments in or upon the properties hereinafter described, said sums to be payable in gold coin of the United States of America on or before nine months from the date at which the electors of the City and County of San Francisco shall vote to issue bonds for the purchase of said properties."[9]

Along with this letter that offered the sale of the company at an extremely low price, the water company sent a 206-page document that fully described all the properties for sale. Will was never sure what San Francisco's supervisors might do, but he hoped this offer was one they would finally accept.

Knowing that nothing was a sure bet when dealing with San Francisco's Board of Supervisors, Will wrote to George Starr at the Empire Mine. In his letter, he stated: "I had expected to leave this afternoon for Grass Valley, as the last act for the present in the comedy entitled 'Buying Spring Valley' was performed by the Supervisors yesterday."[10]

While Bourn waited for the supervisors to put a bond issue on the next ballot—possibly in March—he divided his time among his business activities, an active correspondence with Arthur and Maud at Muckross, and his offers of assistance to the *Sacramento Union,* which was on the verge of failing. He considered the *Union* one of California's finest newspapers—in Bourn's mind, what a newspaper should be. As Will later wrote in an essay, a newspaper should have ideals that are reflected in "higher standards of expression, higher standards of judgment . . . and a nobler development of wisdom and courage." To Will, the *Sacramento Union* met all these requirements, and he did not wish to see its demise.[11]

On March 8, 1921, a special election was held in San Francisco to decide upon a bond issue for the purchase of the Spring Valley Water Company. For once, all the city's newspapers—including the *Chronicle*—backed the measure to raise money to buy the water company. Out of 220,000 registered voters, only 73,980 made it to the polls. When the vote was counted, 42,898 voted yes, and 31,082 voted no. Since this bill required a two-thirds majority, the issue failed to pass.

The Bourns were in Ireland visiting the Vincents at Muckross when the vote for the bond issue was defeated in San Francisco. Sam Eastman was disgusted with the result of this election, and he expressed his feelings in a letter to Bourn: "One of the most important civic questions ever presented to the people was lost by apathy."[12]

Though the Bourns' 1921 visit to Muckross was of short duration, one item of business—other than the disappointing San Francisco vote—that came up during Will's absence concerned his own search for a water supply for his Portola Woods development in the foothills above Woodside. Spring Valley could not supply this water because control of water for this area was handled by the Bear Gulch Water Company. This firm had been started by Senator Charles Norton Felton in 1900 and now belonged to the University of California.[13] To get permission to apply to this company for water, Eastman wrote to the Railroad Commission on April 15, 1921. Although this was a matter of small consequence, it was yet another example of the growing complications surrounding the water business in California.

By the time the Bourns had returned from Muckross at the beginning of June, Will was faced with union problems at the Empire Mine. A letter from George Starr reported that he had been to three meetings with the Mïners' League committee regarding its grievance. But as Starr wrote: "after lengthy discussions about the cost of living, which resulted in our not being able to arrive at any basis upon which we could adjust wages, and also their firm stand against the differential of 50 cents between the miner and the shoveler . . . we did present them this afternoon the enclosed statement, which was received by them with somewhat of a shock. They will read our statement before the League Sunday afternoon at a mass meeting to be held at the Strand Theatre."[14]

Five hundred miners attended this meeting. Though they were able to recognize that the cost of mining had climbed steadily as the depth of the mine increased to the 5,400-foot level, they did not believe that they should receive a cut in wages. When the letter from the Empire Mine to the Mine Workers Protective League Wage Committee was read to the miners, they made it clear that they did not think that $4.25 for miners and $3.75 for shovelers and car men was a "just and fair wage," whether it was under present conditions or any other conditions.

Miners had been earning $5.50 per shift and shovelers $4.25 per shift during 1920, so the union had a solid argument against a wage cut. Although the Empire Mine had a bullion production of $1,697,929 and a profit of $704,179,[15] George Starr and F. W. Nobs managed to convince the union that a cut in wages was necessary. The final outcome resulted in a daily wage of $4.25 for miners and $3.75 for shovelers.[16]

As the summer of 1921 moved from one hot day to another in Grass Valley, the Bourns traveled to the Empire Mine, where they were met with joy by Katie Moriarity. Katie loved to have the Bourns visit the Cottage, and she was ready to prepare their favorite dishes and cook great dinners. But on August 8, 1921, summer became a winter of despair for the Bourns. That day, sixty-four-year-old Will suffered a stroke, and all his vitality was sapped. By the time Agnes and the servants got him back to Filoli, he had to be carried to his room, where he was put under the care of Dr. Herbert Moffitt of the University of California Medical School in San Francisco and Dr. Walter C. Chidester of San Mateo.[17]

Agnes relied upon Sam Eastman to notify Maud and Arthur and make arrangements for them to come to Filoli. On August 15, 1921, Eastman sent a night lettergram to Bourn's New York broker, James Laidlaw, alerting

Laidlaw about what he called Bourn's "nervous breakdown." In addition, he called upon Laidlaw to meet the Vincent party and make arrangements for them. He wrote: "Mr. and Mrs. Vincent, two children, woman companion and maid will arrive New York August twenty-sixth on *Adriatic.* As they probably will remain in New York only one or two days, Mrs. Bourn will greatly appreciate it if you will have someone meet them on arrival *Adriatic.* Also, will you have drawing room and two adjoining compartments engaged New York to San Francisco covering dates of August twenty-seventh and twenty-eighth. I will keep you advised of Mr. Bourn's progress." [18]

What Eastman did not know was that the Vincent party coming from Muckross was even larger. Along with Arthur, Maud, young Billy and Rosie, there were Arthur's sister, Rosemary Vincent, and Ida Bourn, who was visiting at Muckross when the news of Will's stroke arrived.[19] All were headed for Filoli, and they were worried that Will might die before they arrived.

The family gathered around Will, who truly needed their support. It was very difficult for this proud man, who had been the strong one for all the family for many years. Now he was confined to a wheelchair, his arms and hands made gross movements when he used them, and his speech was slurred. Worst of all, he continued to suffer periodic minor strokes. In a way, the stroke he had suffered at the Empire Cottage was like a major bodyquake. Now, he suffered smaller strokes that were much like the equivalent of aftershocks following a major earthquake.

It upset Will emotionally to have to rely upon others, but it was necessary to have a staff of nurses who tended him around the clock. Two female nurses, Lillian Carlson who worked the night shift and Marie Dunlevy who worked the day shift, lived in the gardener's cottage. A male nurse who worked the day shift but was on call if Will had to be lifted from his bed lived in an upstairs bedroom in Filoli. The male nurse who was with Bourn the longest was George I. Mathisen, but he did not come to work until 1924. From 1921 to 1924 the male nurse who took care of Will was Louie, a Belgian who left the Bourns to become a bootlegger in the area.[20]

Will's physicians also had their scheduled visits. From time to time, Dr. Herbert Moffitt drove down from San Francisco to examine his patient and talk to him, while Dr. Walter Chidester made house calls during the week from the Mills Memorial Hospital in San Mateo. Will's physical condition was extremely difficult for this proud man to bear, and he hated to have anybody see him in bed or in his wheelchair except for those who were very close to him and the nurses who took care of him.

In these first months of his invalid state, Will enjoyed the company of his daughter, Maud, and he liked the lively presence of his grandchildren, two-year-old Billy and six-year-old Rosie. Will relied upon Sam Eastman, who handled the affairs of the Spring Valley Water Company, and business at the Empire Mine continued as usual under the direction of cousin George Starr and his assistant F. W. Nobs. Despite Will's physical handicaps, his mind functioned with its usual brilliance, and he insisted upon keeping up with his business activities. He dictated letters, and he even tried to write them in a scrawl that resembled the first writing efforts of a child. In such attempts he used a pencil. He also had a stamp with the label P.E.P. PLEASE EXCUSE PENCIL, which he applied to an ink pad and then stamped his letters and notes.[21] Among all who encouraged and helped Will in every way possible, it was Agnes who shouldered the greatest emotional and intellectual load, for she stepped into the gap and saw to Will's needs, and in addition she ran Filoli with a sure hand.

4 Before Christmas at Filoli in 1921, good news from Ireland cheered the Bourns and Vincents. On December 6, Britain and Ireland signed a treaty that ended the war. Although hostilities dragged on as a result of Eamon de Valera's refusal to accept the treaty, on December 14, 1921, the Dail met and began the debate on the articles of the treaty. By January 7, 1922, the articles were approved by a vote of 64 to 57. At this, de Valera resigned his position as Ireland's president, and Arthur Griffith was elected in his place.[22] Although Ireland's problems were not solved, the coming of peace to Ireland brightened the New Year at Filoli.

But another event on February 27, 1922, came as a shock to the Bourns. That day, Will's cousin William Bowers Bourn Ingalls died in San Francisco at age sixty-eight. For Will, this was a sad time. Willie Ingalls had been a close companion since that long-ago summer of 1865, when they traveled to the New Almadén Mine beyond San Jose to see the mining of quicksilver and later to White Sulphur Springs and then on to Calistoga. That had been a wonderful summer of boyhood pleasures, and now, as Will sat in his wheelchair, the people who had made that time so happy were all gone. His last tie to that time of innocence was now to be buried.

Even as Will thought about the good times that he and Willie Ingalls had enjoyed, business intruded. Eastman let Will know that once again the rent on the Spring Valley headquarters at 375 Sutter Street was going up, this time being doubled from $1,000 to $2,000 per month. Will thought this was outrageous and told Eastman to seek out new quarters for the company. After some consideration of possible rental sites, Bourn and Eastman agreed to move the Spring Valley headquarters into the Hobart Building at 582 Market Street between Montgomery Street and Sansome Street. However, this was to be a temporary location, because Will decided that it was time to find a San Francisco location for their own office building. Before the end of the year, a site was purchased, and excavations for the Spring Valley Building began at 425 Mason Street. Willis Polk agreed to be the architect for the firm's headquarters.[23]

At the beginning of the spring of 1922, Maud and Rosie headed directly to Europe. Maud intended to take her daughter to Paris and then journey to Italy to introduce her to the classical art of that nation's great cities.

Meanwhile, for young Billy that summer at Filoli was one of great joy. He celebrated his third birthday with a grand cake that Alma had baked, and he watched the field hands at work on Filoli's farm. He was taken for cart rides and was in a child's wonderland as he explored the great house and wandered as far into the garden as a three-year-old could.

In September, Will, Agnes, and young Billy traveled to Grass Valley, where they stayed in the Empire Cottage. This was a break away from confinement for Will, and though he was not able to get around without help, he enjoyed the warmth of the late summer. For grandson Billy, the greatest joy of this time was watching the night watchman–beekeeper work with his bees.

By this time, Will's downstairs study—just off the living room—had been converted into a combination bedroom and bathroom so he could remain on the main floor and not have to be carried upstairs to the bedroom area. He could hear the steady sound of the stamp mill, which was like a great drumbeat that carried with it memories of his years at the Empire Mine. The gold mine inherited from his father had been his first great challenge, when he was told that the mine's gold-producing days had ended. Then he and George Starr had proved the so-called experts wrong. Now, after all these years, the mine had reached a depth of 5,800 feet on the incline; by the end of 1922, it was to show a gross profit of more than one half-million dollars.[24]

Will was visited by old friends and by cousin George Starr, who described the work in the mine at the deep level of almost 6,000 feet. He was also happy to be around Katie, who was as jolly as ever and whose cooking brought back memories of those long-ago summers when she had seen to the great appetites of Will and his many mining friends from Grass Valley and elsewhere. But as the last warmth of September gave way to the coming of autumn, Will suffered more and more small strokes. Then, on October 5, 1922, he had another major stroke. Aided by servants and friends, Agnes, Billy, and Will were driven to Colfax where they caught the train. Word of his coming was relayed to Sam Eastman and to Filoli so that everyone would be prepared for Will's arrival.

5 By the beginning of 1923, Will's poor health severely limited his activities. In January, Samuel P. Eastman became the president of the Spring Valley Water Company. Along with running the water company, he kept Will informed about other business activities and helped the family in many ways during these trying times.

On January 23, 1923, Eastman was faced with the task of replacing Dr. Walter C. Chidester, because Will's immediate physician was not well and announced that he was going to take an extended sea voyage to recapture his strength. At Chidester's suggestion, he was replaced during this time by Dr. Howard Mawdsley. Although young Dr. Mawdsley made house calls at Filoli, he was never comfortable around Will. To Mawdsley, a native of Iowa, Will retained a commanding presence, even though he was confined to his bed or his wheelchair. This, along with the splendor of Filoli, contributed to Mawdsley's uneasiness whenever he made visits. Somehow the good doctor was never able to get beyond what he perceived as Will's gruff exterior. Still, he took good care of Bourn despite his own nervousness.[25]

During the winter and spring of 1923, Will's health was a daily concern for Agnes. Some days he seemed to be improving, and his vitality showed signs of increasing. But just as Agnes was ready to cheer, Will would take a downward turn. These were difficult times for the Bourns, and they became even harder when Maud, Elizabeth Rose, and Billy returned to Muckross at the end of March.

In the early fall, the Bourns tried to recapture something of their way of life before Will's illness. Their chauffeur took them on a driving trip to Monterey, Carmel, and Pebble Beach. While there, they purchased an acre lot at Pebble Beach for Maud. As Agnes later wrote, they wanted Maud to have a place of her own in California. This gave them something to think about other than Will's condition and Agnes's own health—she was suffering from diabetes and was receiving insulin shots.

On November 11, 1923, Maud and the grandchildren arrived in New York after an Atlantic crossing aboard the *Rotterdam.* When they reached Filoli, the holiday season was about to begin. Maud and the children brought joy to the house, and everybody looked forward to Thanksgiving and then Christmas when they would have a huge tree in the rather bare-looking ballroom. With the tree all decorated and a blazing fire in the great fireplace, the family would be able to celebrate as the children opened their gifts.

By the beginning of 1924, Maud, Arthur, and the children were living in the Robert Coleman residence, Glasenwood, in Burlingame, which Maud had rented for eighteen months. Along with the house, the Vincents acquired a staff of Chinese servants and gardeners who worked for the Colemans. There was ample room at Filoli for the Vincent family, but Maud had decided that Filoli was too isolated for any schooling she might want to arrange for the children. Most of all, she believed it would be better for her family if they could lead a more normal existence. Even so, they were close to Filoli, and both families were able to see each other very easily. At this time, Arthur was having back trouble and was under the care of Dr. Baldwin, a bone specialist. Vincent's back had been bothering him for some time, and now he had to remain in bed and not do anything to cause strain.[26]

Meanwhile, Maud was busy with plans for a home to be built on her Pebble Beach property. Her architect was George Washington Smith of Santa Barbara. Working with Maud, he drew up plans for a Spanish-style house with a patio, loggia, and a terrace right above the beach and the line of breakers rolling in from the Pacific. Even its name, "Asilo de la Estrella" or Shelter of the Star, carried a Spanish flavor that suited the location overlooking Monterey Bay.[27]

Life at Filoli began to assume a more normal routine, with the joy of having Maud and the grandchildren nearby. But this interlude of happiness was interrupted by a family tragedy on the 26th of February. After a grand lunch, seventy-six-year-old James Ellis Tucker, Maye Bourn's husband, walked out the doors of the Pacific Union Club, tripped, and fell down the long flight of stairs to the sidewalk. By the time his companions reached him, Tucker was dead. The genial clubman, who had fought through many Civil War battles, including Pickett's Charge, and had witnessed General

Robert E. Lee's surrender at Appomattox, was well liked by all who knew him. Will, who liked Tucker very much and enjoyed his company, was deeply saddened by his death. This was the case with everyone who knew Tucker, and his passing received a big write-up in all the San Francisco newspapers. The *Argonaut* described his Civil War career in detail and gave an account of his presence in Mexico at the time of Emperor Maximilian's execution. There, Tucker and many other southern soldiers had found employment and protection after the Civil War. The newspaper account of Tucker's life noted that he had arrived in California on Christmas Day, 1869, in company with Jefferson Howell, a brother of Mrs. Jefferson Davis. The obituary ended by noting that James Ellis Tucker had been a member of the Pacific Union Club for fifty years.[28]

Two months after Tucker's death, Will pulled himself away from thoughts of death and memories of other times. Agnes had told him that she was in touch with the Peixottos, and Will suggested that she write to Ernest and ask if he would consider doing some paintings of Muckross for the ballroom at Filoli. In an April letter to Ernest Peixotto, Agnes indicated that nothing had been done to the room but that Will wanted him to give an approximate idea of how much such a commission would cost. Then Agnes described the room as follows:

> The room is Georgian in its treatment. About 35 ft × 70 ft and 25 ft in height. Two sides have 3 large windows and the end of the room opposite the fireplace entirely taken up by architectural treatment of windows and doors. On each side asymmetrical panels quite large and two smaller ones, and the over mantel and over doors on the end. . . . It would mean as well as the panels the doing of the entire room. Mantel—fixtures—painting etc. I could have photographs taken and the exact measurements. I believe we must have the working plans. I will look and send them on if I can find them.[29]

In the same letter, Agnes asked Peixotto if he would consider meeting their nephew Francis Bourn Hayne,[30] a young Harvard student who was planning a career in architecture and would be in Paris that same summer as the Peixottos. She implied that both she and Will were fond of his nephew and wished the best for him. In closing, Agnes wrote about Will's health and stated that "he is wonderful in his patience and courage and thoughts of others, and he deserves to attain the ability to lead a normal home life."

In the spring of 1924, Arthur Vincent left for Muckross. He said farewell to Maud and the children, caught the train to New York, and on Thursday, April 16, 1924, sailed for home aboard the *Olympic.* Meanwhile, Agnes was not long in receiving an answering letter from Ernest Peixotto regarding the panels for the ballroom. She told Will that Ernest had written: "What a perfectly bully idea Mr. Bourn has had to bring the beauties of Muckross to Filoli."[31]

Peixotto indicated that he would travel to Muckross to make sketches for the panels, then come to Filoli in September or October to submit the sketches to the Bourns. He then went on to answer Will's question of approximately how much all this would cost.

> This, as you realize, is very difficult to give as I don't know the exact number nor the size of the panels. But from what you say in your letter, I should say that I could do a very handsome series of large decorative paintings for the entire room for $25,000. If this sum is more than you intended, do not hesitate to say so. Let me know what you feel prepared to pay, for the scheme could be adjusted and the truth of its worth is that there is nothing I would like better than to do this work for Mr. Bourn.[32]

In the summer of 1924, Maud took Billy and Elizabeth Rose to the Empire Cottage at Grass Valley, where they spent July and August in the heat of the Sierra foothills. To young Billy, who celebrated his fifth birthday at the Empire Cottage, this was a splendid summer. The noise of the stamp mill was music to a young boy's ears, and the coming and going of miners who went down into the depths on the man-cars that rushed deep into the earth and came to a halt 6,200 feet below the surface and 390 feet below sea level was like watching the first big dip of a roller coaster. But in later years, he was to remember that one of his favorite entertainments at the mine was sailing toy boats on the milk-colored water of Lake Biddle. This reservoir contained the liquid residue from the cyanide plant that removed gold from the stamp mill tailings, which at this time included ore from both the Empire and Pennsylvania mines.[33]

In August, Will was homesick for the old days when he could catch the train to Auburn or Colfax and then be picked up by a driver and ride to the Empire Mine. Now, as he rested in his wicker wheelchair, he could only remember what those days were like. This summer with his daughter and grandchildren spending two months at the Empire Cottage, Will's memories were so much with him that he took time to examine a map of the Empire Mine. Then he sent a memo to Sam Eastman that the following names needed to be added to the map: "Woodpecker Ravine by Lake Biddle (the tailings dump); Pine Porches (F. W. Nobs' house); Ophir Cottage (George Starr's home); Empire Cottage; Club House; Cedar Office (watchman's); Old Office (O'Leary); Tramway to the Pennsylvania Mine; Empire Office; Orleans Hill; Mark Twain highway to Auburn; Bret Harte Inn; Memorial Park."[34]

As September began, Will and Agnes were stunned by the death of Willis Polk at fifty-seven. Will was deeply saddened by the news of his friend's passing. Agnes also felt Willis's loss, and in a September letter to Ernest Peixotto she expressed how she and Will felt: "The news of Willis's death I know you will be sorry to learn—his great gifts—and personal charm are a loss, but the old boyish affection and happy times you all had together are only a memory now. Will always held him in deep affection. The protective love of an elder brother.[35]

A month later, on October 16, 1924, Ernest Peixotto signed a contract to do the panels for the ballroom at Filoli. He also agreed to provide general supervision for the decoration of the room as well as for its furnishings. His fee was accepted as $25,000, and the contract stipulated that he was to receive 10 percent upon acceptance of his designs; 25 percent on January 15, 1925; 25 percent on July 15, 1925, and the balance upon completion of the work. The contract was signed by Peixotto, Agnes Bourn as president of the Filoli Estate, and F. S. Markey, secretary of the Filoli Estate.[36]

While things progressed toward the ultimate completion of Filoli's ballroom, Will decided to sell one of his ranches that had never been profitable. Though he had put his brother-in-law, William Alston Hayne, in charge of it, the San Luis Obispo Ranch was a bad investment. He moved Hayne to another ranch he owned four miles north of Marysville in the Sacramento Valley. This was another of Bourn's attempts to help his sister Maud, but though Hayne was a hard worker and tried his best, he was not successful as a rancher. Worst of all, Maud never lived with him at these ranches. At best, she would visit, but even when she tried to fit into the role of the rancher's wife, she was not successful. She was not a cook, and during one visit to the new ranch outside Marysville, she put together a meal for the ranch hands, but all it consisted of was a salad. Seeing this, the workers threatened to quit if this was the kind of fare they were going to be served.[37]

Will sold the San Luis Obispo Ranch for $16,000 on November 25, 1924. But this was a minor property transaction compared to Will's planned purchase of the Bourn Block in San Francisco. At one time, this property, which was bounded by Market, Pine, and Front Streets, had belonged to his father. However, the senior Bourn had lost title to the land when he borrowed money against it to develop the Empire Mine and then neglected to pay the mortgage. Now, Will entered into the process of buying back this block at a cost of more than one million dollars.[38]

Will's reasons for acquiring this triangular block from the heirs of Robert Sherwood were two-fold. He wanted to reclaim what had belonged to his father, and he wanted to tear down the nondescript buildings that occupied two of the property's three lots. Like other San Francisco capitalists of his day, he wanted to build a large structure that would bear his name, and he hired Arthur Brown Jr. to design a grand building. The plan showed a seven-story triangular base topped by a thirty-one-story pentagonal tower featuring an elaborate, sculptured top resembling a crown.[39]

Though confined to his wheelchair, Will never stopped planning for the future. Even as 1924 came to an end, he was involved in plans for the Bourn Block; he kept Agnes busy with their ideas for the ballroom at Filoli; he was in regular contact with Sam Eastman regarding Spring Valley, including additional work on the Calaveras Dam; and he was in contact on a regular basis with George Starr regarding the Empire Mine. As to the latter, the Annual Report for 1924 showed that the foothill sump cross-cut and the main north drift had reached the 6,200-foot level. Even at this depth, the mine showed a profit of $311,989.86 for the year. Added to this were profits from the Pennsylvania, Sultana, and other mining properties, as well as investment profits earned by the Empire Mines and Investment Company. The total profit for stockholders in 1924 came to $1,069,695.81.[40]

6 In January 1925, Agnes Bourn wrote to Ernest Pexiotto and told him about Maud's Pebble Beach home. She wrote: "It already has a look of having been lived in for a long while. Only the patio of course will take a year or so to get things growing."[41] At this time, the children were at home, and Maud talked to her mother of her forthcoming departure. She planned to sail aboard the *Olympic* from New York in March and return to Muckross and remain there during the good weather. Agnes and Maud also discussed the ballroom at Filoli, and Agnes hoped Maud would be able to join Ernest Peixotto in Paris and look at the lighting fixtures for the ballroom.

Two months later, Agnes heard from Peixotto, who had looked at lighting fixtures and other furnishings at Bagues, Incorporated, in Paris. He was shown four chandeliers made for the Galerie des Glaces in Versailles. He liked what he saw, and after Maud saw them, two of the chandeliers were ordered.

By July 23, 1925, an order of confirmation was sent from Bagues to Mrs. William B. Bourn, Filoli House, San Mateo. Within this form were listed the following items:

2 chandeliers of iron and crystal, Versailles Gallery model	Price $3,200
6 sconces, 9-light, bronze and crystal	Price $4,500
1 candelabra and 1 centerpiece	Price $3,000
1 mantelpiece, marble and bronze, Versailles Hercules Salon model, reduced in size	Price $6,000

Total order amount: $16,700

The above sum covering the merchandise delivered in San Francisco, all expenses included. Transportation from San Francisco to San Mateo is the responsibility of the buyer.

Rob. J. Bagues, President[42]

A month later, an annoying echo was discovered in the ballroom. Bruce Porter and Gardner Dailey worked at finding a way to get rid of it. On September 1, 1925, Porter wrote to Peixotto about it: "It lies in the ceiling, and runs like a mouse under the cove over the cornice and quite around the room. The window hangings will not correct it—we've proved—and after experts and amateurs—we've concluded that the ceiling must be replastered with absorbent 'Sabinile'—and the best estimate is that that will reduce the echo 60%."[43]

In October, Agnes and Will decided to have their chauffeur, James Lowrie,[44] drive them to Maud's "Asilo de la Estrella" at Pebble Beach. This was a shorter visit than they had planned, because Will could not stand the cold wind blowing off the Pacific. Even so, they were gone long enough to miss Ernest and Mary Peixotto, who had been at Filoli to install the Muckross murals in the ballroom.

Upon seeing the murals, the Bourns were overjoyed. Although the ballroom was still not finished, they were beginning to see the final pieces fall into place for the planned grandeur of Filoli.

On the last day of October 1925, Agnes wrote to Ernest Peixotto and expressed her joy about the murals. At last, the ballroom was nearing what she and Will had hoped to see:

> Your lovely murals have given the room something, it did not have in its nudity, in the proportions. They are so satisfying that I can't imagine anything better. I wish Willis might have seen it finished—when it is that. I don't know whether I shall be quite able to understand it is ours. There is something about it that is as though a most wonderful dream had come true. Yesterday afternoon Mary Hallock Foote came over. . . . And when she went in she shouted, "Oh, I could roll on the floor, it is so lovely"—rather a strange way to express it, but she was, as it were "carried off her feet" in the surprize and delight of it. And she . . . a little Quaker . . . replete with the vivacity of youth (though 77 years) and the joy in all that is aesthetic and beautiful.[45]

At the end of November 1925, the lighting fixtures arrived from Paris. As workmen hired by Gardner Dailey entered into the space between the inner and outer walls of the ballroom, they found the steel and wooden beams across the ceiling the strongest they had ever seen. Any concern about hanging the chandeliers vanished when the men found the tremendous beams that Willis Polk had included in his design of Filoli.

A month later, Agnes sent a Christmas letter to the Peixottos in which she wrote of an evening she had enjoyed in the ballroom with a Mr. and Mrs. Fiske. They sat and listened to the "Victrola for an hour and a half—and found the blue lights very restful and sympathetic with the music. A big fire so cheery and carpeting—a rug spread at one side and with agreeable chairs. It was a most enjoyable little concert. The acoustics are perfect."[46]

To Ernest Peixotto, the statement about the acoustics must have come as a relief. Bruce Porter and Gardner Dailey had worked long hours to solve the problem of the echo in the ballroom, and Ernest had contributed his own suggestions. Now, in this letter from Agnes Bourn came the proof of what they had all hoped to accomplish when they had set out to squelch the mysterious echo.

Throughout the first seven months of 1926, the finishing touches for the ballroom at Filoli continued. On April 24, 1926, Agnes telegraphed Peixotto that Bagues of Paris had sent the fireplace mantel, and though she found it superb she thought it "necessitates slight warming of tone of woodwork perhaps some enrichment."[47] In addition, she let him know that the fireplace needed a fireback and andirons.

On September 26, 1926, Agnes wrote to Peixotto in Paris to let him know that the fireback and andirons had arrived and that she was quite pleased with them. She also informed him that Maud had cabled her from Paris to let her know that the material for the curtains had been shipped.[48] Even as the ballroom at Filoli neared completion, Agnes continued to think of other things that might be needed. It was as though she feared that the completion of the ballroom would leave Will and her without a project that they could focus their attention on.

Meanwhile, Maud and the grandchildren set sail aboard the *Majestic* to return to the United States. At the same time, Arthur Vincent was sailing aboard a yacht with the Loefflers, a Swedish family. Their voyage would take them down the west coast of Africa past the Canary and Cape Verde Islands and then west across the Atlantic. As Agnes wrote in her letter to Peixotto, Arthur and his friends planned to visit the West Indies and Central American ports, go tarpon fishing, and sail to Palm Beach, Florida. "Sounds most interesting and delightful," Agnes wrote, "a dream he has long had—but we shall miss him at Christmas for I don't suppose they will arrive here before January or February."[49]

Maud, Elizabeth Rose, and Billy arrived at Filoli in the late fall of 1926, and they stayed with Agnes and Will for a month. This was a time of celebration, and they enjoyed both Thanksgiving and Christmas at Filoli. This was Maud's first chance to see the completed murals of Muckross in the ballroom, and she thought they gave the room a splendid finishing touch. For eight-year-old Billy, one of his greatest joys was being able to ride his pony, Winona.

Christmas was very special at Filoli, and Alma Johnson and her kitchen staff prepared wonderful dishes for the feast of celebration. But the exciting time for the children came in the ballroom. Near the center of the room was a tall, beautifully decorated Christmas tree, and beneath its lower boughs were brightly wrapped gifts that circled its base.

After a month's stay at Filoli, Maud rented a home in Burlingame and hired a Miss Vaisey as governess for the children. This arrangement allowed Maud to be in close touch with her mother and father, while at the same time she was able to give the children a more normal sense of home. By early March 1927, Arthur Vincent and the beautiful Mrs. Loeffler arrived by train from Florida after a long, enjoyable cruise. Arthur regaled the family with stories of his adventures, descriptions of ports of call, and tales of great fishing.

It was very satisfying to Agnes and Will to have all the family nearby, and it gave them an opportunity to see them often. To young Billy, the endless days were filled with wonder. In early summer he watched the Italian farmhands of Filoli cut and bale hay for storage in the large barn, and he saw his grandfather carried downstairs, put in his wheelchair, and then pushed to a favorite spot in the gardens, such as Yew Allee, where he was surrounded by a cagelike framework of netting to protect him from insects. The Vincents also made automobile trips to "Asilo de la Estrella" at Pebble Beach. Here, Billy and Rosie walked on the white sandy beach, watched the breakers roll in and crash, and heard the barking of sea lions from rocky promontories that jutted into the Pacific Ocean. That summer they spent the warm days of July to September at the Empire Cottage.

By October, Arthur had run into his usual passport problem, which never gave him enough time in the United States. He said farewell to the family, told them he would return as soon as possible, and headed home to Ireland.

As 1927 neared an end, Will received the annual report from the Empire Mines and Investment Company. While the mining profit was down to $133,214.40, operating expenses for the year had come to $845,293.38. Costs ran high because of the new depth reached in the mine. The main shaft had been increased by 573 feet, "reaching the 7,000′ level at 928 feet below sea level, with 80 feet of sump below. The 7,000 foot station was cut with 97 feet of hanging wall crosscut and levels were turned north and south."[50]

Working at such depths presented many problems, but the hardest to deal with was the steady flow of underground water, which required constant pumping to the surface in order to keep the working area dry enough for the miners. At this depth, the "7,000 foot south drift was extended 221 feet. The vein, although much shattered and varying from 35 to 65 degrees in dip carries scattered lenses of very good grade ore highly mineralized with galena, iron sulphides and a little zinc blende. The best of the lenses is 15 feet long and 12 inches average width and assays $70.50 per ton in gold."[51]

To Will, this was incredible news. At this depth, and after all these years, the major source of the Bourn family's wealth was continuing to produce. The very mine he had rescued from an ill-advised sale, the mine he and cousin George Starr had full faith in, continued to be an astounding producer of gold. It was without doubt the greatest gold mine in the Grass Valley region.

After the beginning of 1928, time seemed to speed up, and almost before Will and Agnes were prepared for it, Maud and the children departed for Europe. It was hard for Agnes and Will to see their daughter and grandchildren leave again, because they had grown accustomed to having them nearby, but Maud wanted to bring some sense of permanency into their lives. With this in mind, they crossed the United States again and set sail for London.

In London the family parted company again. Arthur and Billy traveled home to Muckross, while Maud and Elizabeth Rose headed for Paris. Agnes had not been back to Europe and Ireland since 1921, and she decided that Will would be able to get along without her if she made a short trip. So mother and daughter agreed to meet in Paris in June. They enjoyed their time there, and Maud and Agnes visited Bagues and other shops to search for additional pieces of furniture for Filoli. When they were through with their Paris vacation, they traveled home to Muckross.

While all this took place, Will began to feel depressed, lonely, and trapped at Filoli. In his memory, he could picture London and Paris, and he wished he could be there. Most of all, he missed the lakes of Killarney and the brilliant green grass on the hills and meadows around Muckross. Something of these feelings came out in a letter that he wrote to Maud and Arthur in late July:

> Cricket mine and Arthur dear, someday show this to Mother, and all be guided by my wishes, which are wise and for the best.
>
> Wind up Empire Mines & Investment Company distributing assets to shareholders as at present outlined and in process of accomplishments, so I am told.
>
> Follow similar proceedings with The Filoli Estate (incorporated), have this company also wound up. All stock belongs to Mother and myself. Sell all real estate, furniture, etc. to Mother, and everything else divide up.
>
> *Get out of business,* and place affairs with Trust companies, so you will have your income and live within your income, putting aside each year a sum for charity, welfare, contingencies, etc.
>
> God bless us all.[52]

Before 1928 came to an end, Will began the process of selling pieces of his holdings. It was as though he were listening to the advice he had given Maud and Arthur. At this time, the Lake Merced lots were sold. Altogether, there were 196 lots that covered 45.75 acres. In the sale, this prime real estate brought a net profit of $325,794.31.[53]

Even as this real estate was sold, Will was aware of the declining profits at the Empire Mine. He had been informed by George Starr that the Annual Report for The Empire Mines for 1928 would show only a gross profit of $121,023.00,[54] and this was not a high enough return to risk further venture capital outlay. For at the 7,000-foot level, neither Starr nor Bourn believed they could expect a yearly return worth the high operating expenses.

In December 1928, Will's health took a turn for the worse. His doctors told Agnes that they were not certain they could save him. Upon hearing this, she began sending a series of telegrams to Maud and Arthur to keep them apprised of Will's condition.

During this period, the Vincents were spending some time at Cannes, France, where they often went to escape the cold winter months at Muckross. As each telegram seemed to report a worsening of her father's condition, Maud decided that she and the children had to return to Filoli to be with her parents at this crucial time. She told Arthur there was no need for him to make the trip and that he should go home to Muckross to look after things during her absence.

In the middle of January 1929, Maud, Elizabeth Rose, Billy, and the children's maid, Annie Doody, booked passage to New York on the *Majestic.* During this winter crossing of the Atlantic, Maud developed a severe case of pneumonia. Upon arrival in New York, she entered a hospital, and the children and their maid were cared for by Mrs. Elizabeth Reid, Billy's godmother and the widow of Whitelaw Reid, publisher of the *New York Tribune.* Elizabeth Reid, the daughter of Darius Ogden Mills of Millbrae, was a friend of Agnes and Will.

When Arthur received Maud's cablegram from the *Majestic* about her condition, he hurried from Muckross to England, where he managed to sail on the *Mauretania,* one of the fastest steamers in the Atlantic trade. Despite his efforts to get to Maud's bedside as quickly as possible, he did not arrive until February 10. On February 12, 1929, Maud Bourn Vincent died.[55]

Already aware of Maud's condition, the Bourns were devastated when they received news of her death. Still, Agnes did not allow herself time to grieve. There were too many things that needed her attention, and she called upon Sam Eastman of the water company to prepare a family cemetery. A five-acre site was chosen on a bare knoll west of Filoli. The area was cleared of brush—at this time trees had not grown back in this logged area—and a road was graded to allow automobiles to drive to the cemetery.

As all this took place at Filoli, Arthur Vincent leased a private railroad car for the grieving family. After a sad farewell to friends and relatives, the funeral party boarded the train. Along with Arthur and the two children and their maid, Horace Moody, Agnes's nephew, joined the family. A nurse came aboard to ride with the coffin as the train crossed the country.[56]

The train pulled out of New York on February 13, 1929. It arrived in Chicago on Valentine's Day—ironically, the day that Al Capone's gangsters massacred rival bootleggers. The next day, the train was in Nebraska, and the day after it pulled into the depot at Ogden, Utah. During the days and nights of February 17 and 18, the train crossed the Great Salt Lake, the Great Basin, and then climbed over the Sierra Nevada.

In the early morning hours of February 18, the train rolled across the Sacramento Valley, down the East Bay shoreline, south into the Santa Clara Valley to San Jose, and then up the Peninsula south of San Francisco. It pulled into the Belmont Station in San Mateo County at 10:00 A.M.

Here they were met by Edward Eyre, one of Will's best friends and vice-president of the Spring Valley Water Company. He had brought a limousine for the family and the others, and there was a hearse to carry Maud's coffin on her last ride to Filoli.[57]

Funeral services for Maud took place before the day ended. Beautiful flowers of the season surrounded the coffin, and there were wreaths and flowers of remembrance throughout the room. The eulogy was delivered by Reverend Cambridge of St. Matthew's Episcopal Church in San Mateo, the church where Maud and Arthur had been married. The gathering for the last goodbye to Maud included Arthur; the grandchildren (Elizabeth Rose and Billy); the grieving Agnes Bourn; Horace Moody; Will's sisters Ida Bourn, Maye Bourn Tucker, and Maud Bourn Hayne; and Mr. and Mrs. William Alston Hayne. Other friends who came to Maud's funeral were the W. H. Crocker family, Mr. and Mrs. Samuel P. Eastman, Mr. and Mrs. George Starr, Edward L. Eyre, Miss Emmy Tobey from the water company's San Francisco office, Mr. and Mrs. Rostaghini, who took care of Maud's Pebble Beach home, and all the servants and other employees of Filoli.[58]

Grief-stricken and ill, Will was not able to attend the services and remained in his room upstairs. After the last farewells, the family and friends accompanied the casket to the grave site in the new cemetery, where they bowed their heads after the graveside services and Reverend Cambridge delivered a final prayer. Then Maud Bourn Vincent, who was only forty-six, was laid to rest on the barren knoll overlooking Filoli to the east and the Crystal Springs and San Andreas reservoirs to the north.

Maud's death was almost more than Will could bear. He blamed himself, for if he had not been ill, there would have been no reason for Maud to make a winter voyage.

Now Will began to turn inward and thought about his own death more and more. He began to think about the fortune he had accumulated and the many years he had devoted to the Empire Mine and the Spring Valley Water Company. His zest for running these businesses was no longer with him, and he began to consider selling them. What constantly ran through his thoughts was the idea of his own mortality and the need to get his financial house in order. He wanted to be sure that Agnes, his grandchildren, and his sisters would be left with an inheritance that would not require knowledge of business.

As Will turned inward, Agnes became stronger, for she had a vacant feeling that had to be filled. She and her daughter had been very close. Their relationship had not been the typical mother-and-daughter affair with many stormy periods. They had enjoyed each other's company, and Agnes knew that she would never feel whole again, now that Maud was gone. The saving factor for Agnes was the presence of Elizabeth Rose and Billy. Arthur had decided to remain at Filoli until September, when he once again would have to return to Ireland. There were many loose ends to clear up associated with his and Maud's finances. At the same time, he worked on Spring Valley problems, because the company appeared to be nearing a time when the City of San Francisco would buy it. During this time, Vincent commuted by train to the city, where he had an office at the water company's building at 425 Mason Street.[59]

While Arthur worked at clearing up loose ends and doing what he could for the water company, Agnes found a saving chore as she attended to her grandchildren's needs. Elizabeth Rose was enrolled in the prestigious Castilleja, a private school for girls that dated back to 1907. Each day Rosie was driven to and from this Palo Alto school by Tom Angus. At the same time, Billy was driven to and from the Shinn School, a private school in Hillsborough operated by Dora H. Shinn. On these rides, he was accompanied by his friend Jimmy Lowrie, the chauffeur's son, who attended the Hillsborough Public School.

It was during Billy's time at Miss Shinn's school that one of his schoolmates asked him about the man who lived in a cage at Filoli. When young Billy asked what the boy meant, he learned that he was referring to his grandfather. During Bourn's restful times in Filoli's gardens, he always had a tent of netting placed around and over him as he sat in his wheelchair. In this way, he was protected from flies, mosquitoes, and other insects as he looked at his surroundings.[60]

By this time in his life, Will had truly become a "man in a cage" in a way that went way beyond the boy's description. It had become difficult for him to speak clearly, and his attempts at writing notes or letters turned into childlike scrawls readable by very few persons. It was Sam Eastman who had the patience and ability to decipher Will's handwriting. Bourn's thoughts were trapped inside an almost useless body, and each day was a struggle for this proud man. Even so, he continued to concentrate upon a future he knew he would not see. Now, days and weeks were the measure of his existence, for he believed his time was running out. Illness and tragedy were foremost in the factors that motivated his plans. It was his desire to close the books on his business ventures, because he wanted to leave his wife, grandchildren, and sisters a guaranteed yearly income. To Will, this meant putting all assets into a trust so the fortune he had acquired would be protected from ill-advised business practices.

By February 1, 1929, an old drama in Bourn's business life began its last act when the City and County of San Francisco agreed to buy the facilities of the Spring Valley Water Company and form its own municipal water district. After all the years of court battles between Bourn and the city, after all the city's threats to condemn the water company lands and force a sale at a price it would dictate, San Francisco was about to realize its goal only because illness and tragedy had become determining factors in William Bourn's life.

The offering price that Will and the board members of the water company had agreed upon was $41,000,000. Though San Francisco would have to raise this money by passing a bond issue, this time there was little doubt of achieving this goal. It was a bargain price, for this included the entire Spring Valley Water Company's system. In addition to the pipelines, tanks, and pumps that formed the water distribution system within San Francisco, the offered properties included Lake Merced within San Francisco, and outside the county the reservoir system of Crystal Springs, San Andreas, Pilarcitos, and Searsville Lakes in San Mateo County and the Calaveras Dam in Alameda County. In addition to these storage facilities, the company also sold its pumping stations on both sides of the bay, the underwater pipelines that carried water beneath San Francisco Bay from Dumbarton Point in Alameda County to the Belmont Pumping Station in San Mateo County, and the Suñol Water Temple and filtering beds in Alameda County.

With the sale of the Spring Valley Water Company only awaiting passage of a bond issue by the voters of San Francisco, William Bourn moved quickly to sell the most personal enterprise in the history of his family. On March 1, 1929, he issued a strong suggestion that the days of the Empire Mine were limited. In the company's 1928 report, Bourn stated that the mine had not shown any improvement. In that same report, he wrote that the name and structure of the company were to be changed: "A new company formed by the Empire Mines and Investment Company, called The Empire Mines, has taken over all the mining property formerly owned by your company."[61] What Will had not indicated was that he intended to sell the company.

Two months later, Will completed a deal for the sale of the Empire Mine through Fred Searls Jr., a native of Grass Valley whom Will had known for many years, who was representing Colonel William Boyes Thompson, owner of the Newmont Mining Company. Early that spring, Will had notified Searls that he was ready to sell the mine. His asking price for the mine and all its buildings and equipment—not including the Cottage—was $250,000, less than the insured value of the Empire Mine's stamp mill. Searls jumped at this tremendous opportunity, and in a letter to Colonel Thompson he wrote: "We had to step quickly, because Billy Mein of San Francisco heard of the deal and immediately offered $300,000 cash. . . . We accepted and Bourn stuck by his offer. We incorporated in Delaware the 'Newmont Empire Mine Co.' to do business and put $150,000 working capital in its treasury and sent out a manager."[62]

Within this same letter, Searls wrote that Bourn was determined to sell the mine quickly, because his only daughter had died, his wife was not well, and he was an invalid. Bourn's misfortunes became the first part of good fortunes for the Newmont Mining Company. Once the sale of the Empire Mine was made public in San Francisco, the Newmont Mining Company was approached by the North Star Mine Company, which offered "to put their property and $150,000 working capital into a new company and take 40 percent of the shares."[63]

This was an unforeseen bit of luck, and the Newmont Mining Company jumped at this opportunity. With both the Empire Mine and the North Star Mine under its ownership, the Newmont Mining Company had the right to work ore shoots in both areas without worry about intruding upon mining claims owned by anybody else. By May 1, 1929, the new Empire Star Mines Company, Ltd., had 3,700 acres of mineral rights. They also were in a position to close the North Star's mill and cyanide plant and process all the ore from both mines using the Empire's machinery.

When Bourn learned of this combined operation, he must have had a sense of irony, for at different times he had been the owner of both mines but had not had the opportunity that the owners of the Empire-Star now enjoyed. This was the kind of operation Will would once have found challenging, but his days of mining glory were over. Now he was not building a future; instead, he was planning a proper ending.

Agnes also was concerned about winding up her earthly affairs. Her declining health forced her to take longer and longer periods of rest each day, and because she knew Will would not have sold both the Empire Mine and the water company if he were on the mend, she decided to plan for her own end. With Maud buried on the hill all by herself, Agnes decided it was time to bring her first-born child to the cemetery at Filoli. In the second week of May 1929, she wrote to Ida Bourn in San Francisco and asked her to help in the removal of her infant son from the Laurel Hill vault to a grave in the Filoli cemetery.[64]

The sadness of this time increased as the months of spring and summer passed and the September departure of Arthur and the grandchildren occurred. More than anything else, it had been the presence of Elizabeth Rose and Billy at Filoli during these months of grieving after Maud's death that had been a source of joy to Agnes and Will. Now, as the grandchildren boarded the train to travel across the United States to New York, where once again they were booked on the steamship *Olympic* to sail to England, the Bourns realized how much they had meant to them at this time.

As September 1929 came to an end, the Bourns were very lonely without the presence of their grandchildren. They heard from Arthur, who had returned to Muckross with Elizabeth Rose, and they learned that Billy had been enrolled in school at Dunchurch Hall near Rugby, England. At this time, Agnes contacted her attorney, and by September 17, 1929, she had drawn up her Last Will and Testament. Like Will, she was putting her house in order.

In October, Will dictated a letter to Judge Olney regarding the Filoli cemetery. He wrote: "We have consecrated a bit of ground, called God's Acre on the Hill. It is our family burial ground. Would it not be wise to deed God's Acre to Saint Matthews Church as I think the time will come when no one will care for it and all is now done with that in mind. If it could be made tax free I do not see how it is humanly possible to better protect it."[65]

By the end of 1929, the Bourns had come to terms with their own fragile lives, and they were dealing with the winding up of their earthly affairs. It was not something they talked about, but it was a final reality that they were taking steps to face.

7 Even though the stock market crash of 1929 made it difficult for the City and County of San Francisco to sell its bond issue and pay for the Spring Valley Water Company, it managed to raise the money. On March 3, 1930, the San Francisco Water Company moved into the Spring Valley building on Mason Street. A new era in the city's water system began with this change from a private to a municipal utility operation. It also ended a long struggle between William Bourn's Spring Valley Water Company and the government of San Francisco. Yet even with the acquisition of Spring Valley, the Hetch Hetchy project was not completed. It would not be until October 24, 1934, that water from the Hetch Hetchy system would flow into Crystal Springs Reservoir.

With both the Empire Mine and the Spring Valley Water Company sold, Will began to look at his other holdings with an eye to putting them in order so there would be no loose ends with regard to his financial holdings. By May 7, 1930, he changed the Filoli Estate into Filoli-Incorporated, a family holding company covering all the enterprises owned by the Bourns. This included all investments, all real properties such as Filoli, San Francisco real estate such as the Bourn Block, and agricultural holdings in the Delta and outside Marysville in the Sacramento Valley.[66]

This same year, Will and Agnes received disturbing news from Arthur Vincent, who informed them that grandson Billy had come down with rheumatic fever and was confined to bed. Worst of all, he often had to use a wheelchair.[67] To Will, this was a distressing report. He was extremely fond of his grandson, and it was hard for him to picture such an active and lively boy forced into bed rest and the use of a wheelchair.

Through the last months of 1930 and into 1931, worry about health haunted the Bourns. They had made great achievements during their lives, but now poor health seemed to be a reward for their success. Will was getting worse as the months and years passed; and now, in 1931, Agnes suffered a terrible stroke that left her unable to speak and confined to her bed or to a wheelchair.

When news of this new disaster at Filoli reached the relatives, Agnes's sister, Louise Moody,[68] and her grandniece, Virginia Blood, came from the East Coast to be with her at this crucial time in her life. What they encountered at Filoli was a very sad state of affairs. Will was beside himself with grief, and Agnes was being watched over by her physician and two nurses, E. B. Weiss and Ellen Meyer.

In this grand home that Will and Agnes had built with such care and vision, the upstairs had turned into an expensive hospital–nursing home. Even as the relatives sat with Agnes, they must have been keenly aware of how ironic life can be. This was a home built to entertain guests. It was to have been a happy combination of everything that cultured, monied people could bring to all the aspects of art that went into the building and interior furnishing of Filoli, and all that they could bring from the outside by their love and knowledge of the natural world. Yet only fourteen years after the Bourns had moved into Filoli, they had become prisoners inside their dream.

The only good news during 1931 came from Muckross. In April, Arthur Vincent was appointed to the Irish Free State Senate by W. T. Consgrave, the president of the Executive Council. Then in the fall of 1931, Vincent was re-elected for a full term of nine years.[69] Upon learning about this, Will and Agnes were happy for Arthur and the grandchildren.

Even so, as 1932 began, Will decided it was time to part with Muckross, because he believed he could no longer afford to contribute to the upkeep of the estate.This news came as a shock to Arthur Vincent, for it meant he was going to have to give up Muckross as his home. He understood Bourn's concern about money, but Arthur was extremely fond of Muckross. More than that, he had worked hard to ease the financial burden his father-in-law had to bear. Bourn's decision was difficult to understand, because it had been Bourn's wish that Arthur and Maud should live there and try to make a go of it. Now, after having called Muckross home for almost twenty-one years, Arthur and the grandchildren were being told—not asked—to leave their home.

Despite Arthur's attempts to get Bourn to change his mind, he was able to get him to agree to only one other possibility. This was to give Muckross and its eleven thousand acres to Ireland as a national park. Even though this would leave Vincent without a home, it was better than seeing the estate put up for sale.

One thing stood in the way of seeing Muckross become a park—the Irish government's reluctance to go along with this idea. Here, it was Arthur Vincent who had to convince the government of the Irish Free State to accept this gift from William Bowers Bourn and Arthur Rose Vincent "of the property commonly known as the Muckross Estate to the Nation for the purposes of a National Park."

The Bourn Vincent Memorial Park Bill of 1932 included an attempt to give employment preference to persons who had been working at Muckross at the time of the acceptance of the gift by the Irish Free State. Vincent also managed to include a price of eight thousand pounds to be paid for the purchase of the furniture and household goods; farming implements; boats and fishing gear; and all the livestock (cattle, horses, sheep, donkeys, etc.).[70]

By December 31, 1932, the Bourn Vincent Memorial Park Bill had been passed. The bill stated that the families had the right to erect a monument in memory of the late Maud Chase Bourn Vincent (however, this was never done). As of January 1, 1933, the ownership of Muckross changed hands. Arthur Vincent and his children no longer could claim this estate as their home, but Ireland now had a national park.

As 1933 began, Vincent found his world changed. He began to divide his time between Ireland and France. It was also during this year that he broke away from the loneliness of being a widower, and before the year ended he married Mrs. Dorothy Sands.

Even though Will and Agnes were largely confined to the upstairs part of Filoli, there were times when each was brought downstairs and outside to see the gardens from their wheelchairs. There were also infrequent parties given at Filoli for old friends of the Bourns. The hostess at such functions was often Will's sister Ida.

In celebration of the repeal of the Eighteenth Amendment, a grand party was given on November 24, 1933. The invitation featured a cartoonlike drawing of a balding, corpulent gentleman sitting next to a fireplace. Beside him, on a round table, were a bottle and glass. On the floor there were a keg, a bottle, a box of bottles, another keg with bottlelike legs and spigots, and in the background a coat rack with a coat and top hat. Blowing in the wind beside it were shreds of paper featuring "Happy Days Are Here Again." The invitation read as follows:

DRUNKS DINNER
Celebrating Repeal of Eighteenth Amendment
—Repeal But No Reform—
Will You Please Come To Dinner
At FILOLI HOUSE
November Twenty Fourth At Eight O'Clock
1933
—Mr. and Mrs. Bourn Being Sober Will Not Be Present—[71]

Twenty guests attended. Miss Ida Bourn was the toastmaster, and her sisters—Mrs. James Ellis Tucker and Mrs. William Alston Hayne—were seated at the big dining table. Before the first toast was drunk, the following poem by Bourn's nephew Francis Bourn Hayne was read to the guests:

Let us stand by our glasses and drink down a toast,
To that merry old soul, who in truth, is our host.
He's not with us in person, I want to speak true,
He's too bashful to drink with so boisterous a crew.
To his gay, giddy sisters he's given the task,
To see that you drain every drop from each flask.
There'er casks in the cellar, dust-covered and old,
And husky young footmen to refill the bowl.
Now Woods is at hand to replenish the wine,
And to see every want is fulfilled as you dine.
While out in the kitchen good Alma is there,
And her ovens give out sweet smells to the air.
So you handsome, old gallants who sit in a row,
What other fine blessings could Fortune bestow?
You've wine and fine victuals now at your command,
And a dazzling young lassie upon either hand.[72]

This was the way 1933 ended for Will and Agnes Bourn. It was a strange celebration with the hosts not in attendance. It was a happy time and a sad time. Good news had come from Ireland to announce the recovery of young

Billy Vincent, but the sad news was the farewell to Muckross. As the guests drank their toasts, as the waiters moved back and forth to bring one tasty dish after another from Alma's kitchen, and as the ever-proper Woods saw to the refilling of glasses, the Bourns of Filoli were at rest in their separate bedrooms. They were pleased that their guests were enjoying this celebration, because Will and Agnes had considered Prohibition a law that intruded upon individual choice and only caused a rise of bootlegger gangsterism.

8 Time was running out for the Bourns, and they were resigned to a routine of trying to get everything in order for the day when they would be resting in the family cemetery on the hill. A break away from thoughts of death came during February and March of 1934, when Elizabeth Rose and Billy arrived from Ireland for a visit. Both were beyond childhood, and Elizabeth Rose at nineteen was engaged to be married to Lord Burgh of Northcourt, Isle of Wight, England—a marriage that was to take place on June 6, 1934, in London.[73]

Billy was a tall fourteen-year-old, and his grandparents were amazed to see how much he had grown since they had last seen him. But the visit of the grandchildren was too short, and after they had gone, a true sense of their own limited time left Will and Agnes with a hollow feeling.

On July 23, 1934, seventy-seven-year-old William Bourn wrote to his sisters about last arrangements:

> Darling Sisters: When my time comes to be taken to our "God's Acre" please make all arrangements.
>
> I hope Mr. Cambridge can officiate and wish nobody invited to the services which are to be held at Filoli House, except my sisters.
>
> Everything to be very private. My Trust Will is in the safe deposit box of Filoli Inc. at The Bank of California, several have copies.
>
> God bless us all,
> Brother Will[74]

A year had passed since the Bourns had seen their grandchildren, and on March 25, 1935, their first great-grandchild was born. When news reached them about the birth of Elizabeth Rose's baby boy, Bourn was informed that the child had been named Alexander Peter.

Upon hearing this, Will exclaimed to his nurse: "Alexander the Great, Peter the Great, why not Caesar, Napoleon?"

The answer came from Will's nurse, who said: "What did you want, Mr. Bourn, William the Conqueror?"[75]

This humorous exchange between William Bourn and his nurse was not unusual for this man in a cage. But it was becoming more and more difficult for Will to see any joy in a life that was running out for Agnes and him.

Less than a year after learning of the birth of a great-grandson, the time for dying began. It was Agnes who went first. This was what Will had wanted; he had often mentioned to his secretary, Emmy Tobey, that he wished Mrs. Bourn would go first. With a body weakened by years of diabetes and many months of pernicious anemia, Agnes was not able to fight off bronchial pneumonia. At 2:35 P.M., January 3, 1936, seventy-five-year-old Agnes Moody Bourn died.

In her diary, Ida Bourn wrote that the funeral service was held on January 5, 1936. She noted that at "11:15 A.M. Agnes lay in state in her bed, looking reasonably well." At 12:30 a buffet luncheon was held for the guests, and at 2:30 P.M. the services were held in the library.[76]

Emmy Tobey described the funeral services and mentioned that Bella Worn had surrounded Mrs. Bourn with the flowers she had loved. On the mantle there was a cross fashioned out of white carnations and lilies of the valley. Dr. Lindley Miller read a short service, and Agnes Bourn was then taken to the family cemetery for burial.

Will made all the arrangements for the funeral but was too grief-stricken to attend. His sisters Ida and Maud were there, and among the other mourners were such old friends as Mr. and Mrs. Samuel Eastman, Mr. and Mrs. Bruce Porter, Mr. and Mrs. Alston Hayne, Judge and Mrs. William Olney, Mr. and Mrs. McLeish, Mr. and Mrs. Gerald Rathbone, Mrs. Willis Polk, Bella Worn, Katie Moriarty from Grass Valley, Edward L. Eyre, Robert Hooker, Louis Monteagle, Mrs. Herbert Moffett, Mr. Markey, Emmy Tobey, Marjorie Josselyn, and the nurses and servants of Filoli.[77]

To Emmy Tobey, who had worked for William Bourn for so many years, the funeral of Agnes Bourn was ironic. Filoli had been built with happiness and love as the driving forces behind the completion of this dream, and it struck her that with fires blazing in the fireplaces, with friends gathered about, this should have been a time of joy and not a time to say farewell. In her letter to Will's sister Maye, she noted the irony of the day when she wrote: "She loved Filoli and had selected its many treasures with such high hopes, it does seem a pity good health should have been a stranger in that house for so many years."[78]

In April 1936, Elizabeth Rose and her husband, Lord Burgh, arrived in San Francisco for a short stay.[79] They visited Will at Filoli and found him in very poor health. On April 1, 1936, he had suffered another stroke. While it was not as bad as the one in 1922, it was severe enough so that his granddaughter realized his condition was deteriorating badly.

During the same month, Arthur Vincent arrived in San Francisco after having sailed through the Panama Canal and up the Pacific Coast.[80] He, too, journeyed to Filoli to visit Will. For Vincent and his daughter, this was a farewell visit. When they left Filoli, they realized that the next news from the home would be of the passing of William Bowers Bourn.

Three months after the visit of Elizabeth Rose and her husband, William Bowers Bourn II, age seventy-nine, died on July 5, 1936. Sister Ida sat with him in the last hours. In her diary she recorded: "6:45 Will's closing hour."[81] The physician in attendance was Dr. Howard Mawdsley; also present were two nurses, Marie Dunlevy and George I. Mathisen. At 7:10 P.M., William Bowers Bourn's heart stopped, and he was pronounced dead. The funeral was held on July 7, 1936, and the last of the Bonanza Kings was laid to rest in God's Acre.

On July 10, 1936, the *San Francisco Argonaut* ran a long story about William Bowers Bourn in which it noted the following:

> The death of William B. Bourn severs one more tie between San Francisco of the present and the City of Bonanza Kings. The son of a pioneering family, Mr. Bourn's career was a record of the building of the West, coinciding in its successive phases with the change of San Francisco from a mining center to a metropolis. He began as a miner, as did many of his contemporaries who later hewed out large names in the national life, and after he had thus established himself, and proved his mining genius by making the famous old Empire Mine in Grass Valley one of the greatest gold producers in the world, he turned his attention to civic enterprises. . . . In his passing California has lost one of the foremost of her builder sons."[82]

The humanity of the man was best expressed by Katie Moriarty, the cook and housekeeper in charge at the Empire Cottage. In a letter to Maud Bourn Hayne, Katie wrote: "I am very sad, but he had been so ill such a long time and suffered so much. I just loved to have Mr. and Mrs. Bourn at The Empire Cottage in my time there. We were always so happy together; they were both lovely to me. I did enjoy being with them and enjoyed all the guests that came to the Cottage. I was there 34 happy years."[83]

William Bowers Bourn II passed into California's history quietly, compared to more flamboyant followers of the California Dream, but he would have wished it to be that way. Although he was a man to match California's mountains, he was more like the Big Trees that he loved so much. William Bourn stood alone in quiet dignity as he labored to create not only a personal fortune but also a state, nation, and world that would exist in beauty and harmony.

NOTES

1. PLANTING THE SEED

1. Charles Edward Banks, *The Winthrop Fleet of 1630* (Boston: Houghton Mifflin Co., 1930), 25, 32, 29–30.

2. Oliver Perry Chitwood, *A History of Colonial America* (New York: Harper & Brothers Publishers, 1948), 129.

3. Frederick Merk, *History of the Westward Movement* (New York: Alfred A. Knopf, 1978), 34.

4. Banks, *The Winthrop Fleet*, 47–48.

5. J. C. Furnas, *The Americans: A Social History of the United States 1587–1914* (New York: G. P. Putnam's Sons, 1969), 59.

6. Augustus O. Bourn, *A Sketch of the Descendants of Jared Bourn Who Settled in Boston About the Year 1630* (Bristol, Rhode Island, 1875), 20, carton 3, Bourn Family Papers, 1845–1985 (BANC MSS 86/94c), The Bancroft Library, University of California, Berkeley.

7. Ibid., 5.

8. Ibid., 1.

9. *The History of the State of Rhode Island and Providence Plantations* (New York: American Historical Society, 1920), 4:75.

10. Douglas Edward Leach, *Flintlock and Tomahawk: New England in King Philip's War* (New York: Macmillan, 1958), 1.

11. Ibid., 30.

12. Ibid., 38.

13. Ibid., 43.

14. John R. Swanton, *The Indian Tribes of North America* (Washington: Smithsonian Institution Press, 1968), 25.

15. Leach, *Flintlock and Tomahawk*, 243, 235.

16. Alvin M. Josephy Jr., *The Patriot Chiefs* (New York: Viking Press, 1961), 47.

17. Leach, *Flintlock and Tomahawk*, 244, 246.

18. Bourn, *A Sketch*, 11.

2. WESTWARD VISION

1. Augustus O. Bourn, *A Sketch of the Descendants of Jared Bourn Who Settled in Boston About the Year 1630* (Bristol, Rhode Island, 1875), 20, carton 3, Bourn Family Papers, 1845–1985 (BANC MSS 86/94c), The Bancroft Library, University of California, Berkeley.

2. Samuel Eliot Morison, *The Maritime History of Massachusetts* (Boston: Houghton Mifflin, 1921), 19.

3. Ibid., 19, 225, 268.

4. Bourn, *A Sketch,* 21.

5. Hiram Martin Chittenden, *The American Fur Trade of the Far West* (Stanford: Academic Reprints, 1954), 2: 958–60.

6. Francis Bourn Hayne, "William Bowers Bourn I and the Empire Mine at Grass Valley, California," 2–3, carton 25, Bourn Family Papers; Bourn, *A Sketch,* 21.

7. Bourn, *A Sketch.*

8. Ibid., 22.

9. Inward Letter Book, 1849, Vol. F.2, Falkland Island Archives, Port Stanley.

10. Hayne, "William Bowers Bourn I," 5.

11. Ibid.

12. Louis Rasmussen, *San Francisco Ship Passenger List* (San Francisco: Historic Record, 1965), 1:147.

13. Oscar Lewis, *Sea Routes to the Gold Fields: The Migration by Water to California in 1849–1852* (New York: Alfred A. Knopf, 1949), 132–33.

14. Rasmussen, *Ship Passenger List,* 147.

15. Ibid.

16. John Walton Caughey, *Gold Is the Cornerstone* (Berkeley: University of California Press, 1948), 90–93.

17. Hayne, "William Bowers Bourn I," 5.

3. BOUND FOR CALIFORNIA

1. John Haskell Kemble, *The Panama Route, 1848–1869* (Columbia: University of South Carolina Press, 1990), passim.

2. Ibid., 167–69.

3. John Walton Caughey, *Gold Is the Cornerstone* (Berkeley: University of California Press, 1948), 61.

4. Ibid.

5. Ibid., 62.

6. Kemble, *The Panama Route,* 169–70.

7. J. S. Holliday, *The World Rushed In* (New York: Simon and Schuster, 1981), 433–34.

8. Oscar Lewis, *Sea Routes to the Gold Fields: The Migration by Water to California in 1849–1852* (New York: Alfred A. Knopf, 1949), 190.

9. Kemble, *The Panama Route,* 176.

10. J. D. Borthwick, *Three Years in California* (Oakland: Biobooks, 1948), 22.

11. Ibid., 24.

12. Ibid.

13. Kemble, *The Panama Route,* 122.

14. Ibid., 123.

15. Lewis, *Sea Routes,* 236.

16. Kemble, *The Panama Route,* 147.

17. Sarah Chase Bourn to Philip Chase, 28 May 1854, carton 2, Bourn Family Papers, 1845–1985 (BANC MSS 86/94c), The Bancroft Library, University of California, Berkeley.

18. Francis Bourn Hayne, "William Bowers Bourn I and the Empire Mine at Grass Valley, California," 5, carton 25, Bourn Family Papers.

19. Ibid., 6.

20. Ibid.

21. Sarah Bourn to Philip Chase, 28 May 1854.

22. Ibid.

4. SAN FRANCISCO: A ROUGH CITY OF GOLDEN DREAMS

1. Sarah Chase Bourn to Philip Chase, 25 September 1854, carton 2, Bourn Family Papers, 1845–1985 (BANC MSS 86/94c), The Bancroft Library, University of California, Berkeley.

2. Ibid.

3. Jack R. Wagner, *Gold Mines of California: An Illustrated History of the Most Productive Mines with Descriptions of the Interesting People Who Owned and Operated Them* (Berkeley: Howell-North Books, 1970), 214.

4. Russell R. Elliott, *History of Nevada* (Lincoln: University of Nebraska Press, 1973), 63–64.

5. Ibid., 64.

6. Ferol Egan, "The Road to Washoe: Crossing the Sierra Nevada," *Motorland* 104, no. 2 (March/April 1983), 24.

7. Ferol Egan, "The Road to Washoe: Part II Crossing the Sierra Nevada," *Motorland* 104, no. 3 (May/June 1983), 24.

8. Ibid., 25.

9. Elliott, *History of Nevada,* 68.

10. Rodman Wilson Paul, *Mining Frontiers of the Far West, 1848–1880* (New York: Holt, Rinehart and Winston, 1963), 66.

11. Ibid., 64.

12. John Haskell Kemble, *The Panama Route, 1848–1869* (Columbia: University of South Carolina Press, 1990), 71, 195.

13. William Bronson, *Still Flying and Nailed to the Mast: The First Hundred Years of the Fireman's Fund Insurance Company* (Garden City: Doubleday, 1963), 189.

14. Ibid., 22.

15. William B. Bourn to the Trustees and other officers of The Imperial Mining Company of Gold Hill, Nevada, letters, 1863–66, carton 1, Bourn Family Papers.

16. Grant H. Smith, *The History of the Comstock Lode 1850–1920* (Reno: Nevada Bureau of Mines, University of Nevada, 1961), 293.

17. Edward F. O'Day, "Grass Valley and the Empire: Notes on a Community and a Mine, 1924," unpublished manuscript with editorial cuts by W. B. Bourn, pp. 43–44, carton 1, Edward F. O'Day Papers, 1847–1928 (BANC MSS 87/187c), The Bancroft Library, University of California, Berkeley.

18. F. W. McQuiston Jr., *Gold: The Saga of the Empire Mine 1850–1956* (Grass Valley: Empire Mine Park Association, 1986), 28–29.

19. P. J. Buckminster, Superintendent of the Imperial Mine, Gold Hill, Nevada, to William B. Bourn I, 24 July 1866, carton 1, Bourn Family Papers.

5. AN INTERLUDE OF FAMILY HAPPINESS

1. William Bowers Bourn I to the President and Trustees of the Imperial Silver Mining Company, 24 September 1865, carton 2, Bourn Family Papers, 1845–1985 (BANC MSS 86/94c), The Bancroft Library, University of California, Berkeley.

2. Jack R. Wagner, *Gold Mines of California: An Illustrated History of the Most Productive Mines with Descriptions of the Interesting People Who Owned and Operated Them* (Berkeley: Howell-North, 1970), 214; F. W. McQuiston, Jr., *Gold: The Saga of the Empire Mine 1850–1956* (Grass Valley: Empire Mine Park Association, 1986), 28–29.

3. John Haskell Kemble, *The Panama Route, 1848–1869* (Columbia: University of South Carolina Press, 1990), 236.

4. Hannah Bourn Ingalls to Zebediah Ingalls, 5 October 1865, Bourn-Ingalls Family Papers (BANC MSS C-B 591), The Bancroft Library, University of California, Berkeley.

5. Kemble, *The Panama Route,* 220, 110, 112–14.

6. Hannah Bourn Ingalls to Zebediah Ingalls, 16 October 1865, Bourn-Ingalls Family Papers.

7. Ibid.

8. Ibid.

9. Ibid.

10. The first Cliff House was a one-story eating and watering stop built by Captain Junius B. Foster in 1863. Adolph Sutro bought Foster out in 1883, and on Christmas of 1894 the Cliff House caught fire and burned. Two years later, Sutro built a new Cliff House that was a seven-story wooden chateau with spires and towers, and though this survived the 1906 earthquake, it caught fire and burned in 1907. Within a year of the destruction of Sutro's magnificent Cliff House, a new and smaller building replaced it.

11. William Bowers Bourn Ingalls, *A Boy's Voyage to San Francisco 1865–1866,* transcribed with notes by F. Bourn Hayne, *California Historical Society Quarterly* 36, no. 3 (1957).

12. Hannah Bourn Ingalls to Zebediah Ingalls, 8 December, 10 December, 15 December 1865, Bourn-Ingalls Family Papers.

13. Hannah Bourn Ingalls to Zebediah Ingalls, 17 December 1865, ibid.

14. A. W. B. Vincent, a great-grandson of William Bowers Bourn I, recalls that Henry Bashford was a New York brother-in-law of the Bourns. Hannah Bourn Ingalls to Zebediah Ingalls, 17 February 1865, ibid.

15. Hannah Bourn Ingalls to Zebediah Ingalls, 25 February 1866, ibid.

16. Kenneth M. Johnson, *The New Almaden Quicksilver Mine* (Georgetown: Talisman Press, 1963), 14–19, 72–73, 81, 91.

17. Ingalls, *A Boy's Voyage,* 293.

18. Mildred Brooke Hoover, Hero Eugene Rensch, and Ethel Grace Rensch, *Historic Spots in California* (Stanford: Stanford University Press, 1948), 220.

19. Hannah Bourn Ingalls to Zebediah Ingalls, 4 March 1866, Bourn-Ingalls Family Papers.

20. William Bronson, *Still Flying and Nailed to the Mast: The First Hundred Years of the Fireman's Fund Insurance Company* (Garden City: Doubleday, 1963), 25.

21. Hannah Bourn Ingalls to Zebediah Ingalls, 8 April 1866, Bourn-Ingalls Family Papers; *St. Helena Star,* 21 March 1974.

22. Hannah Bourn Ingalls to Zebediah Ingalls, 8 April 1866, Bourn-Ingalls Family Papers.

23. Robert F. Heizer and Albert B. Elsasser, *The Natural World of the California Indians* (Berkeley: University of California Press, 1980), 14; Hannah Bourn Ingalls to Zebediah Ingalls, 8 April 1866, Bourn-Ingalls Family Papers.

24. Ingalls, *A Boy's Voyage,* 294–95; *St. Helena Star,* 21 March 1974.

25. Ingalls, *A Boy's Voyage,* 295.

26. Ibid.

27. Ibid., 296.

28. Bronson, *Still Flying,* 26.

29. Hannah Bourn Ingalls to Zebediah Ingalls, n.d., Bourn-Ingalls Family Papers.

30. Jessie Gould Hannon, *The Boston-Newton Company Venture* (Lincoln: University of Nebraska Press, 1969). For a biographical sketch of David Jackson Staples, see pp. 203–7. Bronson, *Still Flying.*

31. Hannah Bourn Ingalls to Zebediah Ingalls, 9 May 1866, Bourn-Ingalls Family Papers.

32. Francis P. Farquhar, *History of the Sierra Nevada* (Berkeley: University of California Press, 1965), 84; Hannah Bourn Ingalls to Zebediah Ingalls, n.d., Bourn-Ingalls Family Papers.

33. "The Mammoth Trees of California," *Hutchings' California Magazine* 3, no. 9 (March 1859); Norman Taylor, *The Ageless Relicts* (New York: St. Martin's Press, 1962).

34. "The Mammoth Trees of California."

35. Hannah Bourn Ingalls to Zebediah Ingalls, 15 May 1866, Bourn-Ingalls Family Papers.

36. The Watkins that Hannah mentions was Carlton E. Watkins, who came from New York to California during the Gold Rush. He became noted for his fine photographs of Yosemite, crumbling missions, the Comstock Lode, and other scenes of the

Far West. See Charles B. Turill, "An Early California Photographer: C. E. Watkins," *News Notes of the California Libraries* (January 1918); Hannah Bourn Ingalls to Zebediah Ingalls, n.d., Bourn-Ingalls Family Papers.

37. P. J. Buckminster to William Bowers Bourn I, 24 July 1866, Bourn Family Papers.

38. Ingalls, *A Boy's Voyage,* 294, 295. Kemble, *The Panama Route,* 227–28.

6. BOURN'S NEVADA ADVENTURES

1. "Litigation over the Estate of William Bowers Bourn I . . . 1898–1899," carton 1, Bourn Family Papers, 1845–1985 (BANC MSS 86/94c), The Bancroft Library, University of California, Berkeley.

2. Richard E. Lingenfelter, *The Hardrock Miners: A History of the Mining Labor Movement in the American West 1863–1893* (Berkeley: University of California Press, 1974), 46.

3. Ibid.

4. Ibid., 46, 47.

5. Ferol Egan, "The Road to Washoe: Part II Crossing the Sierra Nevada," *Motorland* 104, no. 3 (May/June 1983): 24–25.

6. J. Wells Kelly, *First Directory of Nevada Territory,* introduction by Richard Lingenfelter (Los Gatos: Talisman Press, 1962), 73.

7. Ibid., 85. For a complete account of this war and of Major William Ormsby's death, see Ferol Egan, *Sand in a Whirlwind: The Paiute Indian War of 1860* (Reno: University of Nevada Press, 1985).

8. Kelly, *Directory of Nevada Territory,* 192.

9. Eliot Lord, *Comstock Mining and Miners,* introduction by David F. Myrick (Berkeley: Howell-North Press, 1959), 204.

10. Rodman Wilson Paul, *Mining Frontiers of the Far West, 1848–1880* (New York: Holt, Rinehart and Winston, 1963), 67.

11. Lingenfelter, *The Hardrock Miners,* 47.

12. Ibid.

13. Ibid., 48–49.

14. Alfred Doten, *The Journals of Alfred Doten 1849–1903,* edited by Walter Van Tilburg Clark (Reno: University of Nevada Press, 1973), 2:917–18.

15. Wesley S. Griswold, *A Work of Giants* (New York: McGraw-Hill, 1962), 190–91.

16. George Kraus, *High Road to Promontory* (Palo Alto: American West Publishing Company, 1969), 111.

17. Griswold, *A Work of Giants,* 192.

18. Kraus, *High Road,* 308.

19. W. Turrentine Jackson, *Treasure Hill: Portrait of a Silver Mining Camp* (Tucson: University of Arizona Press, 1963), 11.

20. Ibid., 10, and map opposite p. 23; Paul, *Mining Frontiers,* 106.

21. Jackson, *Treasure Hill,* 85.

22. Ibid., 21.

23. Ibid., 23.

24. Ibid., 23, 24.

25. Ibid., 25; Alan H. Patera, *The Rush to White Pine* (Lake Grove, Oregon: The Depot, 1988), 21.

26. Jackson, *Treasure Hill,* 144, 145, 147.

27. Ibid.

7. BOURN'S LUCK

1. Hubert Howe Bancroft, *History of California* (San Francisco: The History Company, Publishers, 1890), 7:668–69.

2. Ibid., 7:585.

3. Richard Dillon, *Great Expectations: The Story of Benicia, California* (Benicia: Benicia Heritage Book, Inc., 1980), 162.

4. Ibid., 162, 163.

5. Ibid., 163.

6. Jacqueline McCart Woodruff, *Benicia: The Promise of California* (Vallejo, California, 1947), 74.

7. Ibid., 73.

8. *Who's Who in Bates: A History by the Journalism Class of 1927* (San Francisco: Bates School, 1927).

9. F. W. McQuiston Jr., *Gold: The Saga of the Empire Mine 1850–1956* (Grass Valley: Empire Mine Park Assocation, 1986), 33.

10. Hank Bergtholdt, "Giant Powder and the Strike," *The Empire Star* (Grass Valley: Empire Mine Park Association) 5, no. 7 (July 1987), 3; McQuiston, *Gold,* 33.

11. Jack R. Wagner, *Gold Mines of California: An Illustrated History of the Most Productive Mines with Descriptions of the Interesting People Who Owned and Operated Them* (Berkeley: Howell-North Books, 1970), 213, 214.

12. Ibid.

13. Rodman Wilson Paul, *Mining Frontiers of the Far West, 1848–1880* (New York: Holt, Rinehart and Winston, 1963), 20.

14. McQuiston, *Gold,* 15.

15. George W. Starr, "The Empire Mine, Past and Present," *Mining and Scientific Press* 81 (18 August 1900): 185, 187.

16. C. A. Logan, "History of Mining and Milling Methods in California," 34; Olaf P. Jenkins, *Geologic Guidebook Along Highway 49—Sierran Gold Belt: The Mother Lode Country* (San Francisco: Department of Natural Resources, Division of Mines, State of California, 1948).

17. Starr, "The Empire Mine," 122.

18. Charles A. Bohakel, *A Brief History of the Empire Mine at Grass Valley* (Grass Valley: Empire Mine Park Association, 1980), 5.

19. Wagner, *Gold Mines of California,* 214–15.

20. "Genealogy of the Bourn Family of San Francisco," carton 1, Bourn Family Papers.

21. Sarah Hayne Simpson, daughter of F. Bourn Hayne, supplied this information.

22. The sources of this information were a February 23, 1974, letter from F. Bourn Hayne to Nancy Levensaler; and Nancy Levensaler, conversation with the author, 1992.

8. TRAGEDY AND RESPONSIBILITY

1. Andy Forde, "History of the Christian Brothers Retreat House Estate and the Bourn Family," unpublished manuscript, p. 6, carton 25, Bourn Family Papers, 1845–1985 (BANC MSS 86/94C), The Bancroft Library, University of California, Berkeley.

2. George W. Starr, "The Empire Mine, Past and Present," *Mining and Scientific Press* 81 (18 August 1900): 14.

3. F. Bourn Hayne to Nancy Levensaler, 22 February 1974, in private collection of A. W. B. Vincent, San Francisco.

4. Ibid.

5. Charles A. Bohakel, *A Brief History of the Empire Mine at Grass Valley* (Grass Valley: Empire Mine Park Association, 1980), 5, 6.

6. "The Dead Millionaire: Results of the Coroner's Inquest in the Case of Wm. B. Bourn," p. 1, carton 21, Bourn Family Papers.

7. Ibid.

8. "Suicide Wm. B. Bourn Shoots Himself Through the Heart," *San Francisco Daily Examiner,* 25 July 1874, carton 21, Bourn Family Papers.

9. Ibid.

10. Ibid.

11. Ibid.

12. Newspaper clippings from the *San Francisco Daily Examiner* and the *San Francisco Chronicle,* 25 July 1874, carton 21, Bourn Family Papers.

13. Coroner's Inquest, p. 1, carton 21, Bourn Family Papers.

14. Ibid.

15. Ibid.

16. Ibid.

17. Ibid.

18. The Last Will and Testament of William B. Bourn, carton 22, Bourn Family Papers.

19. Ibid.

20. Statements Presented by Mr. W. B. Bourn II, August 1874, carton 22, Bourn Family Papers.

9. THE CAMBRIDGE YEARS

1. Zebediah Ingalls to Sarah E. Bourn, 6 January 1875, carton 26, Bourn Family Papers, 1845–1985 (BANC MSS 86/94C), The Bancroft Library, University of California, Berkeley.

2. "A Short History of Cambridge," *Cambridge Official Guide* (Cambridge: Cambridge City Council Tourist Office, 1979), 15–17.

3. George W. Starr, "The Empire Mine, Past and Present," *Mining and Scientific Press* 81 (18 August 1900): 54.

4. W. Turrentine Jackson, *Treasure Hill: Portrait of a Silver Mining Camp* (Tucson: University of Arizona Press, 1963), 167, 190.

5. Russell R. Elliott, *History of Nevada* (Lincoln: University of Nebraska Press, 1973), 104.

6. "A Short History of Cambridge," 40.

7. Ibid., 76.

8. Starr, "The Empire Mine."

9. Jackson, *Treasure Hill,* 193.

10. *St. Helena Star,* 1 March 1978.

11. Chase Family Data, carton 1, Bourn Family Papers.

12. William Bowers Bourn II, "Letters to Sarah E. Bourn, 1878," carton 10, ibid.

13. Sarah E. Bourn to D. Z. Parkhurst, 7 October 1898, carton 2, ibid.

14. William Bowers Bourn II, "Memo," carton 11, ibid.

15. Ibid.

10. YOUNG BOURN AND THE EMPIRE MINE

1. George W. Starr, "The Empire Mine, Past and Present," *Mining and Scientific Press* 81 (18 August 1900): 53.

2. Ibid., 51.

3. Ibid., 54.

4. William B. Bourn II to Sarah Bourn, telegram, 18 July 1879, carton 10, Bourn Family Papers, 1845–1985 (BANC MSS 86/94c), The Bancroft Library, University of California, Berkeley; F. Bourn Hayne, "The Sarah E. Bourn Estate, Madroño," p. 2, carton 4, ibid.

5. *Mining & Scientific Press* 40, no. 24 (12 June 1880).

6. William B. Bourn II to Sarah E. Bourn, telegram, 12 October 1881, carton 10, Bourn Family Papers.

7. Jack R. Wagner, *Gold Mines of California: An Illustrated History of the Most Productive Mines with Descriptions of the Interesting People Who Owned and Operated Them* (Berkeley: Howell-North Books, 1970), 215.

8. John Hays Hammond, *The Autobiography of John Hays Hammond* (New York: Farrar & Rinehart, 1935), 1:179; Wagner, *Gold Mines of California,* 177.

9. William B. Bourn II to Sarah E. Bourn, 8 May 1886, Bourn Family Papers.

10. Hammond, *Autobiography.*

11. Ibid.

12. Ibid.

13. William B. Bourn II to Sarah E. Bourn, 21 July 1887, Bourn Family Papers.

14. Charles A. Bohakel, *A Brief History of the Empire Mine at Grass Valley* (Grass Valley: Empire Mine Park Association, 1980), 8.

15. Sarah E. Bourn, "Correspondence 1888," carton 1, Bourn Family Papers; William B. Bourn II to Sarah E. Bourn, 7 February 1888, carton 10, ibid.

11. THE NAPA VALLEY YEARS

1. Sarah E. Bourn, "Abstracts of Title to Property. . . near St. Helena, Napa County, 1874," carton 3, Bourn Family Papers, 1845–1985 (BANC MSS 86/94c), The Bancroft Library, University of California, Berkeley; Mildred Brooke Hoover, Hero Eugene Rensch, and Ethel Grace Rensch, *Historic Spots in California* (Stanford: Stanford University Press, 1948), 281–82.

2. Sarah E. Bourn to Maud Bourn, 1888, carton 6, Bourn Family Papers.

3. Sarah E. Bourn, "Obituaries and Newspaper Clippings," carton 25, ibid.

4. Rudy Mancini, "The Grandeur of Greystone," MS, 1983, 3.

5. Ibid.

6. Ibid.

7. George W. Perry, "Concrete Construction," *The Engineering Record* (March 1894).

8. Mancini, "The Grandeur of Greystone," 6.

9. Ibid.

10. Charles M. Coleman, *P.G. and E. of California: The Centennial Story of Pacific Gas and Electric Company, 1852–1952* (New York: McGraw-Hill, 1952), 63.

11. Ibid., 64.

12. Idwal Jones, *Vines in the Sun: A Journey Through the California Vineyards* (New York: William Morrow, 1949), 74.

12. SAN FRANCISCO: CITY OF PROMISE

1. William Bowers Bourn II, "The City of Promise," *San Francisco Water* (1922), 1, carton 3, Bourn Family Papers, 1845–1985 (BANC MSS 86/94c), The Bancroft Library, University of California, Berkeley.

2. J. L. Romer, "History of the Spring Valley Water Works from Its Inception to June 15, 1903 . . . ," *Bill of Complaint by the Spring Valley Water Company vs. The City and County of San Francisco (September 14, 1903),* 8–9, carton 43, ibid.

3. Frank M. Stanger, *South from San Francisco: San Mateo County, California, Its History and Heritage* (San Mateo: San Mateo County Historical Association, 1963), 78.

4. Romer, "Spring Valley Water Works," 4.

5. Hubert Howe Bancroft, *History of California* (San Francisco: The History Company, Publishers, 1890), 7:740.

6. Richard Longstreth, *On the Edge of the World: Four Architects in San Francisco at the Turn of the Century* (Cambridge: Architectural History Foundation/Massachusetts Institute of Technology Press, 1983), 51.

7. Ibid., 54, 90, 364.

8. F. W. McQuiston Jr., *Gold: The Saga of the Empire Mine 1850–1956* (Grass Valley: Empire Mine Park Association, 1986), 38.

9. John Hays Hammond, *The Autobiography of John Hays Hammond* (New York: Farrar & Rinehart, 1935), 1:210.

10. Letters concerning 2030 Broadway Street, San Francisco, property, 1892–1952, carton 2, Bourn Family Papers.

11. William B. Bourn to Maud Bourn, 19 January 1893, carton 11, ibid.; William B. Bourn to Sarah E. Bourn, 19 January 1893, ibid.

12. George Ordish, *The Great Wine Blight* (New York: Scribner, 1972), 19; Tom Gregory, *History of Solano and Napa Counties, California* (Los Angeles: Historic Record Company, 1912), 199.

13. F. Bourn Hayne, "The Sarah E. Bourn Estate, Madroño," pp. 2–3, carton 1, Bourn Family Papers.

14. Longstreth, *On the Edge of the World*, 228–29.

15. Ibid., 229.

16. This information was provided by Charles Carpy of St. Helena, the grandson of Charles Carpy I.

17. Longstreth, *On the Edge of the World*, 379, note 21, 381–82, note 21.

18. Zaidee Bourn Moody to Sarah E. Bourn, 8 November 1894, carton 13, Bourn Family Papers.

19. "Printed Document Declaring William Bowers Bourn a Freeholder of the City and County of San Francisco," December 26, 1894, carton 3, ibid.

20. Getting a charter for the City and County of San Francisco was not an easy task. It was not until May 26, 1898, that the voters accepted a charter. Even then, the small margin of acceptance by the voters hardly indicated an expression of belief in the charter. See J. P. Young, *San Francisco: A History of the Pacific Coast Metropolis* (San Francisco: S. J. Clark Publishing Company, 1912), 702.

13. EXPANDING HORIZONS

1. *Pacific Churchman*, carton 3, Bourn Family Papers, 1845–1985 (BANC MSS 86/94c), The Bancroft Library, University of California, Berkeley.

2. Ibid.

3. Gertrude Atherton, *My San Francisco: A Wayward Biography* (New York: Bobbs-Merrill, 1946), 50.

4. Richard Longstreth, *On the Edge of the World: Four Architects in San Francisco at the Turn of the Century* (Cambridge: Architectural History Foundation / Massachusetts Institute of Technology Press, 1983), 211, 215.

5. Ibid., 217.

6. Ibid., 211–12.

7. Lawrence Dinneah, *Les Jeunes: An Account of Some Fin de Siècle San Francisco Authors and Artists*, edited by J. R. K. Kantor (Berkeley: The Friends of the Bancroft Library, 1980), 1. Quoted with the permission of The Friends of The Bancroft Library.

8. Longstreth, *On the Edge of the World*, 212, 215.

9. Charles M. Coleman, *P.G. and E. of California: The Centennial Story of the Pacific Gas and Electric Company, 1852–1952* (New York: McGraw-Hill, 1952), 82.

10. Ibid., 82–83, 84.

11. Longstreth, *On the Edge of the World*, 176.

12. T. H. Watkins, *Gold and Silver in the West: The Illustrated History of an American Dream* (Palo Alto: American West Publishing Company, 1971), 141, 143.

13. George W. Starr, "The Empire Mine, Past and Present," *Mining and Scientific Press* 81 (18 August 1900), 153.
14. Ibid.
15. Ibid., 154.
16. Ibid.
17. Ibid., 155.
18. Coleman, *P.G. and E. of California,* 86.

14. THE NEW CENTURY

1. Laurel Hill Cemetery was bounded by California, Parker, and Presidio Avenues. It was called Lone Mountain Cemetery when it opened on May 30, 1854, and in 1867 it was renamed Laurel Hill Cemetery. On January 17, 1914, owners of gravesites in this cemetery and in the Calvary, Masonic, and Odd Fellow cemeteries were notified that they had to remove all bodies. See Gladys Hansen, *San Francisco Almanac* (San Rafael: Presidio Press, 1980), 199–200; E. J. McCutchen to William Bowers Bourn II, February 1899, carton 11, Bourn Family Papers, 1845–1985 (BANC MSS 86/94c), The Bancroft Library, University of California, Berkeley.
2. Ibid.
3. Ibid.
4. J. P. Langhorne to William Bowers Bourn II, 20 February 1899, carton 11, Bourn Family Papers.
5. George W. Starr, "The Empire Mine, Past and Present," *Mining and Scientific Press* 81 (18 August 1900): 184, 185.
6. Ibid., 186.
7. Ibid., 187.
8. Ibid.
9. Ibid.
10. Ibid., 188.
11. Ibid.
12. William Bourn to Sarah E. Bourn, 12 September 1899, carton 10, Bourn Family Papers.
13. Julia Cooley Altrocchi, *The Spectacular San Franciscans* (New York: E. P. Dutton, 1949), 276.
14. William Bourn to Sarah E. Bourn, 6 February 1901, carton 10, Bourn Family Papers.
15. Charles M. Coleman, *P.G. and E. of California: The Centennial Story of the Pacific Gas and Electric Company, 1852–1952* (New York: McGraw-Hill, 1952), 87.
16. Ibid., 89.
17. Ibid.
18. William B. Ingalls to Abbott Ingalls, 25 August 1903, carton 26, Bourn Family Papers.
19. Ibid.

20. Ibid. Ingalls was referring to Tuxedo Park, a country club near Tuxedo Lake, New York.

21. Ibid.

22. Ibid.

23. Ibid.

24. Prince André Poniatowski was born in Paris, January 24, 1864, a descendant of Polish royalty. A banker by profession, he came to the United States in 1892 to learn about American financial conditions. Through William Crocker and his wife he met Elizabeth Sperry—Crocker's sister-in-law—and they married in Paris in 1894. He was interested in low-cost transportation and the use of electric power. In 1897, he invested in the building of the Sierra Railway from Oakdale to Jamestown, California, a short-line that ran fifty-six miles into Tuolumne County with the end of track at Tuolumne City. Later, a branch was built between Jamestown and Angels Camp in Calaveras County. After this project, Poniatowski joined with Crocker in developing the Standard Electric Company of California and in building the Blue Lakes dams and the Electra powerhouse.

25. Ingalls to Abbott Ingalls, 25 August 1903.

26. Tragedy Springs is on the Carson Pass road, Highway 88, a few miles west of Silver Lake. Here, on approximately June 27, 1848, Daniel Browett, Ezrah H. Allen, and Henderson Cox were murdered and robbed. Former Mormon Battalion soldiers of the Mexican War who had worked on Sutter's sawmill, they were bound for Salt Lake City when they were killed. See Ferol Egan, "Incident at Tragedy Springs," *American West* 3, no. 1 (January 1971): 36–39.

27. Ingalls to Abbott Ingalls, 25 August 1903.

28. Coleman, *P.G. and E. of California,* 167. W. R. Eckart had a broad background in design and the construction of mechanical and hydraulic equipment. He had also worked as a consulting engineer for Mackay, Flood, O'Brien, and Fair in the Comstock Mines of Virginia City, Nevada. See ibid.

29. Claus Spreckels immigrated from Hanover, Germany, in 1848. In 1856 he opened a grocery store in San Francisco, and in 1863 he bought a small sugar refining company. He ultimately controlled San Francisco's sugar refineries, started a sugar beet business, and came to control much of the sugar cane production of Hawaii. He organized the independent gas, light, and power companies of San Francisco, which he sold to William B. Bourn II in 1903.

30. Coleman, *P.G. and E. of California,* 90.

15. GROWING FORTUNES

1. Empire Mines and Investment Company Annual Report for 1905, carton 77, Spring Valley Water Company Records (BANC MSS C-G 189), The Bancroft Library, University of California, Berkeley.

2. Charles M. Coleman, *P.G. and E. of California: The Centennial Story of the Pacific Gas and Electric Company, 1852–1952* (New York: McGraw-Hill, 1952), 228–29.

3. Ibid., 229, 230.

4. Ibid., 232.

5. William Bowers Bourn II to Sarah E. Bourn, 25 August 1905, carton 10, Bourn Family Papers, 1845–1985 (BANC MSS 86/94c), The Bancroft Library, University of California, Berkeley.

6. Ibid.

7. Agnes Bourn, "Diary Book for 1906," 4 and 5 January 1906, A. W. B. Vincent Collection, San Francisco.

8. William Bowers Bourn II to Sarah E. Bourn, 8 January 1906, Bourn Family Papers.

9. Agnes Bourn Diary, 9 January 1906.

10. Biographical information regarding Arthur Rose Vincent, in A. W. B. Vincent Collection.

11. Agnes Bourn Diary, 20 January 1906.

12. Ibid., 29 January 1906.

13. Ibid., 4 February 1906.

14. Ibid., 18 April 1906.

15. Julia Cooley Altrocchi, *The Spectacular San Franciscans* (New York: E. P. Dutton, 1949), 282.

16. William Bronson, *The Earth Shook, The Sky Burned* (San Francisco: Chronicle Books, 1986), 24.

17. Ibid., 24–25.

18. Ibid., 92.

19. Ibid., 83.

20. Agnes Bourn Diary, 19 April 1906.

21. Gladys Hansen, *San Francisco Almanac* (San Rafael: Presidio Press, 1980), 195.

22. Bronson, *The Earth Shook*, 111–13.

23. Ibid., 29.

24. Ibid., 29–31.

25. Agnes Bourn Diary, 11 May 1906. The Nevada County Narrow Gauge Railroad began operations on April 17, 1876. By October 1943 this short-line had been abandoned.

26. Agnes Bourn Diary, 15 May 1906.

27. Ibid., 17 May 1906.

28. Kevin Starr, *Americans and the California Dream 1850–1915* (New York: Oxford University Press, 1973), 292–93.

29. Agnes Bourn Diary, 4 July 1906.

30. Ibid., 2 August 1906.

31. River Mines Company, 1906, carton 78A, Spring Valley Water Company Records.

32. Agnes Bourn Diary, 1 October 1906.

33. Frank M. Stanger, *South from San Francisco: San Mateo County, California, Its History and Heritage* (San Mateo: San Mateo County Historical Association, 1963), 178, 185. Captain Albert H. Payson (1847–1930) was a retired officer of the U.S. Army. In 1883, he married Abby Josephine Parrott, a daughter of John Parrott. During his civilian

career, Captain Payson served as vice president of the San Francisco and San Joaquin Valley Railway Company, the predecessor of the Santa Fe Railroad Company in Northern California. In December 1896, Payson served as one of the first board of eleven directors of the San Francisco Gas and Electric Company; in 1901, he became director of the company. He was also an officer in the Spring Valley Water Company before and after William Bowers Bourn II acquired controlling stock in that company. Payson also served as San Mateo's first mayor when the town was incorporated in 1894.

34. Empire Mines and Investment Company Annual Report for 1906, Spring Valley Water Company Records.

16. WATER, LAND, AND POLITICS

1. William B. Bourn to Senator Francis G. Newlands, 13 February 1909, carton 4, Spring Valley Water Company Records (BANC MSS C-G 189), The Bancroft Library, University of California, Berkeley.

2. Spring Valley Water Company Complaint vs. The City and County of San Francisco, 1 July 1914, carton 20, ibid.; carton 2, ibid.; Bourn to Newlands, 13 Febuary 1909, ibid.

3. William B. Bourn to James Laidlaw, 21 August 1908, carton 1, ibid.

4. Samuel P. Eastman's college major and his date of departure from the University of California were supplied by William M. Roberts, University Archivist, The Bancroft Library, University of California, Berkeley.

5. Sky Farm was built by Prince André Poniatowski. For biographical information, see note 24, Chapter 14.

6. J. L. Romer, "History of the Spring Valley Water Works, Prepared for The City and County of San Francisco, 1903–1910," pp. 1–2, carton 18, Spring Valley Water Company Records.

7. Laurence H. Shoup and Suzanne Baker, *Cultural Resource Overview: Lake Merced Transport, San Francisco Clean Water Management Program* (San Francisco: Archaeological Consultants, 1981), 30.

8. Ibid., 31.

9. George D. Lyman, *Ralston's Ring* (New York: Charles Scribner's Sons, 1937), 272–75.

10. William Chapman Ralston (1826–1875) was born in Ohio. He moved to San Francisco in 1854 after having made a fortune in banking. With Darius Ogden Mills, Ralston founded the Bank of California and became its president in 1872. His business interests included steamship lines, railroads, mines in the Comstock Lode, the Palace Hotel, a theater, and woolen and silk mills. He was also a force in politics and a social figure with a grand home in Belmont. Upon his death, he was broke and left his estate in debt.

11. Shoup and Baker, *Cultural Resource Overview,* 45.

12. Romer, "History of the Spring Valley Water Works," 14–17.

13. Ibid., 18–21.

14. This land near Pleasanton was acquired by the Spring Valley Water Company in 1908. Carton 2, Spring Valley Water Company Records.

15. Edward H. Clark, "The History of the Pacific Union Club 1852–1977" (unpublished manuscript, Pacific Union Library, San Francisco, n.d.), 30.

16. Ibid., 32, 42.

17. Descriptions of the interior of the Pacific Union Club are based on a personal visit and on material in the Clark history. See ibid., 43–45.

18. Letters between William B. Bourn and William Crocker, December 1 and 2, 1908, carton 1, Spring Valley Water Company Records.

19. Cost of construction of the Pacific Union Club, ibid.

20. W. B. Lawrence to William B. Bourn, 23 March 1909, carton 1, ibid.

21. *To Remember Willis Polk* (San Francisco: Printed by John Henry Nash for the Spring Valley Water Company, 1926), 4.

22. Carton 18, Spring Valley Water Company Records.

23. Statement of A. S. Crawford, carton 20, ibid.

24. Ibid.

25. Ibid.

26. Ibid.

27. Lawsuit by the Spring Valley Water Company against the *San Francisco Chronicle,* 9 January 1920. The water company received a judgment against the newspaper for $50,000. Carton 2, ibid.

28. Spring Valley Water Company properties as of December 1, 1909, carton 3, ibid.

29. William Mulholland (1855–1935) immigrated to California from Ireland in 1877. He rose from a ditch tender for the Los Angeles water system to become its chief engineer. Mulholland was the guiding force behind the Owens River aqueduct, which brought water from the eastern Sierra Nevada almost 250 miles to Los Angeles. That project took from 1907 to 1913 to complete. He helped the Spring Valley Water Company with the construction of the Calaveras Dam in Alameda County. Also, he was in charge of the construction of the Saint Francis Dam near Saugus, Los Angeles County, which gave way on the night of March 12, 1928. The flood swept through the city of Santa Paula at a height of at least twenty-five feet. In its flood path to the sea, the water killed four hundred people, destroyed homes, other buildings, bridges, highways, livestock, farms, orchards, and everything else in its fifty-four-mile flood plain.

30. Carton 6, Spring Valley Water Company Records.

31. Ibid., carton 11.

32. Jack R. Wagner, *The Last Whistle: Ocean Shore Railroad* (Berkeley: Howell-North Books, 1974), 9.

33. Carton 43; carton 4, Spring Valley Water Company Records.

34. Carton 4, ibid.

35. William B. Bourn to the Honorable Edward Robeson Taylor, Mayor, and the Honorable Board of Supervisors of the City and County of San Francisco, 29 November 1909, carton 11, Bourn Family Papers, 1845–1985 (BANC MSS 86/94c), The Bancroft Library, University of California, Berkeley; William B. Bourn to the Stockholders of the Spring Valley Water Company, 24 December 1909, ibid.

36. William B. Bourn to Jeannette Gilder, 13 January 1910, carton 1, Spring Valley Water Company Records.

37. F. W. McQuiston Jr., *Gold: The Saga of the Empire Mine 1850–1958* (Grass Valley: Empire Mine Park Association, 1986), 47.

38. *San Francisco Call,* 31 March 1910, carton 3, Bourn Family Papers.

39. Ibid.

40. Timmy Gallagher, *Filoli* (San Mateo: National Trust for Historic Preservation, 1982), 13.

41. William B. Bourn to Gifford Pinchot, 11 January 1911, carton 1, Spring Valley Water Company Records.

42. Hiram Martin Chittenden and A. O. Powell, *Report on the Water Supply System of the Spring Valley Water Company* (San Francisco: Spring Valley Water Company, 1912), 22.

43. John R. Freeman, *On the Proposed Use of a Portion of the Hetch Hetchy, Eleanor and Cherry Valleys Within and Near to the Boundaries of the Stanislaus National Forest Reserve and the Yosemite National Park as Reservoirs for Impounding Tuolumne River Flood Waters and Appurtenant Works for the Water Supply of San Francisco, California and Neighboring Cities* (San Francisco: Published by Authority of the Board of Supervisors, 1912).

44. Frank Morton Todd, *The Story of the Exposition* (New York: G. P. Putnam's Sons, 1921), 1:xiv.

45. Ibid., xv–xvi.

46. S. P. Eastman to William B. Bourn, 27 July 1911, carton 3, Spring Valley Water Company Records.

47. William B. Bourn to S. P. Eastman, 23 January 1913, ibid.

48. Legal Complaint Against the City and County of San Francisco, May 1913, p. 8, carton 19, ibid.

49. Ibid., 12–14.

50. Ibid., 14.

51. Ibid., 15.

52. Ibid., 19.

53. Ibid., 199.

54. Ibid., 204.

55. Ibid., 205.

56. Michael Maurice O'Shaugnessy (1864–1934) was born in Ireland and came to San Francisco as a young civil engineer. He designed a water system for San Francisco after the 1906 earthquake; in 1912 he became San Francisco's city engineer. In this capacity, he laid out the municipal railway streetcar system. He was responsible for the construction of the Hetch Hetchy water system and built the dam—named after him—that flooded Hetch Hetchy Valley.

57. Legal Complaint Against the City and County of San Francisco, May 1913, p. 205, carton 19, Spring Valley Water Company Records.

58. Ibid.

59. Ibid., 232.

60. Ibid., 234.

61. Ibid., 240.

62. Ibid., 283–84.

63. Ibid., 279–80.

64. Ibid., 287.

65. Progress Reports of Work on the Calaveras Dam, 1 July 1913 to 31 December 1913, carton 19, ibid.

66. Ibid.

67. Ibid., 3.

17. THE CHANGING TIMES

1. William B. Bourn to E. J. McCutchen, 29 April 1914, carton 1, Spring Valley Water Company Records (BANC MSS C-G 189), The Bancroft Library, University of California, Berkeley.

2. F. W. McQuiston Jr., *Gold: The Saga of the Empire Mine 1850–1956* (Grass Valley: Empire Mine Park Association, 1986), 48.

3. Charles A. Bohakel, *A Brief History of the Empire Mine* (Grass Valley: Empire Mine Park Association, 1980), 14.

4. Empire Mines and Investment Company Report for 1913, carton 77, Spring Valley Water Company Records.

5. Lease of 150 acres of the Lake Merced Ranch to the San Francisco Golf and Country Club in 1914, carton 4, ibid.

6. William B. Bourn to Willis Polk, 2 July 1914, carton 1, ibid.

7. Barbara W. Tuchman, *The Guns of August* (New York: Macmillan, 1962), 122.

8. Ibid., 173.

9. Solano Irrigated Farms, Incorporated Report, carton 58, Spring Valley Water Company Records.

10. William B. Bourn to Arthur Vincent, 18 March 1914, A. W. B. Vincent Collection, San Francisco.

11. Frank Morton Todd, *The Story of the Exposition* (New York: G. P. Putnam's Sons, 1921), 2:150.

12. William B. Bourn to Willis Polk, 10 March 1915, carton 1, Spring Valley Water Company Records.

13. William B. Bourn to Willis Polk, 15 April 1915, ibid.

14. William B. Bourn to Willis Polk, 24 May 1915, ibid.

15. Carton 9, ibid.

16. Ibid.

17. "During a public subscription meeting on April 28, 1910, to raise money for the Panama-Pacific International Exposition, William Bourn made the first subscription of $25,000. This brought hand-clapping from the gathering and shouts of 'Bully Boy!' Nine minutes later a million dollars had been raised. By the end of the meeting, a total of $4,089,000 had been raised." See Todd, *Story of the Exposition,* 1:75–76. Edward F. O'Day, "Wartime Activities of William Bowers Bourn" (unpublished manuscript in Edward F. O'Day Papers, 1847–1928 [BANC MSS 87/187c], The Bancroft Library, University of California, Berkeley), 20–21.

18. O'Day, "Wartime Activities," 35.

19. These three words were the heart of Bourn's philosophy of life, for his personal

motto was "How to Fight, How to Live, and How to Die." But the more he thought about it, the more he realized that he truly believed in "Fight, Love, and Live." The name *Filoli* first appeared on the working drawings for the home as early as 1915.

20. William B. Bourn to Willis Polk, 13 December 1915, carton 1, Spring Valley Water Company Records.

21. Ibid.

22. O'Day, "Wartime Activities," 30–32.

23. Ibid., 49.

24. Ibid.

25. S. P. Eastman, "Report on the Calaveras Dam," 5 February 1916, carton 59, Spring Valley Water Company Records; William B. Bourn to W. F. Herrin, 16 February 1916, carton 1, ibid.

26. William B. Bourn to Ida Bourn, 16 May 1916, carton 11, Bourn Family Papers, 1845–1985 (BANC MSS 86/94c), The Bancroft Library, University of California, Berkeley.

27. William B. Bourn to Samuel P. Eastman, 15 May 1916, carton 5, Spring Valley Water Company Records.

28. George Dangerfield, *The Damnable Question: A Study in Anglo-Irish Relations* (Boston: Little, Brown and Co., 1976), 3–4.

29. Ibid., 209–10.

30. Spring Valley Water Company Records, carton 77.

31. O'Day, "Wartime Activities," 62.

32. Ibid., 63.

33. Ibid., 66.

34. Ibid., 69.

35. Ibid., 118–19.

36. Ibid., 101.

37. Ibid., 104, 108.

38. McQuiston, *Gold,* 49.

39. "Filoli Incorporated," p. 372, carton 79, Spring Valley Water Company Records.

40. Ibid., 373–79.

41. During his long career, Arthur Brown Jr. (1875–1957) designed buildings for the California School of Fine Arts, the Horticultural Building of the Panama-Pacific International Exposition of 1915; city halls for Berkeley, San Francisco, and Pasadena; buildings for the University of California and Stanford University; the Hoover Tower at Stanford; Coit Tower; the San Francisco Museum of Art; the San Francisco War Memorial Opera House, and the War Memorial Veterans Building. In addition, he was a consulting architect for the San Francisco–Oakland Bay Bridge.

42. "Minutes of the regular monthly meeting of the Board of Trustees of the Leland Stanford University," p. 11, carton 2, Spring Valley Water Company Records.

43. O'Day, "Wartime Activities," 140; Julia Cooley Altrocchi, *The Spectacular San Franciscans* (New York: E. P. Dutton, 1949), 312–13.

44. William B. Bourn to Arthur Vincent, 27 May 1918, A. W. B. Vincent Collection.

45. William B. Bourn to F. W. Nobs, 15 July 1918, carton 1, Spring Valley Water Company Records.

46. William B. Bourn to Arthur Vincent, 28 August 1918, A. W. B. Vincent Collection.

47. This information came from A. W. B. Vincent.

48. Altrocchi, *Spectacular San Franciscans,* 305.

49. O'Day, "Wartime Activities," 5.

50. William B. Bourn to the Department of Interior, United States Geological Survey, 11 June 1919, carton 1, Spring Valley Water Company Records.

51. Empire Mines and Investment Company, carton 77, pp. 11, 23, Spring Valley Company Records.

52. William B. Bourn to Katie Moriarity, 6 August 1919, carton 1, Spring Valley Water Company Records.

18. THE FINAL YEARS

1. A. W. B. Vincent, interview by author, Filoli and San Francisco, California, 1986.

2. Spring Valley Water Company Records, carton 2, (BANC MSS C-G 189), The Bancroft Library, University of California, Berkeley.

3. Ibid., carton 40.

4. Ibid., carton 8.

5. George Dangerfield, *The Damnable Question: A Study in Anglo-Irish Relations* (Boston: Little, Brown and Co., 1976), 316.

6. William B. Bourn to the Secretary of State, 22 March 1920, carton 1, Spring Valley Water Company Records.

7. Dangerfield, *The Damnable Question,* 318–19.

8. Edward F. O'Day, "Wartime Activities of William Bowers Bourn" (unpublished manuscript in Edward F. O'Day Papers, 1847–1928 [BANC MSS 87/187c], The Bancroft Library, University of California, Berkeley), 140–41.

9. Spring Valley Water Company Records, carton 22.

10. William B. Bourn to George Starr, 19 January 1921, carton 1, ibid.

11. William B. Bourn, "The City of Promise," *San Francisco Water* 1, no. 3 (July 1922), carton 30, ibid. The *Sacramento Daily Union* began in 1851. Mark Twain was a traveling correspondent for the *Union* in 1866, and twenty-five of his Hawaiian Islands letters were published in the *Union.* It carried on a campaign against the Central Pacific that caused the Big Four to start the *Record,* an opposition newspaper. The *Union* remained in business until 1994.

12. Samuel P. Eastman to William B. Bourn, 9 March 1921, carton 4, ibid.

13. Carton 7, ibid.

14. George Starr to William B. Bourn, 10 June 1921, carton 1, ibid.

15. Empire Mines and Investment Company Annual Report for 1920, carton 77, ibid.

16. Information supplied by Ranger Donna Jones, Empire State Historic Park, Grass Valley, California.

17. Dr. Herbert Moffitt of the University of California Medical School was William Bourn's principal physician. His local physician was Dr. Walter C. Chidester, who had a private practice in San Mateo and used the facilities of the Mills Memorial Hospital

in San Mateo. The Mills Memorial Hospital became one of Agnes Bourn's favorite projects, and she often donated money to it. Dr. Chidester was to share his responsibilities at Filoli, beginning in 1924, with Dr. Howard Mawdsley of San Mateo. In 1928, Dr. Chidester and Dr. Mawdsley formed the San Mateo Clinic. Information regarding Bourn's physicians was supplied by his grandson, A. W. B. Vincent of San Francisco. Information regarding Dr. Howard Mawdsley was supplied by his son, Dr. Dean Mawdsley of Hillsborough.

18. Samuel P. Eastman to James Laidlaw, 15 August 1921, carton 1, Spring Valley Water Company Records.

19. A. W. B. Vincent, interview by author, 8 March 1994, San Francisco.

20. A. W. B. Vincent, interviews by author, 21 and 22 March 1994, San Francisco.

21. Much of this information was supplied at various times by William Bowers Bourn's grandson, A. W. B. Vincent. In addition, I have seen Bourn's handwritten correspondence and the ink stamp P.E.P. (Please Excuse Pencil).

22. Dangerfield, *The Damnable Question,* 342–44, 349. Though this was the beginning for a free Ireland, it was not until 1937 that Ireland and its twenty-six counties were no longer part of Great Britain.

23. Spring Valley Water Company Records, carton 7. Also, see Gladys Hansen, *San Francisco Almanac* (San Rafael: Presidio Press, 1980), 48. Lewis P. Hobart (1873–1954) attended the University of California and the École des Beaux-Arts in Paris. Among his buildings are Grace Cathedral, the Bohemian Club, and Steinhart Aquarium.

24. Empire Mines and Investment Company Annual Report for 1922, carton 77, Spring Valley Water Company Records.

25. Samuel P. Eastman to F. P. Anderson, Bank of California, San Francisco, 23 January 1923, carton 6, ibid. In my research about William Bowers Bourn II, I spoke to the late Dr. Howard Mawdsley about his doctor-patient relationship with Bourn. Even in the last years of his life, Dr. Mawdsley recalled that he had been ill at ease whenever he visited his patient.

26. A. W. B. Vincent, interview by author, 8 March 1994; Agnes Bourn to Mary Peixotto, 20 January 1924, Filoli Center, Woodside, California.

27. Agnes Bourn to Ernest Peixotto, 6 April 1924, Filoli Center.

28. Carton 2, Bourn Family Papers, 1845–1985 (BANC MSS 86/94c), The Bancroft Library, University of California, Berkeley.

29. Agnes Bourn to Ernest Peixotto, 6 April 1924. Ernest Peixotto (1869–1940) was one of five children of a distinguished family of Sephardic Jews. His older brother Edgar was an attorney; his brother Eustace was an army general; his brother Sidney was a social worker; and his sister, Jessica, was a professor of economics at the University of California. Ernest was a distinguished artist, book illustrator, and author. Bourn first met Peixotto in 1895 when he was one of those San Francisco artists and writers who called themselves "Les Jeunes" and who published *The Lark,* a thin "magazinelet" published by Gelett Burgess and Bruce Porter. Peixotto contributed fifteen drawings to *The Lark.* Others who were involved at various times in this venture were Willis Polk, Porter Garnett, and Yone Noguchi.

30. Ibid. Francis Bourn Hayne (1903–1988) was the son of Maud Eloise Chase

Bourn Hayne and William Alston Hayne II. Bourn Hayne was a Harvard graduate, an architect, and a keeper of historical records regarding the Bourn family and the Hayne family. From 1986 until his death in 1988, I interviewed Bourn Hayne extensively at his St. Helena home. His greatest service in keeping alive the history of the Bourn family was his collection of family letters and business records, which he donated to The Bancroft Library of the University of California, Berkeley.

31. Ernest Peixotto to Agnes Bourn, April 1924, Filoli Center.

32. Ibid.

33. A. W. B. Vincent, interview by author, 8 March 1994.

34. Spring Valley Water Company Records, carton 1.

35. Agnes Bourn to Ernest Peixotto, 13 September 1924, Filoli Center.

36. Contract between Ernest Peixotto and The Filoli Estate, 16 October 1924, ibid.

37. Nell Hayne (widow of F. Bourn Hayne), interview by author, 2 April 1994, St. Helena, California.

38. Spring Valley Water Company Records; *The Empire Star* 2, No. 11 (November 1993) (Grass Valley: Empire Mine Park Association), 7–8; Spring Valley Water Company Records, carton 2.

39. Michael Robertson, "In The Beginning," *San Francisco Chronicle,* 19 February 1986, pp. 34–36.

40. Empire Mines and Investment Company Annual Report for 1924, carton 77, Spring Valley Water Company Records.

41. Agnes Bourn to Ernest Peixotto, 23 January 1925, Filoli Center.

42. Robert J. Bagues to Mrs. William B. Bourn, 23 July 1925, ibid.

43. Bruce Porter to Ernest Peixotto, 1 September 1925, ibid.

44. James R. Lowrie followed Thomas Angus as a regular driver for the Bourns. Lowrie served twelve years in the British Army, first as a cavalryman, then he shifted to the motorized division where he learned the trade of auto mechanic. He came to the United States in 1912. This information came from his daughter, Alice Estrada of San Mateo.

45. Agnes Bourn to Ernest Peixotto, 31 October 1925, Filoli Center. The friendship of Agnes Bourn and Mary Hallock Foote dated back to 1896 when Foote's husband, Arthur De Wint Foote, was hired as superintendent of the North Star Mine.

46. Agnes Bourn to Mary and Ernest Peixotto, Christmas 1925, ibid.

47. Agnes Bourn to Ernest Peixotto, 24 April 1926, ibid.

48. Agnes Bourn to Ernest Peixotto, 26 September 1926, ibid.

49. Ibid. Additional information about this voyage came from an interview with A. W. B. Vincent.

50. Empire Mines and Investment Company Annual Report for 1927, carton 77, Spring Valley Water Company Records.

51. Ibid.

52. William B. Bourn to Maud and Arthur Vincent, 29 July 1928, carton 1, ibid.

53. Carton 43, ibid.

54. Empire Mines and Investment Company Papers, carton 77, ibid.

55. All information regarding Maud Bourn Vincent's last weeks came from her son, A. W. B. Vincent, interview by author, 8 April 1994.

56. Ibid.

57. Ibid.

58. A. W. B. Vincent, interview by author, 11 April 1994.

59. The Spring Valley Water Company Building at 425 Mason Street in San Francisco was Willis Polk's last project for William B. Bourn. The lower part of its façade was designed to give the impression of flowing water. Inside the building, a mural painted by Maynard Dixon in 1923 covers the space above the entrance to the elevator; it shows a landscape with Polk's Water Temple at Suñol.

60. A. W. B. Vincent, interview by author.

61. Empire Mines and Investment Company Annual Report for 1928, carton 77, Spring Valley Water Company Records.

62. Fred Searls Jr. to Colonel William Boyes Thompson, Picket Post House, Superior, Arizona, 1 May 1929, carton 11, Bourn Family Papers. Newmont also agreed to pay an additional $10,000 for taxes, stores, and supplies.

Fred Searls Jr. was born in the mining community of Nevada City, California, in 1888. He attended the University of California, where he studied mining geology and wrote a thesis titled "Economics of Recycling the Empire Waste Rock." After his graduation in 1906, he worked for the Goldfield Consolidated Mines in Nevada. In early 1917, he was involved in geological exploration in some of China's remote provinces. He returned to the United States to enlist in the engineering regiment of the 1st U.S. Army Division during World War I, where he rose from private to lieutenant by the end of the war. He was Colonel William Boyes Thompson's top engineer at the time of the purchase of the Empire Mine from William B. Bourn.

Colonel William Boyes Thompson grew up in Montana's mining camps. He ultimately became a promoter of mining properties in New York. When he started the Newmont Mining Company, he coined its name by combining *New* from New York, and *mont* from Montana. He always hired top-rate mining engineers, and one of his best men was Fred Searls Jr. Thompson made Searls president of the Newmont Mining Company, which Thompson had formed in 1921.

63. Ibid.

64. Agnes Bourn to Ida Bourn, 15 May 1929, carton 11, Bourn Family Papers.

65. William B. Bourn to Warren Olney Jr., 2 October 1930, carton 1, Empire Mine Records (BANC MSS 92/841C), The Bancroft Library, University of California, Berkeley.

66. The Filoli Estate, carton 79, Spring Valley Water Company Records.

67. A. W. B. Vincent, interview by author, 8 March 1994.

68. Soon after Louise Moody returned home, she died, and news of her passing added to Agnes Bourn's grief. Ibid.

69. "Arthur Rose Vincent," A. W. B. Vincent Collection.

70. "Bourn Vincent Memorial Park Bill," *Saorstat Eireann* (1932), 2, 19, in ibid.

71. Bourn Family Papers, carton 24.

72. The poem by the late Francis Bourn Hayne comes from the A. W. B. Vincent Collection.

73. Lord Burgh, an eighth baron, was Alexander Leigh Henry Leith, a former officer in the Black Watch, Highland Regiment.

74. William B. Bourn to his sisters, 23 July 1934, carton 11, Bourn Family Papers.
75. A. W. B. Vincent, interview by author, 12 May 1994.
76. Ida H. Bourn Diary, 5 January 1936, carton 4, Bourn Family Papers.
77. Emmy Tobey to Mrs. Maye Bourn Tucker, 5 January 1936, ibid.
78. Ibid.
79. A. W. B. Vincent, interview by author, 20 April 1994.
80. Ibid.
81. Ida H. Bourn Diary, Bourn Family Papers.
82. Obituary, *The Argonaut,* 10 July 1936, in carton 3, Bourn Family Papers.
83. Katie Moriarity to Maud Bourn Hayne, 7 July 1936, carton 23, ibid.

SOURCES AND ACKNOWLEDGMENTS

In writing this biographical history of the William Bowers Bourn Family, I have had the use of the extensive collections of primary documents, letters, and papers of the Bourn Family. In addition, I have used primary materials related to the business affairs of the Bourns and their associates; correspondence with friends and relatives; and the key collections of papers regarding the Empire Mine, the Spring Valley Water Company, Filoli Incorporated, and the Edward F. O'Day Family Papers. Most of these papers are in the manuscript collections of The Bancroft Library, University of California, Berkeley. Other key sources may be found at the Filoli Center, Woodside, California; the library of the Pacific Union Club, San Francisco, California; and the private collection of Arthur William Bourn Vincent, San Francisco, California.

In addition to having had access to these papers, I have also interviewed many people whose memories of the Bourns, the Empire Mine, Filoli, Madroño, and Muckross helped to give me a sense of personalities, events, and places. People who helped in this way were Arthur William Bourn Vincent, who, as the grandson of William Bowers Bourn II, was able to provide me with striking word-pictures of the Bourns, life at Filoli, the Empire Mine, and the visits of the Bourns to Muckross, County Kerry, Ireland. Added to Vincent's memories were those of the late Francis Bourn Hayne, a nephew of William Bowers Bourn II, who provided me with many hours of good conversation and storytelling as he recalled life at Madroño during Sarah Esther Chase Bourn's time. But Hayne's major contribution was saving the Bourn Family Papers, which he donated to The Bancroft Library.

Other family members who provided assistance during the years of research and writing of the story of the Bourns were Nell Hayne (widow of F. Bourn Hayne), St. Helena; Sarah Hayne Simpson (daughter of F. Bourn Hayne), Hood; and Fleur Melvill-Gardner (daughter of Elizabeth Rose Vincent Gardner), London, England.

Additional personal memories of the Bourns were provided by Alice Estrada (daughter of James R. Lowrie, Bourn's chauffeur), San Mateo; Nancy Levensaler (granddaughter of George Starr), Kentfield; the late Downey Clinch, Grass Valley; the late Samuel Eastman (son of Samuel P. Eastman), Portola Valley; and the late Dr. Howard Mawdsley (one of Bourn's physicians), Hillsborough.

Once again, as in my other works of history, the major part of my research was done at The Bancroft Library, University of California, Berkeley. For all their aid, I wish to thank the following scholar-librarians: Anthony Bliss, Walter Brem, Lawrence Dinnean, Peter Hanff, Bonnie Hardwick, and William Roberts.

In addition, I wish to thank Arthur William Bourn Vincent for his many considerations and for the use of papers and photographs from the A. W. B. Vincent Collection, San Francisco; the Filoli Center, National Trust for Historic Preservation, Woodside; the Pacific Union Club, San Francisco; the law firm of McCutchen, Doyle, Brown and Enersen, San Francisco; and The Friends of The Bancroft Library, University of California, Berkeley.

I wish to thank other institutions for answers to some of my questions during my research. These are: the Empire Mine State Historic Park, Grass Valley; San Francisco Room, San Francisco Public Library, San Francisco; Sutro Library, San Francisco; San Francisco Maritime Museum, San Francisco; Benicia Historical Society, Benicia; California Historical Society, San Francisco; San Mateo County Historical Society, San Mateo; Huntington Library, San Marino; Department of Special Collections and University Archives, Stanford University Libraries, Stanford; and the Wells Fargo History Museum, San Francisco.

Many friends, fellow historians, and other knowledgeable persons helped me during my work on this book, and I wish to thank the following: Peter Blodgett, Huntington Library, San Marino; Marilyn Bronson, Emeryville; Bradford Casoly, Berkeley; Charles Carpy, St. Helena; Katherine French, San Francisco; Timmy Gallagher, the Filoli Center, Woodside; Evelyn Gardiner, Grass Valley; Robert Hawley, Ross Valley Book Company, Berkeley; Donna Jones, Empire State Historic Park, Grass Valley; Margaret J. Kimball, Department of Special Collections and University Archives, Stanford; Rudy Mancini, Calistoga; Dr. Dean Mawdsley, Hillsborough; Robert Miller, Berkeley; Russell Pearce, Orinda; Thomas M. Rogers, the Filoli Center, Woodside; the late Charles Steinfeld, Grass Valley; Brother Timothy, Christian Brothers Winery, St. Helena; Ted Wurm, Oakland; Pat Dawson, Muckross House, Killarney County, Kerry, Ireland; and Tony Roche, Photographic Section, Office of Public Works, Dublin, Ireland.

I especially wish to thank fellow California historians Richard H. Dillon, Mill Valley, and Kevin Starr, State Librarian, California State Library, Sacramento, who took time from their busy lives to read my manuscript.

I owe a debt of gratitude to my editor, Margaret F. Dalrymple, who had many suggestions for tightening the flow of the manuscript. She devoted a tremendous amount of time and care, for which I am truly grateful.

As in all my books, the major force behind the scene is my combination editor, computer operator, and constant source of support in this lonely craft—my wife, Marty.

Berkeley, California
Fall 1997

INDEX

The notations Bourn I and Bourn II refer to William Bowers Bourn I and William Bowers Bourn II, respectively.